Microsoft

Take Back Your Life!
Special Edition:
Using Microsoft® Outlook® to
Get Organized and Stay
Organized

Sally McGhee

PUBLISHED BY
Microsoft Press
A Division of Microsoft Corporation
One Microsoft Way
Redmond, Washington 98052-6399

Library of Congress Control Number: 2005923732
Printed and bound in the United States of America.

7 8 9   QWT 9 8 7 6

Distributed in Canada by H.B. Fenn and Company Ltd.
A CIP catalogue record for this book is available from the British Library.

Microsoft Press books are available through booksellers and distributors worldwide. For further information about international editions, contact your local Microsoft Corporation office or contact Microsoft Press International directly at fax (425) 936-7329. Visit our Web site at www.microsoft.com/learning/. Send comments to *msinput@microsoft.com*.

Acquisitions Editor: Alex Blanton and Juliana Aldous
Project Editors: Kristine Haugseth and Sandra Haynes
Editorial and Production: Steve Sagman

Body Part No. X10-82952
Section Part No. X11-22769

To my clients, who continually inspire me.

Contents at a Glance

Table of Contents

Chapter Nine   Processing and Organizing Your E-Mail 180

Part Four

The Prioritizing and Planning Phase

Chapter Ten

Prioritizing and Planning 220

Acknowledgments

This book is the culmination of a long and extraordinary journey of listening, learning, and sharing. When I was 19, a dear friend of mine, Michael Wolff, told me, "You sure can organize, but you sure can't spell!" Michael helped me start my first company, designing paper time-management systems. That was the beginning of a journey I'm still traveling today.

I've been extremely blessed to work with many special individuals, all of whom have contributed to me personally and to the philosophies in this book: Jinny and Tim Ditzler, Ben Cannon, Tony Buzan, Graham Alexander, Sir John Whitmore, Werner Erhard, Tim Gallwey, Iain Somerville, Teri Belf, Pam Tarrantine, Dean Acheson, Leslie Boyer, Kelly Forrister, Brian Smiga, Steve Terry, Ron and Mary Hulnick, and Steve and Carol Moore. Special thanks go to Russell Bishop, who many years ago created a company called Productivity Development Group (PDG). David Allen and I were partners in this company, and some of the core philosophies in this book are consistent with the foundation philosophies that we created together at PDG.

I'm extremely grateful to my partners at work who allowed me to focus on this project, and let me continually change our curriculum to find the best approach. I'd like to thank Annie McGhee Stinson and John Wittry, two of my greatest cheerleaders, along with Cindy Whiston and Eric Osterloh. Special thanks go to Jennifer Wilmoth, my assistant, for her unconditional support, encouragement, and laughter, and without whom this book would not have happened.

Tremendous appreciation goes to my family and friends who also understood my commitment to this project and my declining so many social engagements: Leslie Spees McGhee, Judy Goldfader, Kim Musselman, Nicole Terry, Merle Dulien, and all the McGhee family. All the while, they continued to send me supportive and loving communications.

I would also like to thank my spiritual teachers, John Roger and John Morton, who inspire me to be present, live in my heart, and remember what's truly important in life.

I'm most appreciative of all my clients who have been, and still are, the feeding ground for all of my learning. They continue to be the inspiration for the changes we're making as a company. Special thanks go to Rich Kaplan for suggesting I write this book, to Steve Sagman at Studioserv for his editing expertise, and to Alex Blanton, who calmly and patiently guided me through the process of publishing a book.

God bless all those who have contributed to this book. It's the result of a journey with many amazing experiences, shared with many extraordinary people.

Introduction

How many times in the last five years have you told yourself, "This year, I'm going to get more organized and improve my work/life balance?"

Perhaps you went to your office for the weekend and cleaned off your desk, cleared out your e-mails, filed papers, and even threw things away. It was a great start to your year! However, three months later, or maybe three days later, you noticed yourself relapsing. Your e-mail had begun mounting up, papers were collecting on your desk, and Post It notes were stuck all over your screen. Maybe you've been through this several times, like dieting, trying this program or that, but never finding anything that worked.

Then, you tried listening to a friend's advice about a great, new Microsoft Outlook feature—Adding tasks to the Task list—and you found it useful. But after a few months, you noticed that you'd stopped reviewing the Task list and it was getting bigger and bigger, and things weren't getting completed. You felt overwhelmed, and you couldn't bear to look at the list anymore.

Maybe you bought a Palm Pilot, a Pocket PC, or a sexy little device that promised to make your life easier. Perhaps this was helpful or perhaps your life got more complicated because you couldn't figure out how to use it. Now it's on the credenza, collecting dust! And a few of you still haven't taken it out of the packaging! The thought of going digital can be exhausting, and who has the time, anyway?

Then, there are those of you with anywhere from 200 to 4,000 e-mail messages in your Inbox! I'm not kidding! Some of you (and you know who you are) have that much e-mail. You'd be surprised how organized a person can be with that many e-mails! However, having that many messages does hold a high level of distraction that nags away at you, and it's also an energy drain. Let's put it this way, do you go into the office in the morning and say "Yippee! I just can't wait to open my e-mail?" Most of you are not chomping at the bit to see what's "new and exciting" in your Inbox. I've heard clients say, "I've haven't seen white space in my Inbox since I joined the company. My first day was the last day it was empty!"

Just stop for a moment, pause, and imagine one central system that synchronizes with your Pocket PC and organizes information that you can easily access whenever you need it. You'd have no reminders clogging your head, no e-mails, no voice mails, and everything in one system, at your fingertips, 24/7. Your personal and business life integrated and balanced. Seems impossible? Absolutely not. That's why I wrote this book.

It takes a combination of three simple ingredients: From you, a willingness to observe what you're doing and make behavior changes; from McGhee Productivity Solutions, methods and models that work; and from Microsoft, the best tool there is to organize information, Microsoft Outlook. When you combine these ingredients you can create an Integrated Management System that will help you increase your productivity and work/life balance.

If you bought this book, you've already demonstrated your willingness to change. What comes before change is awareness. When you start to notice what you're doing, you can begin to evaluate what you need to do that's different to get the results you want.

For example, it's Monday, and Mary is sitting at her desk with her soy latte, working on a budget report. Her e-mail dings, and Mary stops what she's doing to look at her mail. She scans the first two or three sentences, but isn't sure what the sender wants. Befuddled, Mary doesn't have the time to figure it out, so she closes the message, and it joins the other 327 e-mails waiting in her Inbox. She turns to continue with the budget report, and there goes the ding again! An urgent request comes in. Mary stops to handle it. In the middle of that fire drill, one of Mary's team members pops her head around the door and asks, "Got a minute?" Mary thinks, "No, I haven't got a minute!" but answers, "Well, I suppose I have a minute." Fifteen minutes later, Mary and her team member are still in her office, Mary's e-mail is still dinging, the fire drill is still pending, and her budget report is due in fifteen minutes.

Mary tries hard to take care of everyone, but in the end, she didn't get her budget report done, and no one was taken care of. Much like Mary, all of you want to make a difference and care deeply for the people at home and at work. However, when you take care of everyone else your work will suffer and, ultimately, you're going to disappoint the people around you, not to mention yourself.

To solve this problem, Mary needs to reset the expectations of her team, enabling her to get more done during the day, and honor her commitments. However, for this situation to change, Mary has to be willing to do something differently.

"If you always do what you've always done, you'll always get what you've always got."
—Unknown Author

The second ingredient is the McGhee Productivity Solutions models and protocols which address common situations that clients have, such as "I've got too much information coming at me too fast," "My e-mail is out of control," "I need to find a way to track delegated items more effectively," "It's taking me too long to file and find things," "I'm getting too many interruptions and tasks are slipping through the cracks," "I'm not using technology effectively," and "I need a better work/life balance."

Our methods consist of either a series of steps for you to follow or a series of questions to ask that will help you solve your productivity challenges. All of our solutions can be implemented immediately, and they relate to real-time circumstances that you're experiencing today.

We use "results surveys" to evaluate our clients' before-and-after progress. This enables us to measure if the education we're providing is creating meaningful change. Employees complete a survey before a work team implements one of our integrated productivity programs, and they fill it out again one month after we finish the project.

As an example, I recently worked with the CIO of a bank and his entire staff. Eight months after we finished working with the department, we completed a results survey. The amount of e-mail in employees' Inboxes dropped by 80 percent, the time it took to find and file information dropped by 61 percent, and interruptions dropped by 40 percent. This demonstrates that productivity education combined with willingness to change and Microsoft Outlook produces extraordinary results.

The third ingredient in our trilogy is the use of Microsoft Outlook. We weren't taught to use Outlook as a productivity tool. If we had training at all, we learned specific features and benefits. Similarly, if I gave you a bag of coffee beans, a grinder, an espresso machine, boiling water, soy milk, and caramel flavor, what would you do with these if you didn't know how to make coffee? They are all individual ingredients. The question is, how do you put them together to make a great soy latte?

Microsoft Outlook has many individual features and benefits, but knowing how to put them together to increase productivity is an important tool that we teach. In this book, you'll learn simple methods and processes that you can combine with Microsoft Outlook to increase your performance and quality of life.

I've chosen Microsoft Outlook because I sincerely believe that it's the most effective productivity tool for individuals and teams today. Whether you're working at home or in an office, whether you're a busy housewife or a college student, Outlook can be customized to work for you. Even if you consider yourself an Outlook power user, I guarantee that before the end of this book, you'll learn better ways of using the technology.

I've been a productivity consultant for more than 24 years, and my clients have been my greatest teachers. I've coached and trained hundreds of thousands of people in corporate environments all over the world and had the privilege of working with some of America's top corporate leaders. I've tested the processes and methods described in this book at many different levels and with many different industries. And I've consistently refined our content to better serve our customers. Throughout the text, I'll refer to these client experiences to give you real-life examples that you can relate to.

I want you to jump into this book, test the processes and methods for yourself, and learn how they'll work for you. Don't believe me; believe your own experience. I guarantee that you'll get value from these techniques and you'll be surprised at how easy it is to become productive.

Who This Book Is For

Those of you reading this book will fall into three categories:

- You're struggling to get more organized, to make your life easier, and be more productive.
- You're fairly organized, but you've fallen off the wagon and need help getting back on!
- You love to be productive and want to improve your skills and techniques.

How to Use This Book

All of us want quick solutions that we can implement right away. We don't want to read the instruction manual. We want to use the tool now, now, now.

This book is designed for immediate results, but it's important to set the stage so you understand the kind of changes that you'll need to make to maintain results over time. Increasing productivity and quality of life involves changing habits, which doesn't happen instantly.

Be sure, to read the first two chapters in Part 1, "Laying the Foundation," before you jump into the following chapters. This will help your understand how to build your Integrated Management System to maintain change over the course of your life.

However, if you just can't wait to get going, you can head straight to Chapter 3, "The Three Phases for Creating an Integrated Management System." Make sure you have Microsoft Outlook running on a computer next to you so you can start implementing these solutions right away!

You'll be able to read this book over and over and learn new pieces. It'll be a permanent reference book for increasing your productivity in the electronic age. But it won't be possible for you to integrate everything in this book in one sitting. As you master one area, you'll want to go back and review another skill, so you can keep fine tuning what you're doing.

Have fun reading the book, and don't be afraid to spill your coffee or tea on it! We much prefer a hot beverage than dust! That just says it's been used and used well.

The Step by Step Quick Reference section on page xxiii is excerpted from *Microsoft Office Outlook 2003 Step by Step*, by Online Training Solutions, Inc. (Microsoft Press, 2003). For more detailed information on using Outlook, please refer to this Step by Step book or *Microsoft Office Outlook 2003 Inside Out* by Jim Boyce (Microsoft Press, 2003).

Step by Step Quick Reference

Working with Outlook

To toggle AutoPreview on and off
- On the View menu, click AutoPreview.

To view the contents of a message in the Reading Pane
- With the Reading Pane visible, in the Inbox or other message folder, click the message you want to view.

To display the Reading Pane
- On the View menu, click Reading Pane and then Right or Bottom.

To hide the Reading Pane
- On the View menu, click Reading Pane and then Off.

To open a message
- In the Inbox or other message folder, double-click the message you want to open.

To open an attachment
1. Open the message containing the attachment.
2. In the message header or body, double-click the attachment.

To open an attachment without opening the message
1. With the Reading Pane visible, click the message containing the attachment.
2. In the Reading Pane, double-click the attachment.

To reply to the sender of a message
- With the message you want to reply to selected or open, on the toolbar, click the Reply button.

To reply to the sender and all recipients of a message
- With the message you want to reply to selected or open, on the toolbar, click the Reply to All button.

To forward a message
- With the message you want to forward selected or open, on the toolbar, click the Forward button.

To create a new message from the Inbox
- On the toolbar, click the New Mail Message button.

To create a new message from any Outlook folder
1. Click the down arrow to the right of the New button.
2. On the drop-down menu, click Mail Message.

To display the All Mail Folders list
● On the Navigation Pane, click the Mail icon.

To address a message
● Type the recipient's e-mail address in the To box, or click the To button and select a name from the Address Book.

To send a message
1. Compose and address the e-mail message you want to send.
2. On the message form's toolbar, click the Send button.

To add an entry to the Address Book
1. On the Tools menu, click Address Book.
2. Click the New Entry button.
3. In the New Entry dialog box, click New Contact.
4. In the Put this entry drop-down list, click the address book to which you want to add the contact, and then click OK.
5. In the Untitled – Contact dialog box, type the information you want to save for this contact, and then click Save and Close.

To create a distribution list
1. On the Tools menu, click Address Book.
2. Click the New Entry button.
3. In the New Entry dialog box, click New Distribution List.
4. In the Put this entry drop-down list, click the address book to which you want to add the distribution list, and then click OK.
5. In the Untitled – Distribution List dialog box, in the Name box, type the name of the distribution list.
6. To add distribution list members from an existing address book, click the Select Members button. In the Select Members dialog box, select the contacts you want to add to the distribution list, and then click OK.
7. To add new distribution list members, click the Add New button. In the Add New Member dialog box, type the display name and e-mail address of the new contact, select the Add to Contacts check box if you want, and then click OK.
8. Click Save and Close.

To attach a file to a message

1. With the message open, on the toolbar, click the Insert File button.

2. In the Insert File dialog box, browse to the file you want to attach, click the file, and then click the Insert button.

To check for new messages

- On the toolbar, click the Send/Receive button.

To delete a message

1. Select the message.

2. On the toolbar, click the Delete button.

To print a message

1. Select or open the message you want to print.

2. On the toolbar, click the Print button.

To turn on smart tags for instant messaging

1. On the Tools menu, click Options.

2. In the Options dialog box, click the Other tab.

3. In the Person Names area, select the Enable the Person Names Smart Tag and Display Messenger Status in the From field check boxes.

4. Click OK.

To send an instant message from an e-mail message

1. Open a message to or from your instant messaging contact.

2. In the message header, click the Person Names Smart Tag next to the contact's name, and then on the shortcut menu click Send Instant Message.

Managing E-Mail Messages

To select the message format

- On the Message form's toolbar, click the down arrow to the right of the Message format box, and click HTML, Rich Text, or Plain Text.

To format messages by using stationery

1. On the Tools menu, click Options.

2. In the Options dialog box, click the Mail Format tab.

3. In the Use this stationery by default list, select the stationery you want.

4. Click OK.

To customize message stationery

1. On the Tools menu, click Options.

2. In the Options dialog box, click the Mail Format tab.

3. Click the Stationery Picker button.

4. In the Stationery Picker dialog box, click the stationery you want to customize, and then click the Edit button.

5. Apply the formatting you want, and click OK in each of the open dialog boxes.

To format a message using a theme

1. Compose a new e-mail message.

2. With the insertion point in the message body, on the Format menu, click Theme.

3. In the Theme dialog box, click the theme you want.

4. Select the Vivid Colors, Active Graphics, and/or Background Image check boxes if you want.

5. Click OK.

To respond to voting buttons in a message

1. Preview the message in the Reading Pane or open the message.

2. Click the Infobar, click the voting option you want, and then click OK.

To set message delivery options

1. Compose a new e-mail message.

2. On the Message form's toolbar, click the Options button.

3. In the Delivery options area of the Message Options dialog box, select the check boxes for the options you want.

4. Click Close.

To set the importance of a message

1. Compose a new e-mail message.

2. On the Message form's toolbar, click the Options button.

3. In the Message settings area of the Message Options dialog box, click the down arrow to the right of the Importance box, and then click Low, Normal, or High.

4. Click Close.

To sort messages

● Click the heading of the column by which you'd like to sort messages.

To group messages

- On the View menu, point to Arrange By, and then click the field by which you'd like to group messages.

To turn off message grouping

- On the View menu, point to Arrange By, and then click Show in Groups.

To change the message view

- On the View menu, point to Arrange By, point to Current View, and then click the view you want.

To customize the message view

1. On the View menu, point to Arrange By, point to Current View, and then click Customize Current View.

2. In the Customize View dialog box, click the button of the element you want to customize.

3. In the resulting dialog box, make the changes you want, and then click OK.

4. Repeat Steps 2 and 3 for each element you want to change.

5. Click OK to close the Customize View dialog box and save your changes.

To color-code messages

1. On the Tools menu, click Organize.

2. In the Ways to Organize pane, click Using Colors.

3. Select the type of messages you want to color-code and the color you want them to be, and then click the Apply Color button.

To create a message signature

1. On the Tools menu, click Options.

2. In the Options dialog box, click the Mail Format tab.

3. In the Select the signatures to use with the following account list, click an account, click the Signatures button, and then click the New button.

4. In the Create New Signature dialog box, type the name of your signature, and then click the Next button.

5. In the Signature Text box, type and style your signature, and then click Finish.

6. Click OK to close the Options dialog box.

To flag a message with the default flag color

- In your Inbox, click the message's Flag Status icon.

To flag a message with a flag color other than the default

1. In your Inbox, right-click the message's Flag Status icon, and then click Add Reminder.

2. In the Flag for Follow Up dialog box, in the Flag color list, click a color.

3. Click OK.

To mark a flagged message as complete

● In your Inbox, click the message's Flag Status icon.

To view all your flagged messages

● In the Favorite Folders list, click For Follow Up.

To flag a message you are composing

1. On the message window's toolbar, click the Message Flag button.

2. In the Flag for Follow Up dialog box, in the Flag To list click a label.

3. In the Due by lists, click a date and a time.

4. In the Flag color list, click a color.

5. Click OK.

Finding and Organizing E-Mail Messages

To find messages

1. On the toolbar, click the Find button.

2. In the Look for box in the Find pane, type a word you know is in the message you are looking for.

3. Click the Find Now button.

To assign a message to a category

1. Select the message, and on the Edit menu, click Categories.

2. In the Item(s) belong to these categories box, type the name of a new category, or, in the Available Categories list, select the appropriate category for the message.

3. Click OK.

To create a Search Folder from a template

1. On the File menu, point to New, and then click Search Folder.

2. In the Select a Search Folder list, click a template.

3. If a Choose button appears in the Customize Search Folder area, click it, specify the criteria to use, and then click OK.

4. Click OK to close the New Search Folder dialog box.

To rename a Search Folder

1. In the Navigation Pane, right-click the folder, and then click Rename on the shortcut menu.

2. Type the new name, and then press Enter.

To create a custom Search Folder

1. On the File menu, point to New, and then click Search Folder.

2. In the Select a Search Folder list, click Create a custom Search Folder.

3. In the Customize Search Folder area, click Choose.

4. In the Name box, type a name for the Search Folder.

5. Click the Criteria button, specify the search criteria, and then click OK.

6. Click OK in each of the open dialog boxes.

To create a view to filter messages

1. On the View menu, point to Arrange By, point to Current View, and then click Define Views.

2. In the Custom View Organizer dialog box, click New.

3. In the Create a New View dialog box, type the name of the new view, select the type of view, select the folders on which the view can be used, and then click OK.

4. In the Customize View dialog box, click the button of the element you want to customize.

5. In the resulting dialog box, make the changes you want, and then click OK.

6. Repeat Steps 4 and 5 for each element you want to change.

7. Click OK to close the Customize View dialog box and save your changes.

8. Click Apply View, and then click Close.

To create a rule to filter messages

1. On the Tools menu, click Rules and Alerts.

2. In the Rules and Alerts dialog box, click New Rule.

3. In the Rules Wizard, follow the instructions to create the new rule.

4. When you are done, click Finish, and then click OK.

To filter junk or adult content messages

1. On the Actions menu, point to Junk E-mail, and then click Junk E-mail Options.

2. Select a level of protection, and then click OK.

To create a folder

1. On the File menu, point to New, and then click Folder.
2. In the Create New Folder dialog box, in the Name box, type the name of the folder.
3. In the Folder contains list, click the kind of items you want to store in the folder.
4. In the Select where to place the folder list, click the mailbox or folder in which you want to create the new folder.
5. Click OK.

To move a message to a folder

1. Right-click the message, and on the shortcut menu, click Move to Folder.
2. In the Move Items dialog box, click the folder to which you want to move the message, and then click OK.

To move a folder

- In the Folder List, drag the folder to the location you want.

To rename a folder

1. In the Folder List, right-click the folder, and click Rename.
2. Type the new folder name, and then press Enter.

To delete a folder

1. In the Folder List, click the folder you want to delete.
2. On the toolbar, click the Delete button.

To share a folder

1. In the Folder List, right-click the folder, and on the shortcut menu, click Sharing.
2. Click the Add button.
3. Select the person with whom you want to share your folder, and then click OK.
4. Click Apply, and then click OK.

To make someone a delegate

1. On the Tools menu, click Options.
2. On the Delegates tab, click Add.
3. In the Type Name or Select from List box, select the person you want to make a delegate, and click OK.
4. In the Delegate Permissions dialog box, select the permissions you want to grant the delegate, and then click OK.
5. Click OK to close the Options dialog box.

To save a message as an HTML file

1. Select the message, and on the File menu, click Save As.

2. In the Save As dialog box, browse to the location where you want to save the file.

3. In the Save as type drop-down list, click HTML.

4. Click the Save button.

To save a message as a text file

1. Select the message, and on the File menu, click Save As.

2. In the Save As dialog box, browse to the location where you want to save the file.

3. In the Save as type drop-down list, click Text Only.

4. Click the Save button.

To specify global archive settings

1. On the Tools menu, click Options.

2. In the Options dialog box, click the Other tab, and then click the AutoArchive button.

3. In the AutoArchive dialog box, choose the global archive settings you want, and click OK to close each of the open the dialog boxes.

To specify archive settings for a folder

1. In the Folder List, click the folder you want to archive.

2. On the File menu, point to Folder, and then click Properties.

3. In the Properties dialog box, click the AutoArchive tab.

4. Select the settings with which you want to archive the folder, and click OK.

Managing Your Calendar

To view your schedule for a specific date

- In the Date Navigator, scroll to and click the date you want to view.

To select a calendar view

- On the View menu, point to Arrange By, point to Current View, and then click the view you want.

To schedule an appointment

1. In the Calendar, double-click the time slot during which you want to schedule the appointment.

2. In the Appointment form, enter the relevant information about the appointment, and click the Save and Close button.

To schedule a recurring appointment

1. In the Calendar, double-click the time slot during which you want to schedule the first occurrence of the recurring appointment.

2. In the Appointment form, enter the relevant information about the appointment, and then click the Recurrence button.

3. In the Appointment Recurrence dialog box, enter the recurrence settings you want and then click OK.

4. Click the Save and Close button.

To schedule an event

1. In the Calendar, right-click the day on which you want to schedule the event, and click New All Day Event on the shortcut menu.

2. In the Event form, enter the relevant information about the event, and click the Save and Close button.

To assign a category to an appointment

1. At the bottom of the Appointment form, click the Categories button.

2. In the Categories dialog box, select the category, and then click OK.

To move an appointment

● In the Calendar, drag the appointment to the new time or date.

To copy an appointment

1. Right-click and drag the appointment to the new time or date.

2. On the shortcut menu that appears, click Copy.

To delete an appointment

1. Click the appointment you want to delete.

2. On the toolbar, click the Delete button.

To create a calendar folder

1. On the File menu, point to New, and then click Folder.

2. In the Name box, type the name of the new calendar.

3. In the Folder contains list, click Calendar Items.

4. In the Select where to place the folder list, click the folder under which you want to create the new calendar.

5. Click OK.

To view multiple calendars

1. Make sure the Calendar is displayed.

2. In the My Calendars area of the Navigation Pane, select the check boxes for the calendars you want to view.

To view your schedule for the work week

1. Make sure the Calendar is displayed.

2. On the toolbar, click the Work Week button.

To view your schedule for a full week

1. Make sure the Calendar is displayed.

2. On the toolbar, click the Week button.

To view your schedule for a month

1. Make sure the Calendar is displayed.

2. On the toolbar, click the Month button.

To change your work week

1. On the Tools menu, click Options.

2. On the Preferences tab of the Options dialog box, click the Calendar Options button.

3. In the Calendar work week area of the Calendar Options dialog box, select the check boxes for your work days.

4. Click OK in each of the open dialog boxes.

To change your time zone

1. On the Tools menu, click Options.

2. On the Preferences tab of the Options dialog box, click the Calendar Options button.

3. In the Calendar Options dialog box, click the Time Zone button.

4. In the Time Zone dialog box, click the time zone you want, and then click OK in each of the open dialog boxes.

To manually label an appointment

1. Double-click the appointment.

2. In the Appointment form, click the down arrow to the right of the Label box, and then click a label.

3. Click Save and Close.

To label appointments with color

1. On the toolbar, click the Calendar Coloring button, and then click Edit Labels.

2. In the Edit Calendar Labels dialog box, select the label you want to edit and rename it as you like.

To print your calendar

1. Make sure the Calendar is displayed, but no appointment is open.

2. On the toolbar, click the Print button.

3. In the Print dialog box, select a print style, and click the Print button.

Scheduling and Managing Meetings

To plan a meeting

1. On the Actions menu, click Plan a Meeting.

2. In the Plan a Meeting dialog box, click the Add Others button and then click Add from Address Book.

3. In the Select Attendees and Resources dialog box, select the Required and Optional attendees and the Resources, and then click OK.

4. In the Free/Busy area, drag the red and green bars to set the meeting time, and then click the Make Meeting button.

5. In the resulting meeting form, complete any additional information, and then click Send.

To set or remove a reminder

1. In the meeting form, select or clear the Reminder check box.

2. If setting a reminder, select the amount of time before the meeting that you want to be reminded.

3. Close the meeting form and save your changes.

To schedule an online meeting

1. On the toolbar, click the down arrow to the right of the New button, and then click Meeting Request.

2. On the Meeting form, select the This is an online meeting using check box.

3. Complete the remaining meeting information, and then click Send.

To accept a meeting request

1. In the open meeting request or in the Reading Pane, click Accept.

2. Choose whether to edit and send a response, and then click OK.

To decline a meeting request

1. In the open meeting request or in the Reading Pane, click Decline.

2. Choose whether to edit and send a response, and then click OK.

To propose a new meeting time

1. In the open meeting request or in the Reading Pane, click the Propose New Time button.

2. In the Free/Busy area, select the preferred time, and click the Propose Time button.

To automatically respond to meeting requests

1. On the Tools menu, click Options.

2. On the Preferences tab of the Options dialog box, click the Calendar Options button.

3. In the Calendar Options dialog box, click the Resource Scheduling button.

4. In the Resource Scheduling dialog box, select the check boxes for the automatic response options you want, and then click OK in the open dialog boxes.

To reschedule a meeting

1. Open the meeting, and click the Scheduling tab.

2. In the Free/Busy area, select new start and end dates and times.

3. Click the Send Update button.

To invite others to a meeting

1. In the meeting form, click the Scheduling tab, and then click the Add Others button.

2. Click the contacts you want to add, click the Required or Optional button, and then click OK.

To cancel a meeting

1. Open the meeting, and on the Actions menu, click Cancel Meeting.

2. Choose whether to send a cancellation notice to the attendees, and then click OK.

To create a group schedule

1. Make sure the Calendar is displayed.

2. On the toolbar, click the View Group Schedules button.

3. In the View Group Schedules dialog box, click the New button.

4. In the Create New Group Schedule dialog box, type a name for the group schedule, and then click OK.

5. Add the group members you want, and then click Save and Close.

To open another person's calendar directly

1. On the File menu, point to Open, and click Other User's Folder.

2. Click the Name button, click the name of the person whose folder you want to open, and then click OK.

3. Make sure Calendar appears in the Folder box, and then click OK.

To save your Calendar as a Web page

1. On the File menu, click Save as Web Page.

2. In the Duration area, enter the start and end dates for which you want to save the calendar.

3. In the File Name box, type the name and path with which you want to save the Web page.

4. Click Save.

To start using the Microsoft Office Internet Free/Busy Service

1. On the Tools menu, click Options.

2. In the Calendar area of the Preferences tab, click the Calendar Options button.

3. In the Advanced options area of the Calendar Options dialog box, click the Free/Busy Options button.

4. In the Free/Busy Options dialog box, select the Publish and search using Microsoft Office Internet Free/Busy Service check box.

5. Click OK in the open dialog boxes.

To publish your schedule to an intranet location

1. On the Tools menu, click Options.

2. In the Options dialog box, click the Calendar Options button.

3. In the Calendar Options dialog box, click the Free/Busy Options button.

4. In the Free/Busy Options dialog box, select the Publish at my location check box, and type the name of the server where your free/busy information should be stored.

5. Click in the Search Location box and type the name of the server.

6. Click OK in the open dialog boxes.

To publish your free and busy times

1. On the Tools menu, click Options.

2. In the Calendar area of the Options dialog box, click the Calendar Options button.

3. In the Advanced options area of the Calendar Options dialog box, click the Free/Busy Options button.

4. Select the Publish at my location check box, and in the Publish at my location box, type the server location and file name.

5. Close each of the open dialog boxes.

6. On the Tools menu, point to Send/Receive, and then click Free/Busy Information to publish your free/busy information to your server.

7. To view your published free/busy information, open your Web browser, and in the Address box, type the URL of the file on the server.

Creating and Organizing a List of Contacts

To create a contact entry from the Contacts folder

- On the toolbar, click the New Contact button.

To create a contact entry from any Outlook folder

1. Click the down arrow to the right of the New button.

2. On the drop-down menu, click Contact.

To create multiple contacts from the same company

1. Open a contact entry from the company you want to duplicate.

2. On the Actions menu, click New Contact from Same Company.

To delete a contact entry

1. Click the contact you want to delete.

2. On the toolbar, click the Delete button.

To assign a category to a contact entry

1. Open the contact entry, and click the Categories button.

2. In the Available categories list of the Categories dialog box, select the category you want to assign to the contact entry, and then click OK.

To link an appointment or task to a contact entry

1. Open the appointment or task, and click the Contacts button.

2. In the Look in box of the Select Contacts dialog box, click the contact folder in which the contact entry you want is stored.

3. In the Items list, click the contact entry to which you want to link the appointment or task.

To flag a contact entry for follow up

1. Open the contact entry you want to flag.

2. On the contact form's toolbar, click the Follow Up button.

To send a vCard through e-mail

1. Open the contact entry you want to send.

2. On the Actions menu, click Forward as vCard.

3. Address the resulting e-mail message, and then click Send.

To print a contact entry

1. Open the contact entry you want to print.

2. On the File menu, click Print.

3. In the Print dialog box, select a print style, and click OK.

To import Windows SharePoint Services contact entries

1. In your Web browser, open the SharePoint contacts list.

2. Click Link to Outlook, and then click Yes.

Keeping Track of Information

To create a task from the Tasks folder

- On the toolbar, click the New Task button.

To create a task from any Outlook folder

1. Click the down arrow to the right of the New button.
2. On the drop-down menu, click Task.

To create a recurring task

1. Create a new task.
2. In the task form, click the Recurrence button.
3. In the Task Recurrence dialog box, set the recurrence options you want, and then click OK.

To set or remove a task reminder

1. In the Task form, select or clear the Reminder check box.
2. If setting a reminder, set the date and time you want the reminder to occur.
3. Click OK.

To modify task settings

1. On the Tools menu, click Options.
2. In the Options dialog box, click the Task Options button.
3. Set the task options you want, and then click OK in the open dialog boxes.

To assign a task to another person

1. Create a new task.
2. In the task form, click the Assign Task button.
3. In the To box, type the address of the person you want to assign the task to, and add any comments in the comments area.
4. Click the Send button.

To change your task view

- On the View menu, point to Arrange By, point to Current View, and click the view you want.

To sort Tasks

- Click the column heading by which you want to sort.

To assign a category to a task

1. Open the task, and click the Categories button.
2. In the Available categories list, select the check box for the category you want, and then click OK.

To view your tasks in the TaskPad

1. In the Navigation Pane, click the Calendar icon.

2. If you don't see the TaskPad, on the View menu, click TaskPad.

To accept a task request

1. Open the task request or preview it in the Reading Pane.

2. On the task form toolbar, click the Accept button.

To decline a task request

1. Open the task request or preview it in the Reading Pane.

2. On the task form toolbar, click the Decline button.

To send a status report on a task

1. Open the task.

2. On the toolbar, click the Send Status Report button.

3. In the message form, type a message if you want, and then click the Send button.

To mark a task as complete

1. Open the task.

2. On the toolbar, click the Mark Complete button.

To stop a task from recurring

1. Open the task, and click the Recurrence button.

2. In the Task Recurrence dialog box, click the Remove Recurrence button.

To delete a task

1. In the Tasks list, click the task you want to delete.

2. On the toolbar, click the Delete button.

To create a note from the Notes folder

1. On the toolbar, click the New Note button.

2. Type the note content.

3. Click the Close button to save the note.

To create a note from any Outlook folder

1. Click the down arrow to the right of the New button.

2. On the drop-down menu, click Note.

3. Type the note content.

4. Click the Close button to save the note.

To delete a note
1. In the Notes folder, select the note.
2. On the toolbar, click the Delete button.

To change your Note view
●   On the View menu, point to Arrange By, point to Current View, and click the view you want.

To assign a category to a note
1. Open the note, click the Note icon in the upper-left corner, and click Categories in the drop-down list.
2. Select the check box next to the category you want, and then click OK.
3. Close the note.

To forward a note
1. Open the note, click the Note icon in the upper-left corner, and click Forward in the drop-down list.
2. In the To box, type the address of the person to whom you will forward the note, and then click Send.

To link a note to a contact
1. Open the note, click the Note icon in the upper-left corner, and click Contacts in the drop-down list.
2. In the Contacts for Note dialog box, click the Contacts button.
3. In the Look in box of the Select Contacts dialog box, click the contacts folder where the contact entry to which you want to link the note is stored.
4. In the Items list, click the contact entry you want to link to the note.
5. Click OK, and then click Close.

Working from Multiple Locations

To set up a new Outlook account
1. Click the Start button, and then click Control Panel.
2. In Control Panel, double-click the Mail icon.
3. On the Server Type page, select the type of server to which you are connecting, and then click Next.
4. On the Internet E-mail Settings page, enter the user information for the account you're setting up, click Next, and then click Finish.
5. To set up a new e-mail account or change an existing account, click E-mail Accounts.

6. To change the location in which Outlook stores your data files, click Data Files.

7. To set up multiple user profiles or change an existing profile, click Show Profiles.

8. Click Close.

To set up a dial-up connection

1. On the Tools menu, click E-mail Accounts.

2. Select the View or change existing e-mail accounts option, and click Next.

3. Click your e-mail account, and then click the Change button.

4. Click the More Settings button.

5. In the dialog box that appears, click the Connection tab, and select the Connect using my phone line option.

6. In the Modem area, click the Add button.

7. On the Type of Connection page of the wizard, select the Dial-up to private network option, and click Next.

8. On the Phone Number to Dial page, type the phone number of your ISP in the Phone Number box.

9. If appropriate to your situation, select the smart card option you want, and then click Next.

10. In the Type a name you want for this connection box, type a meaningful name for the connection you are creating (for example, *Company Dial-Up Connection*), and click Finish.

11. In the Use the following Dial-up Networking connection list, click the connection you just created, and then click OK.

12. In the E-mail Accounts Wizard, click Next, and then click Finish.

To download messages

- On the toolbar, click the Send/Receive button.

To turn Cached Exchange Mode on or off

1. On the Tools menu, click E-mail Accounts.

2. Select the View or change existing e-mail accounts option, and click Next.

3. Click Microsoft Exchange Server, and then click the Change button.

4. Select the Use local copy of Mailbox check box.

To change the Cached Exchange Mode connection setting

1.   On the Tools menu, click E-mail Accounts.

2.   Select the View or change existing e-mail accounts option, and click Next.

3.   Click Microsoft Exchange Server, and then click the Change button.

4.   Click the More Settings button.

5.   In the Microsoft Exchange Server dialog box, click the Advanced tab, and select the option you want.

6.   Restart Outlook.

To create an offline folder

1.   On the Tools menu, click E-mail Accounts.

2.   Select the View or change existing e-mail accounts option, and click Next.

3.   Click your e-mail account, and then click the Change button.

4.   Click the More Settings button.

5.   Click the Advanced tab, and then click the Offline Folder File Settings button.

6.   Click the Disable Offline Use button, and then click Yes.

7.   Click the Offline Folder File Settings button again, and then click the Browse button.

8.   Click the down arrow to the right of the Look in box, and then navigate to the folder you want to use.

9.   Click OK. If Outlook prompts you to create the *outlook.ost* file, click Yes.

To switch between working online and offline

●   On the File menu, click Work Offline.

To synchronize an offline folder

1.   While working online, display the contents of the folder.

2.   On the Tools menu, point to Send/Receive, and click This Folder.

Customizing and Configuring Outlook

To create a desktop shortcut to a specific Outlook pane

1.   Right-click the Outlook program file (usually in *C:\Program Files\ Microsoft Office\Office2003*), and click Create Shortcut.

2.   Right-click the shortcut, and click Properties on the shortcut menu.

3.   In the Target box, type a space after the end of the path, type /select outlook:, type another space, and then type the name of a pane to which the shortcut will be directed.

To customize Outlook Today

1. On the Advanced toolbar, click the Outlook Today icon.

2. Click Customize Outlook Today.

To add a shortcut to the Shortcut pane

1. In the Navigation Pane, click the Shortcuts icon.

2. Click Add New Shortcut.

3. Click the folder for which you want to create a shortcut.

To display or hide a toolbar

● On the View menu, point to Toolbars, and then click the toolbar you want.

To set menu and toolbar options

1. On the Tools menu, click Customize.

2. On the Options tab, select the check boxes of the options you want, and then click Close.

To add a command to a toolbar or menu

1. On the Tools menu, click Customize.

2. Click the Commands tab.

3. In the Categories list, click the command's category.

4. In the Commands list, click the command, and drag it to the toolbar or menu.

To remove a custom command from a toolbar or menu

1. On the Tools menu, click Customize.

2. Drag the command off of the toolbar or menu.

To create a Personal Folder

1. On the File menu, point to New, and then click Outlook Data File.

2. Select Office Outlook Personal Folders File, and click OK.

3. Type a file name, and click OK.

4. Type a name for the folder, and click OK.

To create a Personal Address Book

1. On the Tools menu, click E-mail Accounts.

2. Select the Add a new directory or address book option, and click Next.

3. Select the Additional Address Books option, and click Next.

4. In the Additional Address Book Types list, click Personal Address Book, and then click Next.

5. Type the address or browse to the location where you want to add the new address book, and click the Open button.

To create a personal distribution list

1. On the Tools menu, click Address Book.

2. Click the down arrow to the right of the Show Names from the box, and click Personal Address Book.

3. On the toolbar, click the New Entry button.

4. In the Put this entry area, click the down arrow to the right of the In the box, and then click Personal Address Book.

5. In the Select the entry type list, click Personal Distribution List, and then click OK.

6. Type a name for the new distribution list, and click the Add/Remove Members button.

7. In the Show Names from the list, click Personal Address Book.

8. Hold down the Ctrl key, click the names of the contacts you want to add to the list, and then click the Members button.

To encrypt a message

1. On the message form's toolbar, click the Options button.

2. In the Security area, click the Security Settings button.

3. Select the Encrypt message contents and attachments check box.

To digitally sign a message

1. On the message form's toolbar, click the Options button.

2. In the Security area, click the Security Settings button.

3. Select the Add digital signature to this message check box.

To send an e-mail with restricted permissions

- On the message form's toolbar, click the Permission button.

To change the way Outlook handles external content

1. On the Tools menu, click Options.

2. In the Options dialog box, on the Security tab, click Change Automatic Download Settings.

3. In the Automatic Picture Download Settings dialog box, select the check boxes for the options you want.

4. Click OK in each of the open dialog boxes to save your settings.

To view the blocked content in an individual e-mail message:

1. In the message, click the InfoBar.

2. On the shortcut menu, click Show Blocked Content.

To set advanced e-mail options

1. On the Tools menu, click Options.

2. Click the E-mail Options button.

3. Click the Advanced E-mail Options button.

4. Set the options you want, and then click OK in the open dialog boxes.

To turn off desktop alerts

1. On the Tools menu, click Options.

2. On the Preferences tab, click the E-Mail Options button.

3. Click the Advanced E-mail Options button.

4. Clear the Display a New Mail Desktop Alert check box.

5. Click OK in the open dialog boxes.

To customize desktop alert settings

1. On the Tools menu, click Options.

2. On the Preferences tab, click the E-Mail Options button.

3. Click the Advanced E-mail Options button.

4. Click the Desktop Alert Settings button.

5. Change the settings as you want.

6. Click OK in the open dialog boxes.

To flag, delete, or mark a message as read by using a desktop alert

1. In the desktop alert, click the Options button.

2. Click Flag Item, Delete Item, or Mark as Read.

To manage Windows SharePoint Services alerts

1. On the Tools menu, click Rules and Alerts.

2. Click the Manage Alerts tab.

About the CD

The companion CD that ships with this book contains many tools and resources to help you get the most out of the book.

What's on the CD

The companion CD includes the following:

- Electronic version (eBook) of *Microsoft Office OneNote 2003 Step by Step*

- Links to Web resources, including online resources from Microsoft and Microsoft Office

- Links to Time Management Web Resources on the Microsoft Office Online site

Sample chapters from other books from Microsoft Press:

- *Laptops and Tablet PCs with Microsoft Windows XP Step by Step: Stay in Touch and Stay Productive–At Work, At Home, and On the Go!* (Chapter 4, "Using Your Mobile PC at Your Desk")

- *Beyond Bullet Points: Using Microsoft PowerPoint to Create Presentations that Inform, Motivate, and Inspire* (Chapter 2, "Setting the Stage for Your Story in Act 1")

- *Microsoft Small Business Kit* (Chapter 15, "The Outlook is Bright: E-Mail and Your Business")

- *Microsoft Office System Inside Out–2003 Edition* (Chapter 39, "Managing Contacts, Tasks, and Other Kinds of Information")

- *Microsoft Office System Step by Step–2003 eLearning Edition* (Chapter 20, "Managing Your Calendar")

- Microsoft eLearning Library Course Core Training for Microsoft Office Outlook 2003

Using the CD

To use this companion CD, insert it into your CD-ROM drive. If AutoRun is not enabled on your computer, run StartCD.exe in the root of the CD to display the starting menu. The menu provides you with links to resources that are available on the CD and a link to the Microsoft Learning Technical Support Web site.

Important If your computer is running Windows XP Service Pack 2, you will need to update the Microsoft eLearning Library product by following the instructions at *http://support.microsoft.com/default.aspx?scid=kb; en-us;883083*.

System Requirements

The following software is required to view the software and files on the CD:

- Pentium II PC, 400-megahertz (MHz) or equivalent
- 128 megabytes (MB) of RAM
- Super VGA display at 800 x 600 resolution with high color (16-bit/65K color)
- Microsoft Mouse or compatible pointing device
- Windows-compatible sound board and headphones or speakers (required for audio)
- Microsoft Windows 98 or later
- Microsoft Internet Explorer 5.01
- MSXML Parser 3.0
- Windows Script Host 5.6
- Macromedia Flash Player 6.0 or higher ActiveX control

Note Some of the documentation on this CD is provided in Portable Document Format (PDF). To view these files, you will need Adobe Acrobat or Adobe Reader. For more information about these products or to download the Adobe Reader, visit the Adobe Web site at *http://www.adobe.com*.

Support

Every effort has been made to ensure the accuracy of this book and the companion CD. Microsoft Press provides corrections for books and CDs through the Web at the following address:

http://www.microsoft.com/learning/support/

To connect directly to the Microsoft Press Knowledge Base and enter a query regarding a question or issue that you might have, go to

http://www.microsoft.com/learning/support/search.asp

If you have comments, questions, or ideas regarding this book or the companion CD, or if you have questions that are not answered by querying the Knowledge Base, please send them to Microsoft Press using one of the following methods:

E-mail:

mspinput@microsoft.com

Postal Mail:

Microsoft Press
Attn: Take Back Your Life Editor
One Microsoft Way
Redmond, WA 98052-6399

Please note that product support is not offered through the preceding mail addresses.

Note For the user's convenience, this CD might include third-party software or links to third-party sites. Please note that third-party software and links to third-party sites are not under the control of Microsoft Corporation. Microsoft is therefore not responsible for their content, nor should their inclusion on this CD be construed as an endorsement of the product or the site. Please check third-party Web sites for the latest version of their software.

Part One
Laying the Foundation

In this part

Chapter One

Change Your Approach, Change Your Results

Long before you can increase your productivity and quality of life, you'll want to learn about the misconceptions that hold you back, even before you start. These beliefs affect the way you think about productivity, and they dictate your attitude and approach, persuading you that you'll fail before you've begun! In this chapter, you'll learn all about these beliefs.

I've learned that if you don't change these limiting beliefs, the positive behavioral changes you make will never hold up. They'll crumble under your negative points of view.

My own, personal, limiting belief used to be, "I don't have the time to do all the things I want." I was convinced of this belief, and I clung to it righteously because it appeared to be true. I was stressed out and tired, my work suffered, and my family life and body suffered, too. Without realizing it, I was letting my own belief hold me hostage and force me to sacrifice the things I cared about most.

I'm sure you're aware that there are only 24 hours in a day. No matter how well you manage them, they won't become 25. Conversely, they won't become 23 if you mismanage them. However, the 24-hour day wasn't the reality that was operating in my head, and I managed my life from a to-do list. Each day, I decided what I was going to do. I imagined myself completing the list, and then started the marathon to get it all done. But the list never fit into my calendar. I broke agreements, got home late, and ran myself ragged. But "by George," I was going to get that list finished, even if I had to pull an "all-nighter."

I pretended I could do more than was possible, because I had no respect for the limits of the calendar. I ran over all the boundaries, thinking my to-do list was more important than anything else. I kept hearing myself say, "I don't have the time to do all the things I want," and I was determined to stick to that belief because it seemed so true. Talk about banging my head against a brick wall and wondering why I had a headache!

As I supported my clients to get a better grip on the reality, I began to do the same. I came to respect the calendar that millions of people worldwide use to manage their lives. I learned that there are only 24 hours in a day, and that I can only do what 24 hours will allow. After years of struggling against this limiting belief, my life began to turn around. I stopped breaking agreements. I fulfilled a life-long dream to buy a horse. I created unstructured quality weekends with my husband, and I reduced my work week to four days, only to see my business grow by 40 percent.

As a result, I'm more productive than ever before and my life is wonderfully balanced. And that's what I want to help you achieve.

Ten Beliefs that Limit Productivity

When I work with clients, the first question I ask them is, "What's stopping you from being more productive?" Here's a list of the ten most popular beliefs I hear from clients.

1. There's too much information coming at me too fast.
2. I get too many interruptions.
3. I don't have the discipline to be organized.
4. I have to keep everything.
5. I can't find what I need when I need it.
6. It takes too much time to get organized.
7. Organization cramps my freedom and creativity.
8. I'm no good with technology.
9. There's not enough time in the day.
10. I'm not organized by nature.

Take a moment and evaluate which of these statements rings most true for you. It's only when you can acknowledge these negative beliefs that you can set about changing them!

I still deal with the negative belief, "I don't have enough time to do all the things I want." However, I've learned this is just a point of view, so when it rears its ugly head I can respond to it differently. I tell myself, "I have all the time I need to do all the things I want." Therefore, I've gotten smarter about choosing what I want, and making sure it integrates with my calendar, and not the to-do list in my head. I tell myself, "I can do anything, but I can't do everything," so I've gotten better at deciding what's important to me and focusing on those activities first. These steps have taken discipline, but they've given me tremendous freedom and peace of mind.

Let's take a look at these beliefs one by one, and see how you can turn them around. This will be a critical step to supporting you in maintaining your Integrated Management System over time.

1. There's Too Much Information Coming at Me Too Fast

Belief   My e-mail is overwhelming me. I can't keep up with it.

Reality   The volume of e-mail isn't the issue. *How you process and organize the volume* is the issue. Learning how to use the "Four D's for Decision Making" will transform this belief.

Each year we receive more and more data from a growing array of devices, which can be accessed from an increasing number of locations. It's both exciting and overwhelming at the same time. If you're not careful, the quantity of data starts to drive you instead of the other way around. Remember, the whole idea here is for you to be in charge and take back your life.

Jeff Price, a VP at a mortgage company, talked to me the other day about how to handle his overwhelming volume of e-mail. In response to the question, "How many messages do you have in your Inbox?" he grimaced and rolled his eyes, "1500!" As I watched Jeff process and organize his e-mail, I noticed him opening messages and commenting to himself, "This doesn't make sense. I can't handle this right now. It's too complicated, and I'll look at it later." He then proceeded to close each one of these e-mails back into his Inbox! When you process and organize your e-mail this way, it doesn't take long to accumulate 1500 messages in your Inbox.

"The greatest revolution of our generation is the discovery that human beings, by changing the inner attitudes of their minds, can change the outer aspects of their lives."
—William James

In order for Jeff to process his e-mail more effectively, I taught him how to use the Four D's for Decision Making. This model helped Jeff make strategic decisions for each and every e-mail, enabling him to empty his Inbox. All Jeff needed was a little education about how to process and organize his e-mail more effectively.

I've found that individuals can reduce the quantity of e-mail stored in their Inboxes by as much as 81 percent using the Four D's of Decision Making. This is a powerful model that will help you successfully manage your e-mail.

2. I Get Too Many Interruptions

Belief   I can't get work done during the day because I get too many interruptions.

Reality   It is possible to reduce the number of interruptions you receive and get your "real work" done during the day. The solution is to implement personal boundaries that allow you and your staff to create scheduled, uninterrupted work time.

Small things done consistently in strategic places create major impact.

We all get interruptions throughout the day, but are all of them completely necessary?

Ben Smith, a Financial Manager, is working on an Excel spreadsheet in his office. Kathie Flood, a team member, walks in to ask a question about the company's health policy. Ben stops what he's doing and goes to an intranet site to answer her question. When Kathie leaves, he returns to his Excel spreadsheet to find his place and start over. Joel, another team member, pops his head around the door and says, "Got a minute?" "Sure," Ben replies and leaves his spreadsheet once again. By the time Joel leaves, Ben has lost 30 minutes and now has to head off to a meeting, postponing work on the spreadsheet until an evening or weekend.

Because Ben consistently allowed these interruptions, he actually trained his staff that it was OK to disturb him. Some of these interruptions were necessary, but not all of them were, and unfortunately they had become a habit for his team.

The solution was for Ben to meet with his staff and create new expectations and ask for their help in supporting him. Ben called a meeting and let them know he wanted to get more uninterrupted work done during the day. He explained that he'd set up a recurring two-hour "work time" appointment on his calendar, and during that time he wanted them to avoid interrupting him or booking other meetings. Ben was pleased at how respectful and supportive his staff were to this request. They understood his predicament and wanted to support him in making positive changes.

As a result of creating and reinforcing boundaries, our statistics show that you can reduce your time dealing with interruptions by as much as 61 percent, allowing you to get more of your work done during the day

3. I Don't Have the Discipline to Be Organized

Belief   I'm not a disciplined person so I'll never be able to make a system work.

Reality   Discipline is a skill that you already possess; you demonstrate it every day. The key to discipline is creating the appropriate motivation to make the specific changes you want. This enthusiasm then drives you to be disciplined.

You will be setting up an Integrated Management System later in this book, which will help you improve your productivity and quality of life. This system requires discipline to maintain, so being motivated is an important and necessary step for your success.

There are two kinds of motivation, negative and positive. Both work equally well, but they're quite different. Negative motivation starts when you're sick and tired and tired and sick of an area in your life. Maybe you're fed up with doing e-mail in the evenings, frustrated listening to your to-do's rattling around your head, and weary of working long hours. This kind of negative energy can be a compelling driver for change.

The other type of motivation is positive and will require some digging on your part. Ask yourself the question, "Why do I want to improve my productivity and work/life balance? What is the benefit to me?" When you answer these questions, keep asking yourself "Why?" until you find the underlying motivation. You'll know when you've found it because you'll feel more inspired to make changes. When you discover that core desire, nothing will stop you from getting what you want.

When you start to use Microsoft Outlook in a more disciplined way, you'll find remarkable freedom. You'll create quality time at home, reduce your e-mails, honor your agreements, and feel more relaxed and in control.

4. I Have to Keep Everything

Belief   I have to keep everything. You just never know when you might
need it!

Reality   Okay, prepare yourself. On average, the clients we work with throw
away 50 percent of their stored information, with no ramifications.
They feel lighter, happier, and have more time.

Our clients invest huge sums of energy filing and finding data. Of course,
some of this filing is entirely appropriate, *but* we've discovered that a large
proportion of it isn't. So if you're a "keeper," and you know who you are,
hold on to your hats!

You "keepers" are a proud and experienced breed! There's nothing quite
like laying your hands on a file that no one else can find. It justifies all of
your filing and keeping efforts. Every department has a keeper who
retrieves critical documents no one else can find. You probably know who
the keeper is in your department!

Keepers learned to be keepers. At some point in their lives they made a
decision to hang on to information, and they've have been hanging on to it
ever since. If you're a keeper, you might recognize yourself in one of these
statements:

- I got badly burned when I couldn't lay my hands on an important
document. Now, I'm afraid to let go of information.

- I want to be able to justify the decisions I make, so I keep everything.

- If my system crashes, I want backup information.

- I felt so good when no one else could find "that document." As a
result, I decided to keep everything so I could continue being useful.

At some point, you made a decision about keeping, and that decision has
been driving you ever since. These decisions are very powerful, but they
may not be appropriate in your current situation.

For example, I worked with a doctor who needed help with the paperwork
in his office. I asked him if there were any other areas we needed to clean up
while I was there. He said, "Yes," and promptly showed me a room that
looked like a storage closet and was full of boxes. He said, "That was my old
office, and when it got filled up, I moved into another one!" I must say I was

a little surprised and realized this was a bigger project than I thought! He told me, "I'm a doctor and I might need this information to save someone's life." It was a powerful justification. The only problem was that he stopped being able to find anything a long time ago!

We ordered a dumpster and spent two days getting rid of 80 percent of his papers. After we finished working together, he said to me, "You know, when I first started, I was scared I wouldn't be a good doctor, so I kept all of this information to help me feel more confident. Now I know I'm a good doctor, and I don't need all of it any more!" I will always remember this man because it took a great deal of courage for him to let go of all those papers he'd been holding on to for so many years.

I don't know your reasons for being a keeper, but it's worth taking a long hard look to determine whether they still apply today, and whether they still serve you.

The truth is, most people use only 15 percent of what they file, and this makes the other 85 percent ineffective. By clarifying what is useful and letting go of the rest, you can reduce your filing and save valuable time and energy that you can direct to more meaningful tasks.

5. It Takes Too Much Time to Get Productive

Belief   I don't have the time to set up a system. I've got too much to do.

Reality   You can save one to two hours a day using an Integrated Management System, so there's no justification for not making the time.

Here are some interesting statistics: On average, customers spend two to three hours a day working in e-mail and 60 minutes a day finding and filing information. After setting up an Integrated Management System, they spend one to two hours a day working in e-mail and 10 minutes a day finding and filing information. That's a savings of one hour and 50 minutes a day, which is almost 12 weeks a year! These time savings are nothing short of extraordinary.

Now multiple those savings by the number of people in your team, and then expand that to the number of people in your organization. That will really take your breath away! The bottom line is: You can't afford not to create an effective Integrated Management System.

Take a moment and consider the time you spend

- Finding and filing information.

- Writing a to-do list, and then rewriting it a week later on another list, and then another.

- Opening e-mail, reading the message, closing the e-mail and then coming back to the same e-mail to read it again tomorrow!

- Going to the store to pick up something like dog food, only to arrive at the store and forget the brand name.

- Finding yourself at the office and in need of the proposal for a meeting but having left it at home.

- Needing to read the *Leadership and Self-Deception* book at home, only to find that you left it at the office.

- Arriving at a meeting to find that you don't have the notes you need.

- Walking out of a meeting and remembering a critical point you needed to raise during the meeting! Too late now!

These are just a few examples of how we waste time by not having an Integrated Management System to help us remember what, where, and when.

Take the time to set up your system. You're worth it, and you can't afford not to.

6. I Can't Find What I Need When I Need It

Belief   I waste too much time finding and filing stuff. It's frustrating.

Reality   Setting up a Reference System is a skill that anyone can learn, and it's a skill that can save you 50 minutes a day.

There are so many places to store information today that it's easy to fall into the trap of wanting to use all the tools at your disposal. You may be storing information in multiple and duplicate locations, such as Personal Folders, Inbox, My Documents, Archive folders, Sent Items, or Offline folders, to mention just a few. Can you feel your head spinning thinking about where to find that critical document?

Robert Brown, an account manager at a telecommunications company, was having problems keeping track of the information he needed. He had papers all over his desk, 1,023 messages in his Inbox, and 106 documents in his My Documents folder. A surprising 80 percent of the e-mail in his Inbox was reference material. He didn't know where else to put it, so he kept it in his Inbox. That might sound familiar to you.

Robert wanted to clean up his e-mail first, so I coached him through creating an *E-mail Reference System* in his Personal Folders list. The first step was creating a Folder Hierarchy. Robert created 10 top-level folders that related specifically to his Meaningful Objectives, and he created additional subfolders that related to his Supporting Projects. He then dragged his e-mail messages from his Inbox into these new reference folders, and by the end of the process, he could barely contain his smile. He grinned and said, "I had no idea how easy it would be to file and find information based on my objectives."

Robert then created a *Document Reference System* in his My Documents folder, and also a *Paper Reference System* in his file cabinet using the same Folder Hierarchy that he used in his E-mail Reference System.

Robert duplicated the same Folder Hierarchy across all his storage locations: Personal Folders, My Documents, and paper. This made it easy for him to remember where to file and find his data. Robert didn't realize how simple it was to set up a Reference System that mapped directly to his objectives. All he needed was a little coaching to point him in the right direction. He did all the rest himself.

Most of you weren't taught how to set up an effective Reference System. When you have one, you'll be amazed at how simple it is to find and file information and how much time you'll save.

7. Organization Cramps My Freedom and Creativity

Belief   Being organized blocks my creativity, and there's nothing spontaneous about it.

Reality   Organization actually fosters and supports creativity and spontaneity.

You may find your creativity being disrupted by the non-stop flood of reminders spinning around your head.

- Call Kevin for his birthday
- Review the P&L spreadsheet
- Call Northwind Traders about the meeting schedule

- Review PowerPoint slide deck
- Decide on a Valentine's Day present

Imagine if you could clear your mind of all these lists and transfer them to Outlook. This would create space for new ideas and creative thinking.

Being disorganized can also stifle your creativity. Imagine you're an artist and decide to paint the Colorado autumn colors in Aspen. You drive for three and a half hours from Denver to Aspen to find the perfect spot. When you arrive, you realize you've forgotten to pack your paint brushes. That can make being creative really hard! Preparation does support your creativity.

Another example has to do with your scheduling. When your calendar is booked and leaves no time to be spontaneous, this can be frustrating. However, if you pre-plan, you can block out large chunks of time with no organized events. This provides down time, allowing you to be impulsive and spur-of-the-moment.

After you've set up your Integrated Management System, you'll find that it will support your creativity and spontaneity. The best result is being able to close your system, knowing that everything's taken care of so you can relax and let go!

8. I'm No Good with Technology!

Belief   It takes me too long to figure out how to use technology, and I get incredibly frustrated with it.

Reality   Using technology is a skill anyone can learn with the right kind of education. You'll be surprised at the personal satisfaction that comes from using technology more effectively.

For many of us, technology is frustrating because we expect it to be intuitive. When computers don't respond the way we want, we get irritated. I've heard clients yelling profanities at their computers and have seen them walloping their PCs in hopes of intimidating them into cooperation! Needless to say, this technique seldom works.

Some of us spend hours trying to figure out how to use tasks, set up Internet connections, and deal with errors. We wonder if we're ultimately saving any time at all. Fortunately, just a little bit of technical education can go a long way!

Katie Jordan, a VP of a finance company, was a paper-based organizer who loved her papers. She used Microsoft Outlook only for e-mail because she hadn't been able to figure out how to use it to effectively track her objectives, projects, meeting agendas, and tasks.

She tried using tasks, reminders, and flagging e-mails, but always gave up in frustration. However, when Katie's company decided to move all of their paper-based systems to digital systems, Katie knew it was time to get some help with Outlook because she could no longer avoid it!

After a full day of coaching, Katie managed to eliminate at least two thirds of her papers, transferring the contents into Microsoft Outlook. She learned how to set up Categories to track all of her objectives, projects, meeting agendas, and tasks. Katie also learned how to insert e-mails into tasks and calendar appointments, and how to drag and drop e-mail directly into her Task list. She was consistently amazed at what Outlook could do, and reluctantly admitted that her new Integrated Management System might even work better than her old, paper-based system. This was a huge step forward for Katie given how frustrated she'd been with technology, and how much she had loved her paper.

What Katie was missing in her previous attempt to switch to Outlook was the right type of education. Most technical training classes focus on individual features and benefits, which help you use the basic software, but they don't help you use Outlook to increase productivity and improve your work/life balance. Once you've set up your Integrated Management System, and learned how to use it, you can increase your overall usage of Outlook features by as much as 50 percent.

9. There's Not Enough Time in the Day!

Belief   I just don't have the time to do all the things I want.

Reality   Time is not the issue. The issue is deciding what you can do given the time you have.

As you know, managing your time with Olympian skill doesn't create more hours in the day. We all have the same 24 hours, so the issue isn't managing time; it's managing what you can do with the time you have. I always say to my clients, "You can't do everything, but you can do anything, as long as it fits into your calendar." Therefore, you have to be very careful about what choices you make.

Phil Spencer, an executive in a software company, told me how he didn't have enough time in the day to get his job done. I gently reminded him that he couldn't create any more time, and that the issue was more along the lines of how he was managing his commitments.

Phil kept his to-do lists in multiple locations—in e-mail, on a calendar, on paper, in an Excel spreadsheet, on a running list in his head, and on a few sticky notes here and there. Phil first needed to learn how to centralize and prioritize this list. Then, he needed to find out how to schedule it effectively on his Outlook Calendar so he would know what he could and couldn't do.

Phil transferred his various commitments into the Outlook Task list. He then compared the list with the available time on his Calendar and, right away, saw what his problem was. He was overcommitted and had more to do than time would allow. Yet another over-achiever trying to expand his daily, 24-hour quota!

Phil had to make some tough decisions because he couldn't complete all his agreements with the time he had. He was going to have to reprioritize, renegotiate, and, in some cases, cancel his commitments. Even though these were hard decisions, Phil had a much clearer idea now of what he could and couldn't do.

It was a humbling experience for Phil, but now he has a system that supports him in being realistic so he can make well-informed decisions. This was a powerful change. It put Phil in a position of control instead of reaction, and increased his sense of personal integrity, honesty, and self-esteem.

10. I'm Not Organized by Nature

Belief   Organization is a mysterious talent that only a chosen few are born with. It's a gene that's passed down the family line, but not one I got!

Reality   Organization is an exceptionally simple skill that you *can learn* just like any other. In fact, it's a skill that's easier to pick up than most of the skills you learned in your current career!

Consider for a moment; organization techniques were not taught in school. Most of us learned what we know today through trial and error, picking up tips and tricks here and there, often coming up with stopgap solutions that haven't served us effectively in the long run.

I can point to my own history as an example. When I was little, my dad used to tell me that if I could forget to put my head on in the morning, I would! I was incredibly forgetful and disorganized. I left for school each day with very good intentions, but always forgot something I needed. I realized that I was relying on memory to keep track of things, but that wasn't working. I quickly learned that if I was going to be more successful and feel more in control of my life, I needed to be more organized. I started using a paper organizer to write things down. It was the only way for me to remember things consistently! It made a significant difference, so I continued learning about productivity, going to various time-management courses and trying different systems.

I never found a system that quite fit all my needs, so in 1989, I designed and manufactured my own system in England. Today, these organization skills are just part of who I am. Clients have referred to me as an "Olympic Gold Medal organizer." However, my closest friends know my history better! The fact that I wasn't organized drove me to develop my system and gain the ability to be organized.

Organization is a skill that you can learn. Give yourself the time to be a student and learn some new techniques. They'll help improve your life and they'll be among the greatest gifts you can give yourself.

What Are You Willing to Let Go Of?

When clients like Jeff, whom you read about earlier, embark on changing behaviors, they often have to let go of their beliefs and habits to make room for new approaches. This isn't always easy to do, and it often involves a high degree of trust and courage.

Linda Moschell, a Program Manager at a software company, had 3,983 e-mails in her Outlook Inbox. One of her goals during our coaching was to get to zero e-mails so she could start off with a clean slate. Linda was fed up with having to manage so much e-mail and fed up with her compulsion to keep everything, without which, she feared, she could not operate. By the end of our session, Linda had successfully reduced her e-mail by half. I asked her, "What are you willing to do to eliminate the remaining e-mail?" The thought of eliminating the remaining 1,991 messages was more than Linda could bear. However, a week later, I received this e-mail.

"Change. It has the power to uplift, to heal, to stimulate, surprise, open new doors, bring fresh experience, and create excitement in life. Certainly it is worth the risk."
—**Leo Buscaglia**

Dear Sally,
Yesterday, I deleted every single e-mail in my Inbox. I sent a message to all my
staff and customers and informed them that my mail had been deleted and if
there was anything I'd missed to get back to me ASAP!

Three months later she e-mailed me again.

Dear Sally,
I feel great. I have 25 e-mails in my Inbox and nothing happened as a result of
deleting the backlog of 2500 messages!!!! I took the leap and it worked! I realize
that I can do my job without keeping so much information. What a relief!

Letting go and changing behaviors sometimes takes a leap of faith and a
great deal of courage. Linda wanted to get to zero e-mail, but to do it she had
to recognize that her current system wasn't serving her. She needed to
change her approach in order to obtain a more manageable Inbox. Linda
did something different because she really wanted to make her life simpler.

Clients like Linda hire me because they have problems they haven't been
able to fix. They say, "If I had more time, if I got less e-mail, if my boss had a
clue, if only Microsoft Outlook would do this, if I didn't get interrupted,
then I could be productive, and *then* I could have the life I want."

If only I could just wave a magic wand and give clients what they want.
However, over the years, I've learned that *the problems clients are identifying*
aren't the problems that need fixing! The problem isn't "out there" with
technology, with co-workers, or with e-mail. It's with us and how we're
approaching these issues.

Over the last several years, I've heard increasing complaints about e-mail
from sources such as clients, newspapers, business magazines, and even
television. The people who make these complaints present convincing
arguments, and it sure sounds like e-mail is a huge problem. However, the
problem is our *approach* to e-mail. We've allowed it to become an issue and
we've allowed ourselves to become the problem!

Our company has thousands of clients who consistently finish their days
with empty Inboxes! We have statistics to prove that with the right kind
of education, you can reduce the number of messages in your Inbox by
81 percent and you can reduce the volume you receive by 50 percent.

One of my favorite expressions is, "If you always do what you've always done, you'll always get what you always got." If you're not as productive as you'd like, if your e-mail is not working for you, and if you don't have the life balance you want, you'll have to do something different, otherwise nothing's going to change and you'll keep getting the same results.

If I did have a magic wand, I wouldn't use it to give you more time, to solve your Outlook problems, or to whack your boss over the head. I'd use it to give you the motivation and the discipline to change your approach so you can experience different results, and I'd use it to give you practical solutions that you can easily implement to make your life more enjoyable and productive.

Take the time to reevaluate your beliefs and the way in which you approach productivity. Remember, you can take back your life and create a new reality for yourself.

"I used to say, 'I sure hope things will change.' Then I learned that the only way things are going to change for me is when I change."
—**Jim Rohn**

Chapter Two
What Is Personal Productivity?

The purpose of this book is for you to increase personal productivity while maintaining balance in your life. Accomplishing these goals can be difficult if you don't know what productivity and balance really mean, or if you don't know how to improve them. In this chapter, I'll introduce a clear definition of both of these concepts. You'll be surprised how simple they are, and you may even wonder why achieving them has been so hard.

To define productivity and balance, I'll highlight two core principles throughout the book: *Meaningful Objectives* and *Strategic Next Actions*. These principles are the foundation for productivity, and they're the cornerstones you'll be using to build your own Integrated Management System.

I'll introduce *The Cycle of Productivity*, which diagrams how to increase and measure productivity. I'll also describe what an Integrated Management System (IMS) is, and why it's critical to maintaining and improving efficiency in your personal and professional life.

Defining Personal Productivity

sonal productivity may seem like an easy enough term to understand, it actually means very different things to different people. When I ask its what productivity means to them, I get a variety of responses.

Getting more done

Meeting my objectives more effectively

Using my resources more wisely

■ Experiencing work/life balance

- Feeling in control and relaxed
- Delegating more effectively
- Spending more time being proactive, not reactive
- Going home each day feeling complete
- Getting more of the right things done
- Focusing more on my objectives
- Spending more time with my kids

When you review these comments carefully, you'll discover that there's an underlying theme that links them all together. That theme is "action."

I define personal productivity in its simplest form as *completing action*. However, you can cheerfully complete actions until you are blue in the face (and some of you are) and still not experience productivity. I'm sure you've had days that were really busy and you got a lot done, but on reflection, you didn't feel as effective as you wanted to be. So what was missing?

Meaningful Objectives

When I've observed clients who are extremely productive, I've found that simply completing a list of actions isn't enough for them. What's important is that their actions are linked and driven by their *Meaningful Objectives*. These clients rarely do anything that doesn't relate to one of their objectives.

Meaningful Objectives are your North Star, your guiding light, and your reference point for success or failure. Without meaning, objectives become dry and nothing more than text on a to-do list that you might (or might not) look at every now and then. You won't be motivated to work on your objectives, but you'll feel guilty when you don't.

I often say to my clients that, "Your productivity is only as good as your objectives." It's very important to have Meaningful Objectives because productivity is impossible to direct and measure without them. Meaningful Objectives are the first core principle you'll use in this book to increase your productivity.

Examples of Meaningful Objectives are:

- Sales—Sell three million dollars of online learning products by December. (Mark receives a 5% commission on revenue when he makes this goal, and money is a major motivator for him.)

- Career Development—Complete a certification program for coaching at the senior management level by May 1st. (Joe has had a dream to provide effective coaching services at this level for many years.)

- Health—Run Pikes Peak under my personal-best time of 3 hours and 15 minutes. (Bob suffered a mild heart attack two years ago, so this represents a major accomplishment to him.)

- Home—Build a 500-square-foot dog run. (Sally wants to protect her landscaping from two rather large, 11-month-old puppies.)

If you don't have clear objectives, you can easily fall into the trap of completing actions just for the sake of doing something. You'll feel as though you're getting a lot done, but deep down you know you aren't being as effective as you can be.

You'd be amazed at how many people I've coached, at every organizational level, who don't have Meaningful Objectives. Even if they do, their objectives are often unclear. Identifying objectives that are meaningful, and clarifying them so that they're specific, is a critical step in helping you manage your life. As Lily Tomlin once said, "I always wanted to be somebody. I guess I should've been more specific!"

The other trap that you might fall into is having too many objectives. The results can have a cumulative, negative effect. You feel that no matter how productive you are, it's never enough. You miss deadlines, you experience an unusual number of "911" situations, your work is mediocre, your life isn't in balance, and your priorities conflict. It's normal to want to please others and demonstrate that you're part of the team by taking on more work, but in that context, it's also easy to over-commit. Your intention is honorable but your results may not be so glowing. You ensure that your performance at work isn't harmed, but the consequence is that your personal life ends up suffering. When you have too many objectives, ultimately something goes out of balance.

It's important to manage both the number and the content of your objectives so you can maintain equilibrium in your life. In Chapter 10, "Prioritizing and Planning," you'll learn more about how to identify and manage your Meaningful Objectives while maintaining balance.

> "You've got to think about the big things while you are doing the small things, so that all small things go in the right direction."
> —**Alvin Toffler**

Strategic Next Actions

After I learned how important Meaningful Objectives are to productivity, I expanded my definition of productivity from *completing actions* to *completing actions that link to meaningful objectives.*

However, I noticed another situation that was impeding clients' productivity. They were adding tasks to their to-do lists that couldn't be completed, and they'd learn this only when it came time to take action. At that point, they'd realize that a to-do item involved multiple steps and couldn't be finished without several other preceding actions, and in many cases, they realized these tasks weren't the most strategic to take, anyway.

My most productive clients spend considerable time planning and thinking through their tasks. They ensure that each task they've listed is the most strategic action they can take and it doesn't have any dependencies. (A task that has a dependency means additional steps must be completed before you can begin the task.) I'll be referring to these well-thought-out actions as *Strategic Next Actions.*

A Strategic Next Action is a step that links to your Meaningful Objective, and is the most critical step that can be taken without a dependency. When you take the time to think through your Strategic Next Actions, watch out because your productivity will soar! Strategic Next Actions is the second core principle you'll be working with throughout the book.

After I discovered the importance of Strategic Next Actions to productivity, I expanded my definition to *consistently completing Strategic Next Actions that link to Meaningful Objectives.* This statement encapsulates what I saw my most successful clients doing. They consistently completed Strategic Next Actions that were driven by Meaningful Objectives. After you incorporate these two principles into your Integrated Management System, I think you'll be quite enthusiastic about how useful they are and how much value you'll receive.

> *Productivity: Consistently completing Strategic Next Actions that link to Meaningful Objectives.*

Work/Life Balance

Do you remember a time in your life when you experienced a sense of well-being and had a healthy relationship between work and home? What did that feel like, and what were you doing? It's important to have a personal reference point for balance, otherwise you can't create or maintain it.

The American Heritage Dictionary defines balance as "A weighing device, consisting essentially of a level that is brought into equilibrium by adding known weights to one end while the unknown weights hang from the other." I define balance as *a consistent focus or influence that creates a sense of well-being*. If you're not feeling good and you're out of sorts, you need to find a way to increase your sense of well-being and bring yourself back into balance so the scales are equally weighted. I hear you saying, "Easier said than done!" and you're correct. The challenge is to determine what you can do to increase your well-being.

When you review your personal and business Meaningful Objectives, focus on them collectively and ask yourself, "Do these objectives create balance for me?" It's important to include both personal and business because you can't create balance in a vacuum; you need to evaluate the whole picture and not just a piece of it. Once you've done this a few times, you'll start to discover what balance is for you.

Balance is subtle and it's different for each one of us. Sometimes all it takes to acquire it is one great vacation with your family, consistently exercising three times a week, or having unstructured time on weekends. The most unexpected events can create a high degree of well-being, so bringing your life back into balance doesn't necessarily require time-consuming activities. It does require quality activities like being alone for a day, getting a massage, or reading a great book. You may not immediately recognize what these are, but by trying different things, you'll find out.

We're all so busy "getting things done" that we often don't think about making balance a consistent focus. Balance might seem like an inappropriate word to use in conjunction with work, and many of my clients think that if they approach work with balance, they'll slow down, get less done, lose their edge, and ultimately reduce their productivity. However, watching my most productive clients, I see them using balance to *increase* productivity, not *decrease* it. When they exercise early in the morning, they start their day being more centered and having a clearer head. When they make time during the week to watch a sports game or go to the theater, they awake the next morning with the great idea they've been searching for. Sometimes I see clients working long hours for days back to back, but then they balance that work with a three-day vacation, or take time in the middle of the week to play golf or work in the yard.

It's important to identify what allows you to successfully create balance. The key is to simultaneously review your personal and business objectives while asking yourself "What do I need to do to maintain balance?" Chapter 10 discusses how to accomplish this goal in detail.

The Cycle of Productivity

The Cycle of Productivity shows you how to increase effectiveness by consistently completing Strategic Next Actions that link to Meaningful Objectives. This cycle is the foundation of your Integrated Management System, so it's important to understand how to use it, and why it's so significant.

Over the years, I've noted that my most successful clients repeat a distinct set of behaviors over and over, achieving their objectives effectively while maintaining balance. The Cycle of Productivity is a very simple, four-step model that highlights these behaviors.

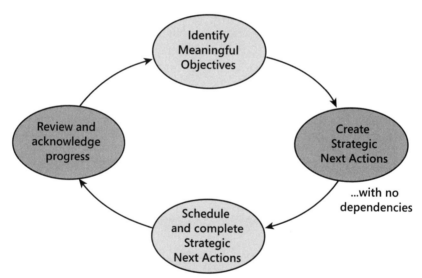

Figure 2-1 The Cycle of Productivity demonstrates how to increase productivity.

Step One: Identifying Meaningful Objectives

Identifying your Meaningful Objectives is the first step in the Cycle of Productivity. Whether you're a homemaker, a college student, a small business owner, or a worker in the corporate world, identifying clear Meaningful Objectives for both your business and personal life is essential. Without them, productivity can't take place.

Objectives assist you in measuring progress, making course corrections, and focusing on strategic activities. They're also powerful filters that support you in making effective decisions.

You probably receive a non-stop flood of information that requires your immediate attention. If the information you receive directly relates to your objectives and assists you in moving forward, the decision to take action is clear. However, if it doesn't relate to an objective, you'll need to evaluate how to handle it because working on actions that don't link to objectives isn't productive. You'll learn more about managing objectives in Chapter 7, "Processing and Organizing Your Task List."

Without objectives, it's easy to become directionless and fall into the trap of "any road will do," which is not a very satisfying long-term strategy. It takes time to clarify objectives but the value you receive from having them is enormous. Take the time to create objectives on the front end because, ultimately, this will save you time on the back end.

Step Two: Creating Strategic Next Actions

The next step in the Cycle of Productivity is to create Strategic Next Actions that link to your Meaningful Objectives. You need to ensure that these actions are critical and don't have any dependencies. You can only move forward in the cycle with an action item that can physically be *completed in one, simple step*.

The sidebar about Henry and his car is just a small example of how seemingly "simple" next actions can end up having multiple, unexpected dependencies.

The Case of Henry and the Car

Consider the case of Henry Miller, a client whose objective was to sell his car so he could buy the one he really wanted. To accomplish this, he needed to define a Strategic Next Action, which he thought was to fix the brakes. That task seemed pretty simple until Henry and I had a conversation.

When I asked Henry, "What do you need to do to fix the brakes?" he replied, "Take my car to the dealership on Broadway." When I asked him, "What do you need to do to take you car to the dealer?" he answered, "Book an appointment to have them look at the brakes." And when I asked, "What do you need to do to book the appointment?" he said, "Go online to look up the phone number." So Henry's Strategic Next Action wasn't to get the car's brakes fixed; it was to get on the Internet and get the phone number for the dealership.

Henry found that fixing his car's brakes had multiple dependencies. In order to fix the brakes, he needed to take the car to the dealer. To take the car to the dealer he had to book an appointment. To book an appointment he needed the phone number, and to get the phone number, he needed to go on the Internet. His real Strategic Next Action was to go online and get the phone number for the dealer on Broadway. All the other steps had dependencies and couldn't be done.

When I look at the to-do lists of my clients, 80 percent or more of their lists are made up of steps that have dependencies. This means that they're creating lists that *can't be done*. That's why a lot of our task lists seem overwhelming and unrealistic; they often are. If you have a Strategic Next Action that you can't start because it has multiple dependencies, then it's not a Strategic Next Action; you can't continue the Cycle of Productivity and therefore nothing will happen. You'll have a big old to-do list that's going nowhere fast! The key is to create Strategic Next Actions without dependencies, ensuring you can complete them easily and quickly. Once you start breaking down your actions in this way, you'll be amazed at how easy it will be to keep the Cycle of Productivity going.

Step Three: Scheduling and Completing Strategic Next Actions

Once you decide what your Strategic Next Actions are, you can move to the third step in the Cycle of Productivity, which is *scheduling and completing* these actions.

Most clients I work with are profuse "creators," writing long lists and agreeing to numerous activities. The problem lies in completing what they've agreed to do. Even though their day contains only 24 hours, they don't plan their activities to that time frame. They say "yes" to agreements and sincerely believe everything will work out, but without realistic scheduling, they sacrifice balance and break agreements.

The key to accomplishing tasks is to plan Strategic Next Actions on your calendar so you can ensure that they get completed without your surrendering balance or missing important deadlines. My company's statistics prove that there's a 75 percent greater chance of a task being completed if it's scheduled on your calendar rather than tracked on your task list or in your head. Placing a task on your calendar ensures that you see it and have the time to complete it. When it's on your task list, you may not look at it, and if you don't allocate time to do it, it probably won't happen.

When you begin to schedule your Strategic Next Actions onto your calendar, you'll dramatically increase the likelihood that you'll complete these actions. This kind of completion releases energy and gives you the motivation and inspiration to continue moving forward.

You might just be one of those people who's starved for completion. Your objectives span months or years, giving you no daily sense of achievement. By redirecting your focus to implementing a Strategic Next Action without a dependency, you will experience a daily sense of accomplishment that leads to renewed energy.

Step Four: Reviewing and Acknowledging Progress Toward Objectives

Because my clients are so busy reacting to the world around them, they rarely take time to review and acknowledge the results of the tasks they've completed. Their time is spent dealing with the volume of information they receive, and desperately trying to keep their heads above water.

When you acknowledge the completion of a Strategic Next Action, you can then evaluate if it successfully moved you closer to one of your Meaningful Objectives, and if you were able to maintain balance. If it did, you can create a subsequent Strategic Next Action to continue the Cycle of Productivity. However, if completing an action didn't move you forward, you'll need to create an alternative Strategic Next Action to get you back on track. In either scenario, you're acknowledging completion and reviewing progress towards Meaningful Objectives and balance.

Acknowledgement is critical because it's the fuel that motivates you to keep completing the Cycle of Productivity. Reviewing is essential because it keeps you on course with your Meaningful Objectives. Much like steering a ship, you have to continually adjust the helm to ensure you reach your destination.

The Cycle of Productivity enables you to simultaneously maintain your focus on the big picture and complete small, tactical steps. All of your actions will be determined by your Meaningful Objectives, so if you continually create and complete Strategic Next Actions, you'll achieve your goals.

This is a simple concept, but it delivers profound results. As my grandma used to say, "It's a cinch by the inch and hard by the yard." Turns out she was right!

Introducing the Organizational Hierarchy Model

The Organizational Hierarchy Model demonstrates how Meaningful Objectives align with the company Mission and Goals and then break down to Supporting Projects, Tasks and Subtasks, and Strategic Next Actions. This ensures that your Strategic Next Actions truly map to your Meaningful Objectives. The clear hierarchy guarantees that all levels of an organization are aligned with the company Mission and Goals.

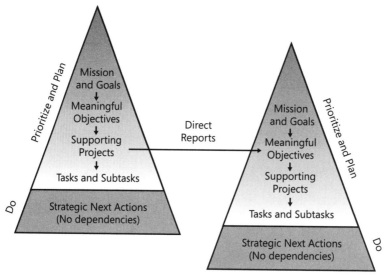

Figure 2-2 The Organizational Hierarchy Model shows you how to align Strategic Next Actions with Mission and Goals.

In this model, I use a certain set of terms—Mission and Goals, Meaningful Objectives, Supporting Projects, Tasks and Subtasks, and Strategic Next Actions. Your company, division, or group may use alternative terms that mean the same thing, so you can translate this model to fit the nomenclature that exists within your company.

The Cycle of Productivity integrates with the Organizational Hierarchy model. When you complete a Strategic Next Action, you unlock a dependency that was keeping a subtask inactive. As you continue the Cycle of Productivity, consistently completing Strategic Next Actions, you eventually unlock your Tasks, and then Supporting Projects, and then Meaningful Objectives, and eventually the Mission and Goals of the company.

Obviously, reaching company goals requires completing many cycles of action. If you stay focused on consistently completing Strategic Next Actions that link to Meaningful Objectives, you're on your way to a much more focused, aligned, and productive environment. This is the foundation and philosophy for the IMS that you will be setting up. The idea is to track Meaningful Objectives, Supporting Projects, Tasks and Subtasks, and Strategic Next Actions so you know what cycles of action need to be completed to move toward accomplishing your Meaningful Objectives.

So What's the Big Deal About Productivity?

Productivity sure sounds easy. All you have to do is stay focused on your Meaningful Objectives and complete the associated Strategic Next Actions. My clients stare in amazement at the Cycle of Productivity and say, "Wow! That sure sounds easy, so why does it seem so hard in real life?"

The truth is, of course, that our lives are never that simple! When we're working with a company, community, or family, we have many internal and external distractions that make it more challenging to maintain focus on the Cycle of Productivity. Take a look at the following list and see if you can relate to any of these distractions.

- Unclear objectives
- Too many objectives
- Changing and conflicting priorities
- Multiple people involved
- Daily interruptions
- Unexpected fire drills
- Speed and volume of information coming to you
- Technical problems
- Lack of the right skills, or having to learn them
- Misunderstandings
- Staying up too late!

When you take four or five of these distractions and add them into your day, completing the Cycle of Productivity becomes even more challenging. It's easy to get sidetracked, to react, to forget what you were doing, to spin your wheels, or to give insufficient thought to your decisions. Many people say, "I don't have the time to slow down and think about what I'm doing. I just need to get it done!" Does that sound familiar?

Keeping Your Focus

The key is to create an Integrated Management System that supports you in maintaining your focus so you won't get distracted by numerous interruptions, misunderstandings, technical difficulties, and other obstacles.

To help this focus, you will be building these four questions into your Integrated Management System:

- What are your Meaningful Objectives?
- What are your Strategic Next Actions?
- When will you get them done?
- Where will you get them done?

These questions keep you focused on the Cycle of Productivity and ensure that you consistently complete Strategic Next Actions that link to Meaningful Objectives.

Introducing the Integrated Management System

I'd like to review what an Integrated Management System is in more detail, so you'll know what you're going to create. With an IMS, you have all of your relevant personal and business information managed and tracked in one central location. It enables you to dump your inbox, your voice mail, the papers on your desk, and the items you're memorizing in your head into one spot. With your IMS, you can also see what your objectives are, judge where they are against their plans, and determine what needs to happen to keep them moving forward. The system is centralized, flexible, and accessible so you can use it 24 hours a day, seven days a week.

Setting up your IMS within Microsoft Outlook is an enlightening process for most of our customers. They've been using Outlook for many years, but never realized the value it could offer. After you've set up an IMS, I'm certain you'll be extremely happy with the results. Your life will be more organized, and you'll feel more focused, relaxed, and in control of your world.

A vision without a task is but a dream; a task without a vision is drudgery; a vision and a task together is the hope of the world.
—From a church in Sussex, England

The Integrated Management System consists of these three systems:

- Collecting System
- Reference System
- Action System

The Collecting System

A Collecting System is made up of a series of *approved Collecting Points* where you and others place your commitments and communications. These Collecting Points are physical locations that you use to capture your actions, reminders, meeting notes, and where other people drop off tasks or information for you. Typical approved Collecting Points are your e-mail, voice mail, and a paper inbox. Some time during the day, you'll need to stop to process the information in these Collecting Points, and make decisions about what to do with each item. You'll either throw the item in the trash can, store it in your Reference System, or store it in your Action System. You'll learn, in more detail, how to set up an effective Collecting System in Chapter 4, "Setting Up Your Approved Collecting Points."

The Reference System

The Reference System enables you to track information that *does not require action*, but that you want to keep to access later. You'll store this type of reference information in Contacts or in folders you create in the Folder List in Outlook, in your Windows My Documents folder, or on a Windows SharePoint site. You'll learn how to set up an effective Reference System in Chapter 8, "Setting Up Your Reference System."

The Action System

The Action System will track any information that *requires you to take an action*; for example, your Meaningful Objectives, Supporting Projects, 1:1 Meetings, and Strategic Next Actions. You will track this type of action information in the Microsoft Outlook Task list and Calendar. You'll learn in more detail how to set up an effective Action System in Chapter 6, "Introducing the Planning and Action Categories."

Figure 2-3 shows the three systems in the IMS.

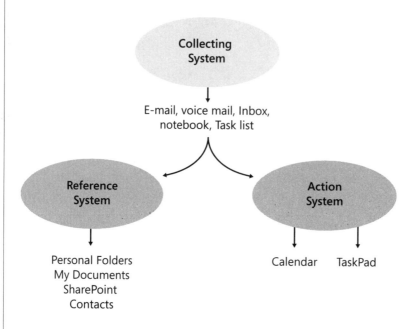

Figure 2-3 The IMS consists of three systems.

Introducing the "ControlPanel"

After your Integrated Management System is set up in Outlook, the
ControlPanel is the quickest way to see an overview of your Action and
Reference Systems. The ControlPanel is a particular arrangement of panes
that you create in the Outlook window, as shown in Figure 2-4. The
ControlPanel gives you immediate access to multiple pieces of information
that support your productivity.

Much like the dashboard of a car, which shows you how fast you are driving,
how much gas is left, what direction you're going, and what time it is, the
ControlPanel in your IMS gives you an overview of how well you're meeting
your objectives. To set up the ControlPanel, first make sure the vertical
navigation pane is open on the left side of the Outlook window. If it's not
visible, click View, and click Navigation Pane. Then click the Calendar icon
in the lower left corner. To complete the ControlPanel, click View again, and
click TaskPad. The final step is to click on the folder icon in the bottom left.
Also on the View menu, you can select Work Week to see the Calendar as
it's shown in Figure 2-4.

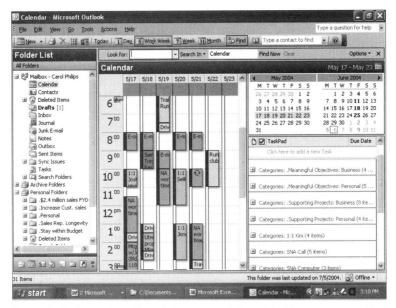

Figure 2-4   The ControlPanel shows your Integrated Management System.

On the far right of the ControlPanel is the TaskPad, and in the middle is the Calendar. The TaskPad and Calendar together make up the Action System. In Figure 2-4, you'll notice that Carol Philips, a Sales Manager from Lucerne Publishing, has grouped her tasks into multiple categories in the TaskPad: Meaningful Objectives, Supporting Projects, 1:1 Meetings, and Strategic Next Actions. You will be setting up these categories later in the book. On the left is Carol's Reference System, where she tracks all of her reference information. In the Folder List, Carol can access her e-mail reference folders and her Contacts folder. On the Start menu, Carol can access her My Documents and SharePoint folders using shortcuts.

The ControlPanel enables Carol to see her Action and Reference Systems simultaneously. This gives her access to all the information she needs to do her job in one place, so it's extremely powerful.

Access—All Day, Every Day

Many brands of personal digital assistant (PDA) can help you take your important information with you. A Pocket PC, which is one type of PDA, synchronizes with Microsoft Outlook, enabling you to view the Task List, Calendar, Contacts, and your Personal Folders. (You can also synchronize office documents if you wish.) The Pocket PC is so small that it enables you to have access to your IMS 24 hours a day. Wherever you go, it goes, making life much easier.

For example, when I go grocery shopping, I look under my Strategic Next Action: Errands list, I find the store I'm going to, I open up that task and there is my grocery list. When I'm at the airport with an hour to spare, I can go to my Strategic Next Action: Call list and see all the phone calls I need to make. Since my contacts are synchronized on my PDA, I have everything I need, when I need it. This is pretty cool! Most people spend sixty minutes a day finding and filing things. Once you have a good system in place, your finding and filing time can be reduced to ten minutes. That's a fifty minute time savings every day, so go buy a PDA and save a lot of time!

Bringing It All Together

You will set up your IMS in Part Two of this book, and build it around the Cycle of Productivity and the definition for productivity: consistently completing Strategic Next Actions that link to Meaningful Objectives. As you work in your IMS, you'll be pleasantly surprised at how much your productivity will improve, and as you "course correct" when your objectives don't support balance, you'll discover how much the quality of your life will increase. The key to all of this is to take the time to set up an IMS and then use it consistently. Like any change in your life, it'll require focus and discipline, similar to what is required to go to the gym. You won't get fit in one workout. It takes an unfailing focus, week by week, to make that happen!

"We are what we repeatedly do. Excellence, then, is not an act, but a habit."
—Aristotle

The unexpected benefit of an IMS is that when you turn it off, you get to turn off this part of your world, enabling you to really "be" in your life instead of just "doing" in your life. You can enjoy counting rain drops, watching the snow fall, and spending time with your family and friends. Remember, the purpose of an IMS is to help you increase productivity and enhance the quality of your life, not necessarily to do more.

Chapter Three

The Three Phases for Creating an Integrated Management System

In order to make setting up your Integrated Management System easier, I've broken down the process into three distinct phases, which I call the Three Phases for Creating an Integrated Management System:

- Phase 1: Collecting

- Phase 2: Processing and Organizing

- Phase 3: Prioritizing and Planning

In this chapter, I'll give you a brief overview of each phase so you'll understand its purpose, what you can expect to learn about it, and how it will help you build your IMS. Don't be fooled by the seeming simplicity of these phases. We've spent thousands of hours in discussions, working one on one with clients, and monitoring and measuring results, to create something that moves the complexity of managing life to the simplicity of managing a system. I believe that by using such a system you'll be able to make your life more cohesive and recapture valuable time, energy, and focus.

Phase 1: Collecting

The purpose of the Collecting Phase is to assist you in developing a seamless *Collecting System* that will capture all of your commitments and agreements. In this phase you'll also complete an exercise called "clearing the mind," which will assist you in transferring the to-do's from your head to Microsoft Office Outlook.

A Collecting System is made up of a set of approved *Collecting Points*. Collecting Points are physical locations where you gather your actions, reminders, and meeting notes, and where colleagues or family members can drop off tasks and information for you. Typical approved Collecting Points are your e-mail, voice mail, and paper inboxes at home and at work. Sounds simple enough, however it's not quite that straightforward in real life!

When I ask clients how many Collecting Points (buckets) they have on average, they say four to six. However, after closer scrutiny, I find that it's really more like 25 to 30, which is a big difference! Having 25 to 30 buckets is a lot more complex and confusing. You may not realize it, but your car seat, the kitchen table, your pockets, and even the notes you scribble on the back of an envelope are all places where you're collecting information and to-do's. Discovering how many Collecting Points you actually have can be an eye opener, not to mention a wee bit overwhelming! When you have a large number of Collecting Points, it's difficult to remember where you put things, and you can spend considerable time sorting through piles to find critical items.

By deciding which buckets are the most useful and practical, you can consolidate your 25 to 30 categories down to 5 to 10. The result is a Collecting System that will help simplify your life and ensure that you're capturing everything you need.

Is Your Head a Collecting Point?

Even as you're reading this book, you've probably wandered off into the recesses of your mind, thinking about actions you have to do? True? This indicates to me that you're collecting actions in your head—ah ha!—another very popular, "unapproved" Collecting Point!

Most of my clients are completely unaware of how much they're tracking in their heads and the kind of impact that this has on their effectiveness. When you're busy remembering to print handouts, download voice mail, and order Valentine's Day gifts, it's hard to focus on anything else. You're in your head recalling what you have to do! I hear clients mumbling to themselves, "Don't talk to me now; I'm trying to remember something!" That's a bit dramatic, but I think you understand my point! It's hard to be present when you're in your head focusing on your to-do lists.

In Chapter 5, you'll do the "clearing the mind" exercise, in which you'll download all the to-do's you've got floating around in your brain and capture them in the Task list in Outlook. The Task list is a great place to track all of your Meaningful Objectives, Supporting Projects, 1:1 Meetings, and

Strategic Next Actions. After your head is free from tracking these lists, you can focus on more creative and meaningful activities, such as strategizing, planning, and improving your work/life balance. Most clients experience a huge sense of relief when they get everything out of their minds and captured into a leak-proof system. I have to scrape my clients off the ceiling because they're so light and relaxed, and some of them even sleep better at night. Now that's fantastic!

Phase 2: Processing and Organizing

The purpose of the Processing and Organizing Phase is to set up Action and Reference Systems, and to understand how to effectively process and organize your Collecting Points using the Workflow Model. By the end of this phase you'll have completed building your IMS; your e-mail, voice mail, and paper inboxes will be empty; and your system will contain all of your actions and reference material. Picture that in your mind—everything empty and organized in one centralized system that you can access easily.

The Processing and Organizing Phase is made up of two individual pieces: processing and organizing. They are intrinsically linked but separate. Processing helps you decide what to do with an item in a Collecting Point, and organizing helps you decide where to file it in your Action or Reference System.

Let's look at a common example. If you open an e-mail message in your Inbox, you must decide *what* to do with it, otherwise it ends up staying in the Inbox. If you decide you need to write a proposal for Alpine Ski House, you then need to decide *where* you're going to capture that task in your Action System so you can complete it.

This sounds easy for some people, but for those with hundreds or even thousands of e-mails in their Inboxes, it's not as straightforward as it appears. Clients often open e-mail messages and can't figure out what to do with them, so they avoid making a decision and leave these messages where they are, only to be re-opened and re-read multiple times. If you do this consistently, you rapidly end up with large volumes of e-mails with a pending decision about each one. Your Inbox then becomes a combined Action and Reference System, and you can feel overwhelmed and stressed!

"It doesn't take a lot of difference to make a difference."
—Sally McGhee

Introducing the Workflow Model

The Workflow Model in Figure 3-1 shows you how to *process and organize* your information from a Collecting Point into your Action and Reference Systems. Processing is a series of questions, represented by the ovals, which help you decide *what to do* with the contents of your Collecting Points. Organizing is a series of files and categories, represented by rectangles, which help you decide *where to store your information*. The Workflow Model supports you in making immediate and meaningful decisions so that you're able to empty your Collecting Points.

In today's electronic world, with anywhere from 60 to 250 e-mails flooding your Inbox each day, it's critical to make rapid, but well-thought-out decisions. There is a contradiction here; you need to make *rapid* decisions but you also need to *pause* to give yourself time to make *effective* decisions. I remind my clients that "you have to slow down to speed up." *I believe strongly that it's in these pauses that effective decisions are made.* When you allow the "noise" in your environment to drive you, what gets lost in the shuffle is effective decisions and, therefore, effective action.

Many of my clients find themselves in a pattern of reacting to the information that comes into their Collecting Points. Information delivery is happening so rapidly they feel the need to respond at the same pace! This creates ineffective communication and unproductive cycles of action. Giving more thought to decisions on the front end results in tremendous time savings on the back end.

The Processing and Organizing Phase is about taking the time you need to make better decisions, and ensuring you have an effective system to track and manage all of your Action and Reference items. The Workflow Model shows you just such a system, and you'll be using it to process and organize your Collecting Points and empty them into your Action and Reference Systems, which you'll set up in Chapter 7, "Processing and Organizing Your Task List," and Chapter 8, "Setting Up Your Reference System."

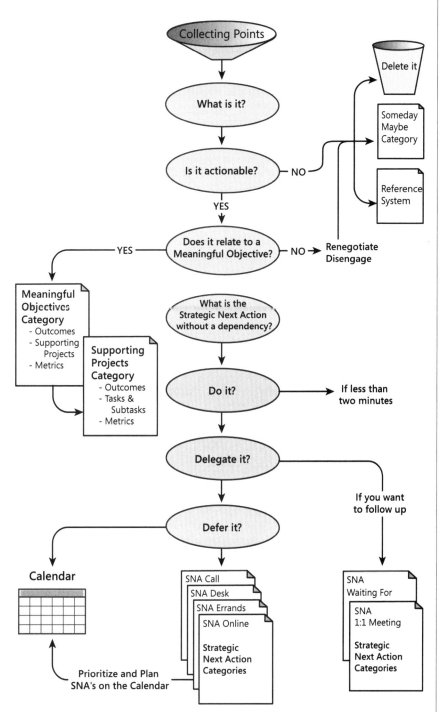

Figure 3-1 The Workflow Model helps you process and organize your Collecting Points effectively. You'll learn about this model in detail in Chapter 6.

Phase 3: Prioritizing and Planning

The purpose of the Prioritizing and Planning Phase is to enable you to sustain and maintain your IMS so you can continue to increase productivity while maintaining balance. This phase also enables you keep your system up-to-date, to stay focused on your Meaningful Objectives, and to routinely prioritize and plan your Strategic Next Actions onto your Calendar to ensure that they get done.

Without a routine maintenance program, your system will become clogged with incomplete actions and rapidly go out of date. Reacting will take the place of well-thought-out planning, and you'll find yourself storing activities in your head instead of using your system to do the work of remembering and reminding. Eventually, you'll abandon your system and revert back to your old ways, saying, "the system never worked anyway, and it was too hard to maintain!" Blasphemy! We just can't have that! I'm being dramatic here, but with good reason. Remember, if you always do what you've always done, you'll always get what you've always got.

After your system is set up, it won't manage itself. It needs you to keep it up-to-date and alive, which requires that you do some things differently. Generating these new routines takes discipline and a *conscious, consistent focus.* Once they become habit, you'll be flying high and you'll never look back.

Introducing the Weekly Review

The Weekly Review is a recurring appointment with yourself that helps you remember to update your system, prioritize, review Meaningful Objectives, and schedule Strategic Next Actions onto your calendar.

Keeping your system up-to-date involves persistence; a lot can happen in a week. You will have completed tasks, moved forward on objectives, agreed to new actions, delegated activities, re-prioritized your focus, and maybe even changed roles. It's important to capture these changes and update your IMS so it represents your current situation. Only then can review your Action System—Meaningful Objectives, Supporting Projects, 1:1 Meetings, and Strategic Next Actions—effectively prioritizing and planning them into your Calendar. Your system needs to reflect all of these weekly changes; otherwise, when you prioritize and plan, it's no longer relevant and it will mirror an out-of-date situation. If you continue to leave your system unattended, your lists will become redundant and they'll grow older and older and finally lose their shelf life. Your list will then become a "moldy oldie to-do list," not an "action list" that's alive and vital.

The ControlPanel, shown in Figure 3-2, is where you'll perform the Weekly Review. The Calendar and TaskPad, on the right, give you access to your Action System, showing your Meaningful Objectives, Supporting Projects, 1:1 Meetings, and Strategic Next Actions. The Folder list, on the left, gives you access to your Reference System, showing all of your e-mail and other folders. This view enables you to see everything you have to do in one place, which makes prioritizing and planning much easier.

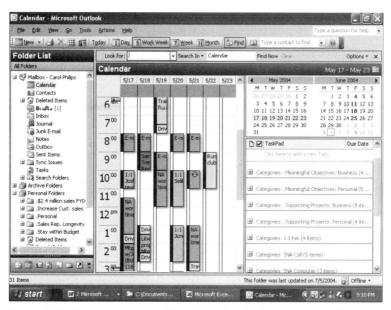

Figure 3-2 You conduct your Weekly Review in the ControlPanel.

Most of my clients open Outlook to their Inbox. I open Outlook to the ControlPanel, enabling me to monitor where I'm going and make sure I'm moving toward my Meaningful Objectives. The Weekly Review ensures that I pry myself away from the trees so I can elevate myself and manage the forest. When I'm in e-mail, I'm hugging a tree and not overseeing the forest. This process enables me to course-correct and make certain I'm on track, and it's incredibly powerful. My clients feel more focused, controlled, relaxed and inspired after completing a Weekly Review. Sounds good to me!

Committing to Change

After you've completed each of the Three Phases for Creating an Integrated Management System, I'll ask you to review the changes you want to make and write them down so you're very clear about what they are. Once you've completed setting up your system, you'll review these changes to see how best to integrate them into your life.

It's very important to engage in this process with a strong commitment to personal change because if you're "wishy washy" or uncommitted, you'll fail before you start. You need to recognize why you want to modify things in your life and understand what's really driving you to make changes. When you can identify the inspiration behind the desire, discipline shows up naturally.

Take a moment to recognize what's motivating you to make changes in your life. Grab a pen and a latte, and take some time to answer these two questions as honestly as you can.

- What do you want to do *differently* as a result of reading this book? (Empty my Inbox regularly, track delegated items, prioritize effectively, or go home earlier?)

- What do you want to *experience* differently as a result of reading this book? (Be more relaxed, focused, and in control?)

It's essential that you understand your motivation for change, because that will make setting up and sustaining you IMS so much easier and more graceful.

The Tools You'll Need to Get Started

In order to get started on the Three Phases for Creating an Integrated Management System, you'll want to make sure you have the following set up and available:

- I recommend using the latest version of Outlook, Microsoft Office Outlook 2003. However Outlook 2002, Outlook 2000, and Outlook 98 will work just fine. The book's screen images will show Outlook 2003, but you can still set up your IMS in an older version of Outlook. Some of the instructions will just be slightly different.

- Ensure that your e-mail is being downloaded directly into Microsoft Outlook.

- I recommend that you use some type of personal digital assistant (PDA) and ensure that it will allow you to synchronize your information with Microsoft Outlook. This book's examples use the Pocket PC. (You can purchase an inexpensive PDA that synchronizes with Outlook on eBay.)

- Verify your corporate policies about storing personal and business information in Microsoft Outlook. It is *essential* to know if you can incorporate your personal data into Outlook. I will be recommending that you integrate the two in order to make your life simpler and to help maintain work/life balance.

Focusing on Small Things First

Most of the changes I recommend are small changes that aren't difficult to make and that create a big difference.

For example, I'm sure you've opened an e-mail, decided you didn't want to deal with it, and closed it back in the Inbox. This is a small thing that takes seconds to do. If you repeat the same thing over and over, it doesn't take long before you have hundreds, or perhaps thousands, of e-mail messages in your Inbox. This is an example of "small things done consistently in strategic places create major impact." Conversely, if every time you open an e-mail you make a decision about what to do with it and where to put it, you can immediately remove it from the Inbox and dramatically reduce your e-mail volume. This is equally as powerful as the previous example, but with more positive results.

There's no way you can make all the changes I'll suggest in one sitting. Modifying behaviors takes time for all of us. However, you can choose two or three changes that would make the biggest impact and focus on them first.

The remaining chapters are dedicated to assisting you in completing The Three Phases so you can effectively set up your Integrated Management System. Creating the system is the most time consuming part, but once it's set up and you've entered all of your Action and Reference information, you'll find that managing it is quite simple. Using the system will quickly become a habit and effective part of your life.

"Small things done consistently in strategic places create major impact"
—**Unknown author**

Part Two

The Collecting Phase

In this part

Chapter Four

Setting Up Your Approved Collecting Points

The first step in creating your Integrated Management System is completing the Collecting Phase. The purpose of the Collecting Phase is to assist you in developing a leak-proof Collecting System, in which you'll effortlessly capture all of your commitments and agreements. This chapter and the next will help you identify where and how you're currently collecting information and assess whether or not it's working for you. You'll review how to reduce interruptions while you're in the process of collecting, and how to successfully combine your personal and business information into one integrated system. You'll also complete an exercise called "clearing the mind," in which you'll transfer your entire to-do list from your head to Microsoft Outlook. The benefits of this phase are simplification, an increased sense of well-being, and a greater experience of personal control.

In this chapter, I'll begin by reviewing how to set up your Collecting System, which is made up of a series of *approved Collecting Points*. Collecting Points are physical locations where you gather your tasks, reminders, and meeting notes, and where colleagues or family members can drop off actions and information for you. Typical approved Collecting Points are e-mail, voice mail, paper notepads, and paper inboxes.

Identifying Your Current Collecting Points

To create an effective Collecting System, you first need to identify the number of Collecting Points that you're currently using, and evaluate whether that number is really working for you. If you were to guess how many Collecting Points you have, how many do you think it would be? You'd probably say four or five. However, you actually have a lot more than five, as you're about to find out!

Where Do You Really Store Your Information?

I'd like you to take a look at how many places you're using to collect information. In Figure 4-1, you'll see lots of collecting boxes. Each box represents a physical or electronic *Collecting Point*. Take a mental walk through your life, from home to work, and write down as many places as you can think of where you're collecting information, commitments, and communications.

Figure 4-1   Where are you currently capturing your commitments and agreements?

If you run out of steam, review the questions below. They'll help you think of additional locations. It's important to identify how many Collecting Points you have so you can evaluate their usefulness.

While you're at work:

- When you're in meetings, where do you record notes and actions?

- When you get stopped in the hallway for a "drive by" interruption, where do you capture the action?

- When your boss sends you an e-mail to "Create a product strategy," where do you track it?

- Where do you collect your paper faxes?

- When you receive an overnight delivery package, where do you put it?

- Where do you put actions that result from face-to-face interruptions while you're in your office?

While you're on a business trip:

- When a client gives you a business card and asks that you call him, where do you put it?
- Where do you collect hotel and car receipts?
- When you're in baggage claim and get a great idea, where do you record it?

While you're traveling home from work:

- Where do you put the dry cleaning receipts after you drop off your laundry?
- When you answer your cell phone and a colleague needs you to call a client about a contract issue, where do you track it?
- On the radio, you hear Bruce Springsteen is coming to town, and you want tickets. Where do you record that?
- When you get a free car wash slip, where do you put it?

While you're at home:

- When the phone rings, and it's a message for your daughter who's not at home, where do you put the message?
- Where do you record that you've run out of breakfast cereal and need to buy more?
- Where do you make note that the gutter is broken and needs fixing?
- Where do you put the paper mail?
- Where do you track soccer practice for your son?
- When friends show up with tickets to a ball game in three weeks, where do you store them?

In general:

- How many e-mail boxes do you have?
- How many voice mail boxes do you have?
- How many note pads do you have?
- How many calendars do you have?

Are Your Collecting Points Working?

After going through this exercise, Carol Philips, a Sales Manager for Lucerne Publishing, said, "Wow! That's a whole lot of buckets. I have over 26!" You may be equally surprised by the number of buckets you've identified. Most of our clients are taken aback to find themselves with 20 to 25 Collecting Points as opposed to just the four or five they thought they had. When you have this many collecting locations, it becomes cumbersome to keep track of your commitments and locate information easily. Your Collecting Points become unorganized and overpopulated storage points and, in some cases, they collect dust as well as actions.

"I am rather like a mosquito in a nudist camp; I know what I want to do, but I don't know where to begin."
—**Stephen Bayne**

If I were to ask, "What are your priorities this week?" you'd need to go to each of your 20 to 25 Collecting Points to identify what you need to do. Only then would you be able to prioritize your list. Hmmm, that sounds time consuming and somewhat complicated, which leads to the question, "Does having so many Collecting Points work for you?"

Carol Philips' response was, "I need to consolidate everything. It's all too overwhelming. No wonder I can't find anything!" After my clients become aware of how many Collecting Points they're using, the realization is always the same: "I need to minimize the number of Collecting Points I have!"

Identifying Approved Collecting Points

If you could consolidate everything into one bucket, I'm sure you would. However, even though that's not possible right now, you can funnel your information into five, approved Collecting Points, as shown in Figure 4-2, which is a dramatic reduction from what you now have. You might end up with a few more than five because of the duplications required to support your personal as well as your business life, but it's still less than 20 to 25.

The five, basic Collecting Points I suggest are:

- A paper inbox and/or a portable paper inbox for road warriors
- A paper note pad and/or digital note pad
- Voice mail
- The Microsoft Outlook Task list
- E-mail

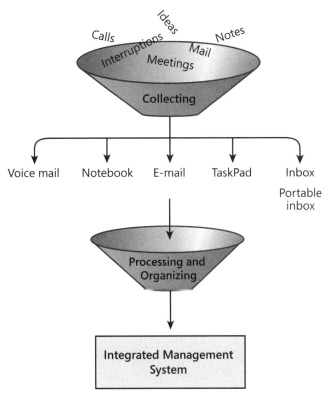

Figure 4-2   The Collecting System shows you how to funnel your information into five approved Collecting Points.

In the next section, you'll learn how to reduce all of the Collecting buckets you identified in the exercise above into these five approved Collecting Points.

Using a Paper Inbox and Portable Paper Inbox

Having a central, paper inbox at work or at home is a simple concept, but it can be a revelation, even if you who don't usually deal with a lot of paper.

Mary Baker, a publishing client, loved her paper. Paper was her business, after all! She had papers on her desk, on the floor, and on her credenza. Wherever there was a surface, there were papers. She was having a hard time finding and filing papers with so many of them placed so randomly about.

We began by getting her a physical paper inbox, clearly labeling it, and putting it on her desk. Then, we stacked all her papers in it. We took all the sticky notes off her monitor and removed the business cards from the window ledge, and we put everything in her inbox. In 20 minutes, her office was surprisingly clean! Mary now had a pile of papers in her inbox that needed to be processed and organized into her IMS. That was her next challenge.

I have two paper inboxes, one at home and one at work. When I pick up the mail at home, I distribute it into my inbox, my husband's inbox, or the trash can. Our home inboxes aren't as professional-looking as the inboxes in the office. Mine is the Martha Stewart wicker basket type with a raffia tie and a label indicating "Sally's Inbox." Snail mail goes directly into these inboxes. It doesn't go on the kitchen counter, the kitchen table, or the dining room table. Using a paper inbox is a simple process, and it makes finding papers much easier because they're in one spot rather than five different places. We now enjoy eating on the kitchen table without using this week's mail as a placemat!

When you first set up your physical paper inboxes at home, gather up all the papers from the various locations you've been using and drop them into your inbox. This might be a bit overwhelming at first, but once you empty this Collecting Point a couple of times you'll start to trust it. Before long, using it will become second nature. The good news is that there'll be no more papers in the kitchen or on the dining room table. That's worth the price of an inbox right there!

At work, all my papers (faxes, overnight delivery envelopes, mail, and internal documents) go into my paper inbox on my desk, and it's very clear where to put them. Many clients I work with don't have paper inboxes; they use their desk, credenza, and any flat surface they can lay their hands on. Their staff members, who want to drop off papers, end up putting them on their chairs or leaving sticky notes on their desks because it's the only way to call attention to these items. Once clients start using a paper inbox, they need to let their staff know where it is and how to use it, otherwise their chair and desk will continue to collect papers and sticky notes. Even though some of us are almost 100 percent digital, we're not 100 percent paper-free so, for now, the paper inbox still has great value and helps to keep a clean desk.

There are many times during the day when I'm not near my paper inbox, but I still need to collect bits of paper, receipts, meeting handouts, meetings notes, and business cards. To solve this problem, I created a portable paper inbox to carry with me. As you know, a quick trip to any office supply store will provide all kinds of wonderful, colorful file folders and expanding folders that you can use to create a portable inbox. My portable paper inbox is an 8 ½ by 11 inch expanding file, including four dividers, an 8 ½ x 11 note pad, and pockets for CDs, pens, and business cards. See Figure 4-3 for a diagram of my portable paper inbox.

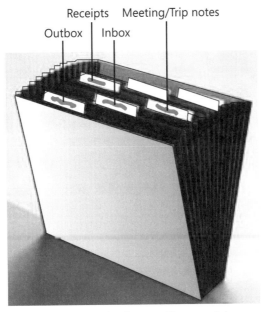

Figure 4-3   Example of a portable paper inbox

The four dividers in my portable paper inbox are labeled as follows:

- **Inbox**   Collects papers I receive while I'm away from my office.
- **Meeting/Trip notes**   Stores printed handouts and agendas I need to take on a business trip.
- **Receipts**   Keeps all of my travel receipts so they're ready for reimbursement.
- **Outbox**   Stores papers I'm given that need to be filed or distributed to other people when I get back to the office or my home.

When I'm on the road, I always carry my portable paper inbox, which enables me to capture receipts, business cards, and meeting handouts in one location. Without the portable inbox, these items would go into my wallet, my briefcase, or my back pocket, often never to be seen again! When I return from the road or a local appointment, I simply empty my portable inbox into my paper inbox on my desk and distribute my outbox. My portable paper inbox is then ready to take to my next meeting or on my next trip. This system ensures that all my paper items are centrally located in one place, ready to be processed and organized into my IMS. If you don't travel much or not at all, a simple plastic file labeled "Inbox," and stored in your briefcase, helps collect papers that need to go back to your office inbox.

The paper inbox still has value today. It helps reduce alternative Collecting Points—a desk, credenza, kitchen counter—and centralizes your papers into one location. I highly recommend that you dust off your inbox or go purchase a new one. It's a simple concept, but it works.

Carrying a Paper Notebook and a Digital Notebook

Having one notebook, rather than multiple notebooks, is a way to instantly minimize the number of your Collecting Points. It's also another great opportunity to visit the office supply store and pick out a fun note pad. You Microsoft OneNote users, I'll be discussing OneNote in a moment.

One of my clients, Katie Jordan, had twelve notebooks. Yup! She had twelve. No kidding! Each notebook tracked one of her twelve different projects. Note-taking worked well for Katie; however, she had one little problem. She often found herself in a project meeting with the wrong project notebook. Katie also kept track of her project tasks in her twelve note pads, and keeping her eye on them each day was becoming cumbersome. She wanted a simpler way to track notes and retrieve action steps.

I recommended that she use one notebook and take notes in chronological order. This way she'd always have the right notebook wherever she went. She'd have only one place to look up notes and she'd have it organized by date. I also suggested that she track action steps on a separate page using clear symbols to distinguish them, such as a square symbol to reflect an action item. When Katie looked back over her notes, she could easily identify the actions by their symbols and transfer them to her Task List.

Katie archived her old notebooks on her bookshelf and put elastic bands around them. She bought herself a spiral bound notebook and when she took notes she separated out her action items on a single page. When she returned to the office, she'd tear out the action page and, you guessed it, put it in her paper inbox. Now all her paper actions were stored in one central location leaving her notepad to track only reference information.

Notebooks are a great place to have fun. Back in the old days, I used to have a round, bright red, leather notepad, and a red ink pen. I hasten to add, it was a pen that didn't leak on airplanes and it had an additional cartridge in the pen so I never ran out of ink! I loved writing in a round notepad with red ink.

Today, however, I use a Tablet PC, which is my latest elegant note-taking device. The Tablet PC allows me to capture handwritten notes directly into OneNote. OneNote is a software product with which you can take meeting notes, either by writing on the screen or by typing. I have a pen that actually writes on my PC screen, which is pretty nifty. With the click of a button, I can transfer action items from my digital notes directly into the Task list in Microsoft Outlook. The Task list is part of my Action System, where I record all of my action items, and OneNote is part of my Reference System, where I store reference information that doesn't require action. OneNote enables me to sort reference information using a simple folder structure, and its search functions are incredibly powerful, making it easy to find handwritten or digital notes quickly. I carry a Pocket PC too, which also allows me to record handwritten notes. With my Tablet PC and my Pocket PC combined, I no longer need to carry notepaper with me. This results in one less Collecting Point and one less item to lug around when I'm traveling.

Using E-Mail

Using e-mail as a Collecting Point is particularly effective. This Collecting Point captures information for you on a continual basis, and captures the information in writing. Most of your family, friends, co-workers, and community use it, so it's a very familiar medium for all of us. The features in Microsoft Outlook that enable you to integrate e-mail messages with the Task list make it especially productive. You'll learn more about using e-mail in Chapter 8.

I'd suggest having one e-mail account rather than multiple e-mail accounts. I've worked with clients who have as many as seven e-mail addresses, so consolidating their e-mail accounts made a huge difference. The ideal situation is to combine all accounts into one. This might not work if you're unable to integrate personal and business e-mail or if you feel uncomfortable about mixing the two. However, I think you'll be surprised to learn how many information workers now combine personal and business into one system! I'm consistently taken aback by it myself. Company policies have relaxed on the topic of mixing personal and business items, and most companies I work with allow employees to receive "appropriate" personal e-mail in their Outlook Inboxes. For some clients, this remains a sensitive area, so I'll discuss integrating personal and business information in much more detail at the end of this chapter.

Another reason for having multiple Inboxes is to support productivity. David Simpson, a bookkeeper, has four clients. He visits them on four different days. David has an e-mail address and an inbox for each client.

David bills by the hour, so he wants to work only on his clients' e-mail requests during the time he's working for them. On Tuesdays, he works with a health club, and only wants to read and sort the club's e-mail that day. In this instance, having separate e-mail addresses actually supports David's productivity.

Take a look at your current e-mail accounts, and if you can consolidate them in a way that will increase your productivity, just do it!

Taking Advantage of the Outlook Task List

The Outlook Task list, and specifically the *Categories: (none)* category, is an ideal Collecting Point for capturing to-do's from your head, and actions from conference calls and voice mail. In Figure 4-4, you'll see that Carol Philips has multiple categories in her Task list. Her first category is Categories: (none), which is the default category Carol uses as her primary digital Collecting Point. You'll set up this category in Chapter 5.

Carol has found that the Categories: (none) Collecting Point helps her stay more focused and assists her in capturing all of her actions items instead of tracking them in her head. When Carol gets distracted by a mental "action reminder" while processing her e-mail, she simply types it into the Task list, where it's automatically placed in the Categories: (none) Collecting Point Similarly, when her mind wanders off in meetings, she captures those thoughts in Categories: (none) as well, mentally bringing her mind back to being present.

Carol also uses a Pocket PC as well as a Tablet PC. Both of these devices run Microsoft Outlook and can be synchronized with each another. Carol captures actions into Categories: (none) using her Pocket PC just as easily as using her Tablet PC. This means that wherever Carol is, she has access to Categories: (none) and can transfer information into it. Whether you're at a hockey game or out to dinner with friends, using a Pocket PC to capture your reminders is pretty slick, not to mention practical. Whipping out your Tablet PC just isn't as handy and cool as whipping out your Pocket PC!

I've also seen clients use Categories: (none) to help them empty their voice mail. If they can't handle a message right away, they transfer the action item into their Categories: (none) Collecting Point and delete the message from their voice mail box. This enables them to completely empty their voice mail and places the actions they can't do in the Categories: (none) Collecting Point, ready to be processed later. This helps them reduce the number of locations where they're storing action information, centralizing the collecting of actions in the Task list.

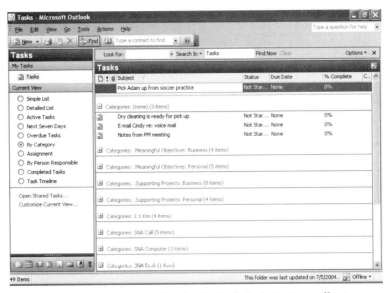

Figure 4-4   Categories: (none) in the Outlook Task List is an effective Collecting Point.

The mind is a powerful system. Left to its own devices, it can be a huge source of distraction, pulling you away from being present and taking you down the mental corridors of your thoughts. A great way to prevent this from happening is to keep emptying the to-do's from your head into Categories: (none) so you can continue to be present in whatever you're doing.

To set up the Categories: (none) Collecting Point, follow these steps:

1. Click the Folder List button in Outlook, and click either the Tasks folder or the Tasks icon at the bottom of the list.

2. Right-click the gray column-heading button labeled Subject, and select Customize Current View, as shown in Figure 4-5.

3. In the Customize View dialog box, click Group By.

4. In the Group Items By section of the Group By dialog box, click the drop-down menu, and select Categories, as shown in Figure 4-6.

5. Click OK.

6. Click OK again.

Figure 4-5   Customizing the current view

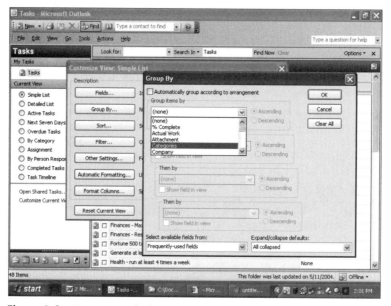

Figure 4-6   Grouping tasks by categories

7. At the top of the Task list you'll see a Subject heading. Under this
    heading is a field with the words "Click here to add a new Task." Click
    this field and type **WEEKLY REVIEW**.

8. Press the Enter key and the task will automatically show up under the Categories: (none) list, as shown in Figure 4-7.

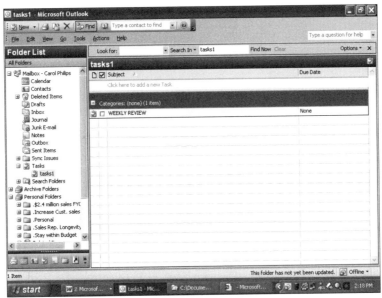

Figure 4-7   Creating a WEEKLY REVIEW Task in Categories: (none)

You will be using the Weekly Review task later in this chapter, so please keep it in the Task list.

Using Voice Mail

Voice mail is another wonderful, mainstream Collecting Point. Some of us have multiple voice mail boxes so there's a lot of opportunity to consolidate. Chris Cannon, one of my clients, had five voice mail boxes. He had:

- a land line at home
- a land line at work
- a cell phone
- a pager
- a client land line on site

Chris liked that his clients, family, and friends knew how to get hold of him. However, he was getting tired of downloading so many voice mail boxes. Chris and I discussed whether or not he really needed five voice mail boxes and how we could consolidate them.

Chris realized that as long as his clients, family, and friends knew how to get hold of him, no one would mind using one number over another. He bit the bullet and consolidated to two voice mail boxes. He eliminated the client landline and the pager. He directed his work landline to his cell phone. He ended up with a personal land line and a cell phone voice mail box. (Redirecting a landline to a cell phone can be a great way to eliminate a Collecting Point.)

You can also use voice mail not only to capture messages from others, but to capture your own to-do's. When you're in the car and remember you need to send Annie updated PowerPoint slides, you can't safely write down a reminder or type it into your laptop, but you can call yourself and leave a message on your own voice mail system. This ensures that you get it out of your head and put it into one of your approved Collecting Points to be processed later.

For some of us, voice mail is being transferred to e-mail. It's called *unified messaging*. Unified messaging helps eliminate the land line at work, condensing two points into one. It takes your voice mail messages and directs them to your e-mail inbox. When you open the e-mail, you can hear the voice mail message directly through your computer's speakers. Some clients use a headset for more private messages.

Carol Philips now has seven approved Collecting Points that she uses; her inbox at home, her inbox at work, her Categories: (none), OneNote, two voice mail boxes, and e-mail. She hopes to eliminate another voice mail box soon and use only her cell phone for all her calls. That would drop her Collecting Points to six. It's a whole lot easier for Carol to manage six Collecting Points than the 26 she started with! The key to consolidating Collecting Points is to decide which ones you want to use, set them up, and consolidate all your other locations into these approved Collecting Points. After you've set them up, all you need to do is use them consistently and train those people around you to use them.

Carol commented that after setting up her Collecting System, "My life is much simpler as a result. Gone are the days of collecting on my desk, fridge, dining room table, sticky notes, multiple note pads, my car dashboard, a white board, shelves, cupboards, floors, on my briefcase, and in my head. From 26 to seven Collecting Points. What's not to like?"

To set up her approved Collecting Points, Carol purchased the following tools:

- two physical, paper inboxes; one for her desk at work and one for her desk at home
- a Pocket PC that synchronizes with Microsoft Outlook
- a travel Pocket PC cable, so she can synchronize her Pocket PC and her laptop while on the road
- a portable paper inbox

Carol then took a number of actions. Without hesitation, she:

- labeled the physical paper inboxes so others knew to use them
- learned how to use the Tablet PC's OneNote software
- learned how to synchronize her Pocket PC with her laptop
- labeled her portable paper inbox sections
- cancelled a voice mail box

To change her habits, Carol also:

- downloaded reminders from her head to Categories: (none)
- avoided using sticky notes or paper
- put her mail in her inbox and not on her desk

After three months, Carol reported that using her Collecting System had now become a habit. She didn't even think about it and was relieved to have reduced her buckets to so few.

You Are *Not* a Collecting Point!

When you review the five, key Collecting Points in Figure 4-2, you'll notice that there isn't a Collecting Point with your name on it. Guess what! You're not an approved Collecting bucket! Most people, however, spend a considerable amount of time during the day collecting information from various kinds of interruptions. In other words, you're using yourself as a "human Collecting Point." All of us get interrupted throughout the day, not only by people, but by technology—the ding of an e-mail, the ring of a cell phone, and the buzz of a pager. When I ask clients "When do you do your best work?" most respond, "First thing in the morning and last thing at night."

In other words, clients aren't getting their real work done in the office. Perhaps you've had the same experience.

"The average
American worker
has fifty interrup-
tions a day, of
which seventy
percent have noth-
ing to with work."
— **W. Edward
Deming**

Dealing with interruptions is part of your job, but it probably isn't your primary job. If you're a receptionist, for example, every time the phone rings, it would be inappropriate to say, "I'm sorry, I'm not taking calls for the next hour. Please call back at two o'clock and I'll help you then." This strategy wouldn't be realistic because, in this example, your job is dealing with interruptions. However, handling interruptions is almost certainly not your principal responsibility, therefore why do you get so many of them?

Why Do You Get So Many Interruptions?

As Ted Morris, a client from a large telecommunications company once said to me when asked why he got so many interruptions, "*Because I allow them!*" It's really that simple. What underlies this comment is that people actually unconsciously train their staff and co-workers to interrupt them and to leave things to the last minute. When you accept interruptions, you're sending a message that says, "It's OK to interrupt me." If you do this consistently, it becomes the culture. In other words, what you allow from others is a form of training others.

The problem with this concept is that most of the time you're unaware of the impact this training has and you're even unaware that you're carrying out this training. The short-term effect of consistent interruptions is that you get distracted, and you end up doing your real work at home or after hours. The long-term effect is that your team becomes less proactive and more reactive, coming to you with issues at the very last minute. We all need to accept interruptions, however I recommend that you consciously retrain your staff to handle interruptions more effectively and, as a result, reduce their volume.

Ted was able to reduce interruptions by 40 percent by resetting expectations and communicating them clearly to his team. Ted recognized that whenever his staff interrupted him, he always stopped what he was doing to help them. They felt respected and honored by this, but Ted wasn't getting his work done at work. He was working two hours every evening at home.

Once, Ted tried to change this pattern. The next time he got interrupted, he said, "I can't take this interruption right now. You'll have to come back." The staff member replied, "But I need to have this data for a meeting in 30 minutes!" What choice did Ted have but to handle the interruption. Once again, he reinforced that he was available and the pattern continued.

I suggested to Ted that he have a meeting with his staff to clearly reset their expectations and to support him in being able to get more work done during the day. He told his team that his work was intruding on his personal life. His solution was to book two hours of uninterrupted time a day so he could get his work done *at work*. This time was scheduled on Ted's calendar so no one could book him for meetings, and his team could see the reserved time and therefore respect it. Ted also clarified that if his team interrupted him during this time, he would ask them to come back later. Ted did a good job of reinforcing his boundaries, which was critical for change to take place. If you don't reinforce the expectations you set, then nothing will change. Remember, "If you always do what you've always done..." You can fill in the rest by now.

Ted's team needed to be more proactive, thinking and planning ahead to get his involvement rather than reacting and leaving things to the last minute. This is a positive result of redefining expectations; it pushes people to move their planning to the front end, ultimately saving time and resources on the back end.

Ted asked his staff to consider the alternative solutions to interrupting him: Incorporating conversation points in 1:1 or staff meetings, sending e-mails with a 24-hour turnaround time, or mulling over how to handle the situation themselves. Ted realized that if he took more time to train his team, not only would he get more done, but they'd be better off. His staff had relied on Ted without his realizing it. Now he wanted to help them help themselves and be more self-reliant. Ted became a leader instead of a manager.

Ted's goal was not to entirely eliminate interruptions. He recognized that they were part of the rhythm of his business. However, he needed to approach them differently because their quantity was affecting the quality of his life. By resetting expectations and reinforcing them with his team, he was able to create a positive change. From this, he began to realize other areas where his actions were unconscious and how to consciously reset and re-clarify his boundaries. When you become more conscious of training your team, continuing the process comes naturally.

By consistently allowing certain behaviors from your team, you might as well be saying "please do it this way." Be careful what you allow, because what you allow becomes what you create. Interruptions are a function of what you tolerate and what you consent to. You've actually trained the people around you without realizing it. Once you become aware of this

"Boundaries help you stop reacting to everyone else's expectations and start living by your own. You aren't being demanding of anyone else, you're simply taking control of your own life. You're choosing more effective choices and better using your most precious resource you."
— **Linda Manassee Buell**

process, it becomes a lot easier to change. I've done studies in departments of two hundred people during which they reduced interruptions by 20 percent as a result of setting and reinforcing clear boundaries.

Resetting Expectations and Holding People Accountable

If you don't create your own expectations, the world around will do it for you, and you may not like what you get! My clients often feel like they can't change expectations, and even that they're imprisoned by them. "You don't understand. That's the way it is around here. I can't change it!" Maybe you're right, maybe you can't. However, you *can* change what you do and how you manage or participate in your team. Take a look at the expectations you've created consciously and unconsciously—e-mail response times, drive-by interruptions, phone response times—and decide what changes you want to make. Then meet with your team to clarify, and align everyone to, these new expectations. You don't have to wait for your boss to drive this action; you can drive it. Everyone is tired of incessant interruptions and will welcome the opportunity to talk about changing them. Go for it!

After you've created new expectations, the next step is ensuring you hold yourself and your team accountable for making them happen. If you don't set accountability, nothing will change and you'll only teach your staff that these "change" conversations are meaningless and ineffective.

When you start to successfully demonstrate new behaviors, others will want to do the same. There's nothing like a little bit of authentic demonstration to spark the minds and hearts of those around you. People want to improve, and when they see others progressing, they're inspired to change themselves. Leadership by example is always more powerful than leadership by edict, and it doesn't have to come from the top. It can start anywhere someone decides to lead.

Ted successfully made a change. What he did was relatively simple. He added "dealing with interruptions" to his monthly staff meeting. During the meeting, he let his staff know that he planned to block out on his calendar two hours, exclusively for work, and he described his purpose for doing so. He asked his staff to plan ahead what they'd need from him so that they could support his request for uninterrupted time. Ted made it very clear that he'd enforce this request, and if someone tried to interrupt him, he'd ask them to come back later, no matter what was going on (except for a real emergency, of course).

Ted reset his expectations up front so that his team would understand why he was behaving differently and then support him. If he'd made these changes without discussing them with his team, his staff could have become confused and frustrated, saying "he's not available and I don't know why!" Ted's staff was most accommodating because they were all in the same boat; they weren't getting their work done either! It's critical to set the stage before you set up new boundaries so your environment can support you.

When Ted consistently kept his two hours of uninterrupted work time, his staff started to work in cooperation with him. There were fewer interruptions and his staff became more proactive. Ted modeled a purposeful change and supported his staff in doing the same.

Changing the E-Mail Culture

Another minefield of bad habits is e-mail. E-mail isn't just a form of communication; it's an opportunity for huge productivity gains or huge productivity losses. If you don't train yourself, and your staff, to handle e-mail productively, you'll watch it take over your lives, reduce your productivity, and become an endless cause of distraction, not only at work but also at home.

E-mail dominates the day-to-day operations of today's companies, so it's time we all addressed it and stopped pretending that we don't have the time or resources to deal with it. My company has client statistics that prove that educating staff regarding best practices for e-mail can cause an 81 percent drop in the total amount of e-mail in each employee's Inbox and a 26 percent reduction in the daily e-mail volume received by employees. These statistics are impressive, to say the least, and they demonstrate that education works. They confirm that employees are starved for knowledge, and when they get it—watch out!—it makes a difference.

E-mail really isn't the problem. The problem is how we've allowed ourselves and our staff to approach it, and how little training we've provided. Much like handling interruptions, the training they have received so far has been somewhat unconscious. When you process e-mail at 10 o'clock on Sunday night and during meetings, you send to others a message that it's fine to do that. However, when your team or colleagues see you in control—going home with an empty Inbox and taking your weekend off—they'll want to do the same. Who wouldn't? First, take the time to get your own house in order, and then you can train your staff and colleagues to do the same.

So where do you start? By clarifying the expectations you have, and holding yourself and others accountable.

Using FedEx is a good example of creating and reinforcing expectations. You can't send a FedEx package in less than three minutes. It takes 12 hours, minimum. FedEx stands behind that boundary, and it's not negotiable. When you call to set your pick up, you talk with a voice-activated service, not even a real person! However, FedEx works, and it's incredibly successful. I don't mind having to call 12 hours before I want my package to arrive, and I don't mind talking to a machine. Why? Because FedEx has established clear expectations and *FedEx always delivers on their response time. I can count on it.* That's what makes FedEx the company it is today.

Take another look at your internal and external customer expectations. It's better to have a 12-hour turnaround time and deliver 100 percent of the time, then have a less-than-three minute turnaround, always be missing deadlines, and feel overwhelmed and out of balance.

Some jobs are designed to support short turnaround times. If you're a receptionist, a fireman, an information technology specialist, or a doctor in an emergency room, your work requires an immediate response. This is not true of most professions. There are very few businesses and job descriptions that can successfully support a less-than-three-minute turnaround time. Technology has enabled us to respond immediately, however most of us have other work activities we need to complete that take longer than three minutes. You attend two-hour meetings, one-hour conference calls, write complex proposals, and create budgets, making it impossible to achieve three-minute response times. If you believe that you have to respond to everything immediately, you'll end up doing e-mail during meetings, conference calls, and the one-hour journey home, which means that you're never really present in any activity you're doing. This can be frustrating and unsatisfying.

Susan Henderson worked for a software company. Her team habitually responded to e-mails in less than three minutes. "They were addicted to the ding, compulsively checking mail on their Blackberries during meetings, on the way to meetings, and even in their cars while driving," Susan said. "Because everyone is e-mailing back and forth in less than three minutes, it's forcing the team to be super-reactive." Her staff justified this behavior, saying, "If I don't reply quickly, decisions and discussions are held without my input, so I have to be on e-mail all day."

The three-minute response time drives environments for reactive and unproductive behaviors. Responding so quickly works occasionally, but maintaining that pace throughout the day is ineffective and unrealistic. Once it gets started, it's hard to stop unless you meet with your team, let them know that you want to change your expectations, and clarify what you want to change them to.

Susan held a staff meeting and, as a team, they came up with the following expectations: E-mail response times will be four hours. Less than two-minute interruptions will take place on instant messaging. And the team will turn off the e-mail ding!

To support the four-hour response time, she asked her staff to be more proactive about communications. She tied e-mail effectiveness to performance reviews to let her staff know that she was serious about making changes. This approach caused her staff to become more proactive, thinking through their projects ahead of time rather than being reactive and shooting e-mails back and forth. Her staff got more work done during the day because they did not have to check e-mail so often. The changes were very positive.

Carol Philips was telling me about her weekend e-mail, "My whole department does e-mail on Sunday evenings!" She sounded a tiny bit frustrated. With a little digging, I found out that when Carol was extremely overwhelmed with e-mail, she started processing it on Sunday nights to catch up. Her staff discovered her online, and when they got immediate responses, began e-mailing one another, and this kept going until it became a "Sunday night habit." I suggested to Carol that she set up a staff meeting and discuss the Sunday e-mail culture. Interestingly enough, everyone wanted to be with family on Sunday night instead of doing e-mail so the team reset its expectations. E-mail sent over the weekend didn't have to be responded to until Monday, and any urgent decisions would be handled over the phone. This caused her team to be more proactive regarding e-mail, and to protect the time they had at home with family. If people wanted to do e-mail they could, but it was no longer a Sunday requirement.

E-mail is not the problem. The problem is how we approach it. If you change your approach, you can change your results. Whether you run a team or participate in one, you can lead these changes.

Reducing Drive-By Interruptions

"Boundary setting is not about getting other people to change (even though at first, it may seem that way). It's really about deciding what you will and won't tolerate any longer in your life, and then communicating this firmly and consistently whenever you need to. Boundaries are essential to becoming a healthy adult and balancing your work and personal life effectively. They demonstrate your commitment to self-respect."
—**Natalie Gahrmann**

I'll bet you never think of yourself as a drive-by interrupter! Drive-bys are when colleagues interrupt you, in the office, in the corridor, or at breaks in meetings. Some of these interruptions are effective, but too many cause you to do your work at home! Imagine you're working on a spreadsheet when someone pops in and asks, "Got a minute?" Usually, that means "have you got fifteen?" If the same thing happens throughout the day, it's hard to get anything done.

I suggest talking with your team about how to decrease these types of drive-by interruptions. Common solutions are to e-mail requests instead of interrupting, add discussion points to meeting agendas, or capture action items in your Outlook Task list to be handled during 1:1 meetings. Whatever the solution, prepare the environment to expect change, and let everyone know how you'll reinforce it. "If you stop me in the corridor, I'll ask you to follow up with an e-mail to ensure that I act on it." This sets the stage and helps you reduce some of the discomfort you might experience redirecting these kinds of interruptions. It's not always easy to ask for what you want and change your behaviors. After you've addressed these issues with your team, you'll feel more comfortable making the changes.

You can make changes to reduce drive-by interruptions with your staff, but you need to be careful how you try to make them outside of your team! The best approach to effect change outside of your group is by personal demonstration. You may not think that by changing your own habits you can affect anyone else's, and it may seem like a small thing to do in comparison to changing a department but *it doesn't take much of a difference to make a difference*. The little changes you make do make a difference and do positively affect the people around you.

Turning Off Ringing Phones and Beeping Pagers

If you always answer your phone, people will always expect you to take their calls. If you always return messages within 24 hours, recipients will always expect a 24-hour response. Set realistic expectations, stick to them, and watch your internal and external customers be happy.

It's important that response time expectations are indicated in your voice mail. This allows people new to you to know what to expect, and it reinforces the expectations of those you consistently interact with. No one said you have to answer your phone every time it rings.

My company has a four-hour response time on cell phone calls and eight hours on landline calls. As long as people stick to these response times, they can choose when they answer their phones and when they turn them off. The key is not that the phone is answered. The key is that people respond to their messages within the response time they've promised.

Whatever the nature of the interruptions you face, the best approach is to clarify your purpose, your expectations, and how you're going to hold people accountable. Everyone can get more done during the day if interruptions are minimized. My experience is that your team will be glad you brought up the topic of interruptions. Believe me, I have been in hundreds of these meetings and people are thrilled to talk about reducing interruptions. We all experience the same problem

Integrating Personal and Business Information into One System

Should you or should you not integrate your personal and business information into one Integrated Management System? Your decision is vital because whether you combine the two affects how you set up your system.

This issue is a very sensitive topic for my clients. Some have integrated personal and business information easily, and couldn't imagine it otherwise, while others are extremely uncomfortable about mixing the two.

A stumbling block for many clients is often their own personal beliefs about mixing personal and business information. In my early twenties, I was told repeatedly not to combine personal and business. It was drilled into me that it would be inappropriate and unprofessional. However, the working environment today is very, very different from the way it was 25 years ago. In those days, my wardrobe was also filled with suits and panty hose, now I wear jeans and socks to work! That took me quite a while to adjust to. Integrating personal and business is just another level of adjustment.

With the introduction of the Pocket PC, a device that you can carry wherever you go, it starts to make more sense to combine personal and business information. When I'm out shopping, I have immediate access to my grocery list. At the video store, my DVD list is handy when I can't remember what I want to watch. You'll find that your life gets easier if you integrate personal and business together. Life itself is integrated so having a system that reflects that is a blessing. You're going to do personal activities at work anyway—making doctor appointments, scheduling car services, and calling to clarify insurance claims—and it's a lot easier to manage all this using one central system instead of two. If you're able to keep your dentist, car service, and insurance contact data in your Contacts list in Outlook, you'll complete these activities faster, which means you'll spend less time at work doing them.

I've consulted with a variety of corporations and most of them allow you to integrate personal data (personal e-mail, personal contacts, and personal folders), as long as the content is appropriate. Your company may not follow this policy, so be sure to find out what your company guidelines are. Knowing that your company would support you in combining the two helps make the decision a lot easier.

What to Do When the Personal Must Stay Personal

In some situations, you may need to keep two systems because company policies say so. If you have a PC or laptop at home, you can run Microsoft Outlook on it and use it as your personal system exclusively. You can either print out the data that you need daily or purchase a Pocket PC and synchronize it with your personal system. You'll then use your work PC for business only and carry a Pocket PC for the personal.

Some clients carry a portable paper management system for their personal information and keep their computer and Pocket PC for work use only. I recommend staying entirely electronic rather than working with paper because our daily lives are increasingly moving into our work world. Of course, you'll eventually discover which system works best for you.

You've now come to the end of this chapter and have almost completed the Collecting Phase. Chapter 5 will finish this phase. Before you move on, pause and reflect on what you've learned and the changes you want to make. You'll record these changes in Outlook in a task called the Weekly Review, which you set up earlier in this chapter.

What Changes Will You Make?

Go to the Task list in Outlook, and open the task you labeled *WEEKLY REVIEW*. In the Notes section of this task, type three headings: Collecting, Processing and Organizing, and Prioritizing and Planning, as shown in Figure 4-8.

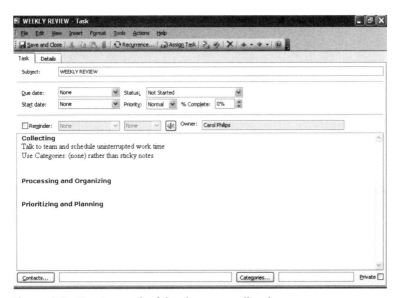

Figure 4-8 Keeping track of the changes you'll make

As you go through the Three Phases for Creating an Integrated Management System and make decisions about the changes you want to make, I'd like you to come back to this task, open it up, and record each of your decisions. These changes will enable you to "live the system" and ensure it works for you and becomes part of your life.

After you've created this task, please take a moment to record what you want to do differently to complete the set up of your approved Collecting Points, consolidating your unapproved Collecting points, reducing interruptions, and integrating your personal and business information into a single Integrated Management System. Please write down these actions under the heading "Collecting." It's very important to record the changes you want to make as this helps you clarify what you're going to do and reminds you to do it! You will be looking at this list once a week. More on that in Chapter 10.

"Success is nothing more than a few simple disciplines, practiced every day."
— **Jim Rohn**

For inspiration, here are a few examples of what my clients have written:

- Use one paper notepad. Take all my additional paper notepads, put elastic bands around them, and archive them on my credenza. Never to be used again!

Elegant Edge of Productivity

As you'll learn through this book, you can use many different and fun tools to help you get and stay organized. Here are a couple of slick tools that work well for me. This list is just a sample of what I have on hand at the moment.

- **Fancy writing tools** Ink pens that are road-warrior proof and fun to write with: visit www.writersedge.com; www.joon.com.

- **Cool notebooks** Great-looking leather Padfolios. Visit the Leather Trip Web site (www.leathertree.com).

- **Tablet PC** The Toshiba Portege. You can read about it at the Toshiba Web site (www.toshibadirect.com). Search on "Tablet PC."

- **Slick inboxes** Leather or plastic inboxes. For more information, visit The Container Store (www.containerstore.com/browse/index.jhtml?CATID=69245).

- **Trendy Pocket PC cases** Cases customized to fit your PDA. You'll find them at CasesOnline (casesonline.com/configurator.php).

- **High-tech portable inboxes** An expanding wallet, available at any office supply Web site.

- **Sexy cell phones** Smartphones that can synchronize with Outlook. You can read about it at the Motorola Web site (www.motorola.com). Search on "smartphone."

You can use this list as a guide for your own online shopping.

- Purchase OneNote software so I can take meeting notes digitally and eliminate paper notepads.

- Set up a paper inbox on my desk at home and work. Put all the papers on my desk, floor, and credenza in the paper inbox.

- Buy myself a PDA so I can use Categories: (none) as a Collecting Point when traveling out and about and combine personal and business information.

- Download voice mail messages when I am at my computer so I can type appropriate actions into Categories: (none) instead of writing them on paper and then having to transfer them.

- Eliminate my landline at home and use only my cell phone.

- Set up an agenda in the next staff meeting to talk about e-mail and phone response times, and drive-by interruptions.

- Find out about company policies that relate to personal and business data storage.

Wrapping It Up!

In this chapter, I discussed how to set up and minimize your Collecting Points to simplify your system, reduce clutter, eliminate chaos and confusion, and give you physical, mental, and emotional breathing room, not to mention a clean kitchen counter! I discussed how to create effective boundaries to reduce interruptions, making it easy to get more work done during the day and spend more quality time at home. And last, I talked about whether or not to integrate your personal and business information into one system.

The last part of the Collecting Phase is clearing the mind, which Chapter 5 is dedicated to. Don't be fooled by the simplicity of improving your Collecting System. It can make a huge difference. If you reduce interruptions by 40 percent, that alone will be worth it. Onwards and upwards!

"If you always do what you've always done, you'll always get what you've always gotten."
— **Author Unknown**

Chapter Five
Clearing the Mind

This chapter completes the Collecting Phase, which is the first of the Three Phases for Creating an Integrated Management System. The purpose of the Collecting Phase is to assist you in developing a leak-proof Collecting System with which you'll effortlessly capture all of your commitments and agreements.

You'll complete an exercise called "clearing the mind," which will enable you to capture all the actions you've been carrying around in your head and transfer them into the Microsoft Outlook Task List. This process is very liberating, and it gives you a more realistic view of how much you can do.

You'll also create Meaningful Objectives in both your personal and business life and transfer them into the Outlook Task list. This is a vital step because your IMS will be built around these objectives,

Finally, you'll learn why it's essential to create a system that supports you in keeping your agreements, and helps you understand when to renegotiate or, in some cases, just say "no" to them. Saying "no" is hard for most of us, but we all could use that word a little bit more. The funny thing is, the more you use "no," the more focused and productive you'll become, and the easier you'll find it to achieve your objectives.

Are You Using Your Mind As a Collecting Point?

We all underestimate how much we use our minds as a Collecting Point, and how this impacts our daily focus and ability to be present. Think about it, when you're in a meeting and remember something you need to do, you start figuring out mentally how you'll get that something done. This takes your focus away from your colleagues so you're no longer listening to what they're saying. Over time, these preoccupations affect the quality of your interactions and you end up spending time *after* meetings, catching up on information you missed. Worrying about what you have to do, when you can't do anything about it, is *not* a productive activity.

Here's another example: Imagine that you're at home and your daughter is talking to you. At the same time, a voice in your head is reminding you to take your car to the garage to have the oil changed. Some part of your daughter knows you're not really present with her; you're already driving your car to the dealership! Yet, if anyone asked you which experience was most meaningful, you'd answer "spending time with my daughter." Thinking about tasks when you're spending time with someone else compromises the relationship.

My clients often say, "I have more to do than I can do, and it's overwhelming!" However, I've discovered that this feeling is often disproportionate to the number of tasks they actually have to do! Mental lists are harder to manage than written lists because they appear much bigger than they really are. With mental lists, it's tough to get a realistic perspective on your priorities and how long they'll take to get done.

Understanding the Conscious and Unconscious Mind

When you understand the relationship between the conscious and unconscious mind, you'll begin to realize why it's critical to get the to-do's out of your head and into the Outlook Task list.

Your conscious mind has limited space and can track only small quantities of data at any given time; on average, four to ten items. The unconscious mind, on the other hand, is unlimited and can track infinite quantities of data, as shown in Figure 5-1. It also has no idea of time, and it's not very organized, as you'll see in the example below.

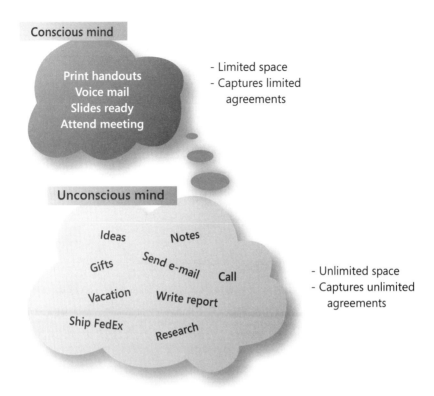

Conscious mind

Print handouts
Voice mail
Slides ready
Attend meeting

- Limited space
- Captures limited
  agreements

Unconscious mind

Ideas   Notes
Gifts   Send e-mail   Call
Vacation   Write report
Ship FedEx
Research

- Unlimited space
- Captures unlimited
  agreements

Figure 5-1   The conscious and unconscious mind

Molly is driving to work, and reviewing her mental to-do list, which includes pick up a soy latte, check e-mail, print handouts for her 3 PM meeting, check with Benny whether the room is set up, and call Karen to sing "Happy Birthday."

As Molly arrives at work, Michael leaps out of his office and shouts, "Molly, just wanted to remind you to call Litware to make sure the presentation is set up!" Molly replies, "Of course. No problem." Molly's *conscious* mind, however, is completely occupied by her current to-do list, and there's no room for another item, so it drops into her *unconscious* mind.

Molly then checks her e-mail, prints handouts, and walks over to her meeting. Her mental to-do list just got smaller so she now has space in her *conscious* mind. While Molly sits in the meeting, her mind wanders and she feels her *unconscious* trying to grab her attention. "Call Litware to make sure the presentation is set up." However, Molly's in a meeting right now and can't do anything about it, so back it goes, into her *unconscious*!

At the end of the meeting, Molly picks up additional action items and records them in her head. She goes back to her office where her e-mail is pinging and her phone is blinking. The next thing she knows, it's 6 PM and she's driving home, safely in the bubble of her car. She sighs and relaxes, her mind wanders off, and there it is again, "Call Litware to make sure the presentation is set up." Her cell phone battery has died and she doesn't have a charger in the car! Ah well, it'll have to wait. Back it goes into the unconscious.

Molly gets home, feeds the dogs, takes a look at the mail, prepares dinner, and at 10:30 PM, she finally relaxes in her easy chair and lets her mind wander off. There it is again! "Call Litware to make sure the presentation is set up." Too late for Molly to do anything about it right now, so back it goes, into her unconscious.

I'm sure you can relate to this experience! When there's room in your *conscious* mind, the unconscious will remind you of incomplete tasks. It works like clockwork! You may have noticed, your unconscious jogs your memory at the most inopportune moments and in the most inconvenient places. It has no concept of time or priority.

Think of the times you've gotten into the shower only to remember that you need to buy shampoo. Of course, the next time you're in the drug store, you'll forget to buy it. Not only is this frustrating, but it doesn't support you in getting things done.

Are You Carrying a Heavy Load?

Carrying lists of incomplete tasks in your mind can create enormous mental, as well as physical, stress. Everything that's incomplete in your life, no matter how old, gets recorded in your unconscious or conscious mind. Fix the gutter, change the lightbulb, repay Terry the $60 I borrowed, and finish reading that book. You get the idea. Each incomplete item that you carry around is allocated a certain amount of your mind's attention, ensuring that you don't forget about it. The more "incompletes" you have, the more overwhelmed and stressed you become.

Imagine, for a moment, that each incomplete in your head weighs one pound, and you have 100 of them. Picture yourself dragging a 100-pound load wherever you go, 24 hours a day, 7 days a week; even in your sleep! How would you feel trying to get things done while dragging this weight around?

Maybe you've grown strong and no longer realize how heavy your load is. The scary part of that is that you've gotten so used to the load that it's become normal. Just to be clear, it's not normal. You'll be amazed by how much lighter you'll feel when you let go of your incompletes.

The best way to manage a mental to-do list is to capture it in a Collecting Point. The Outlook Task list is a perfect location because it's centrally located and designed to carry heavy loads. The Task list will remind you when and where actions need to be done so you remember to buy shampoo when you're at the store. You'll also remember to make your calls when you're near a phone and not in a meeting.

Why use your head and pay the price of lugging around a heavy weight when you can use Outlook to carry it for you? It's time to unshackle the mind and give it some peace. You won't believe how much lighter you'll feel when you let go of all these incompletes. We'll have to scrape you off the ceiling!

Clearing the Mind and Lightening Your Load

The purpose of the "clearing the mind" exercise is to empty your mind of all the to-do's you've been harboring in your head. In order to do this, you need to be ruthless, capturing every incomplete that you can possibly think of. Don't underestimate the mind! It's tricky, and it'll keep hold of your incompletes and then wake you up in the middle of the night, reminding you to do them. I'm sure you've had that experience before!

This exercise is an opportunity to let go of everything that you've been carrying around in your head. Let Outlook manage your lists for you, so you can use your mind for more important activities, such as planning and strategizing, and simply being present.

The palest ink is better than the best memory.
— **Chinese Proverb**

Doing the "Clearing the Mind" Exercise

You'll be using Categories: (none) as your Collecting Point for the "clearing the mind" exercise.

To ensure that you capture as many items as possible, from all areas of your life, I'd like you to allow yourself to think randomly—from work to home, from small to large, and from important to irrelevant. Just allow anything in your mind to surface, in any order it appears. Your job is simple; capture each thought, and type it into a new task. Even if some of the tasks you come up with are connected, please enter them as individual tasks. If you currently use categories to organize your lists, please ignore them for now and only enter items into the Categories: (none) Collecting Point. This is a free-flowing exercise, and you'll organize this list later, in Chapter 7.

"Your system is
only as good as
your mind. If it's on
your mind, it's not
in your system."
— **David Allen**

To begin the exercise, go to the Task list, and use the "Click here to add a new task" field to enter a task, such as "Create a draft budget for 2005." Type your item in the Subject line, press Enter, and watch it instantly show up in Categories: (none). If you are an experienced user, this is normal. However, if you are learning how to use the Task list, this is a pretty cool feature. Now, enter the next item that comes to mind, such as "Buy dog food," and press Enter. Then add the next item, such as "Set up United Airlines travel for Minnesota trip." As you can see, these items are unrelated, random, and a mix of both personal and business. That's OK. This is how clearing the mind works. Allow your mind to flow in the order it wants. Just go with it, and try not to hinder it by organizing it any particular way

Spend at least fifteen minutes clearing the mind and, if you get stuck, you can read through the personal and professional trigger lists in Lists 5-1 and 5-2. These lists are designed to prompt you to remember items that you may have forgotten. If you get to the end of your mind sweep and haven't read these trigger lists, review them carefully to make sure that you've captured everything you can possibly think of. You want to get this "stuff" out of your head and into your system. As a reference point, clients usually enter anywhere from 20 to 35 incompletes at a time.

You'll be building your IMS around the list you've created, so it's critical that you complete this exercise *before* continuing on with the next chapter of this book. Please don't skip this process as it's very important for the integrity of the system. You'll also feel better after you've done it.

Projects started, not completed
Projects to be started
Commitments/promises to
    Others
    Bosses/partners
    Colleagues, subordinates
    Other people in organization
    Outside people
    Customers
    Other organizations
    Professionals
Communications to make/get
Initiate or respond to:
    Phone calls
    Voice mail
    E-mail, pages, faxes
    Letters, memos
Other writing to finish/submit
    Reports
    Evaluations/reviews
    Proposals
    Articles
    Promotional materials
    Manuals, instructions
    Re-writes and edits
Meetings that need to be set/requested
Who needs to know about what decisions?
Planning/organizing
    Formal planning (goals, targets)
    Current projects (next stages)
    Upcoming projects
    Business/marketing plans
    Organizational initiatives
    Upcoming events
    Meetings
    Presentations
    Organizational structuring
    Changes in facilities
    Installation of new systems
    Travel
Financial
    Online banking
    Cash flow
    Statistics and budgets
    Forecasts and projections
    P and L's

Balance sheet
Credit line
Banks
Receivables
Payables
Petty cash
Administration
    Legal issues
    Insurance
    Personnel
    Policies and procedures
Customers
    Internal
    External
Marketing, promotion, sales
Customer service
Systems
    Phones, computers, equipment
Inventories
Supplies
Office/site
    Office organization
    Furniture/decorations
Waiting for...
    Information
    Delegated tasks/projects
    Replies to
      E-mail
      Calls
      Proposals
      Requisitions
    Reimbursements
    Petty cash
    Insurance
    Ordered items
    Items being repaired
    Tickets
    Decisions of others
Professional development
    Training/seminars
    Things to learn/look up
    Skills to practice/learn
    Computer training
Research--need to find out about
Professional wardrobe

List 5-1. Professional triggers

Projects started, not completed
Projects to be started
Commitments/promises to
    Spouse
    Children
    Family
    Friends
    Professionals
    Borrowed items
Projects: other organizations
    Service
    Church
    Volunteer
Communications to make/get
    Family
    Friends
    Professional
Initiate/respond to
    Phone calls
    Letters
    Cards
Upcoming events
    Special occasions
    Birthdays
    Anniversary
    Weddings
    Graduations
    Holidays
    Travel/vacation
    Social events
    Cultural events
    Sporting events
Research
    Things to do
    Places to go
    People to meet/invite
    Local attractions
Administration
    Financial
        Bills
        Banking
        Investments
        Loans
        Taxes
    Legal affairs
        Will
    Filing

Waiting for...
    Mail order
    Repair
    Reimbursements
    Loaned items
    Medical data
    RSVPs
Home/household
    Landlord
    Property ownership
    Legal
    Real estate
    Zoning
    Taxes
    Building/contractors
    Heating/air-conditioning
    Plumbing
    Electrical
    Roofing
    Landscaping
    Driveway
    Walls/floors/ceilings
    Decoration
    Furniture
    Utilities
    Appliances
    Light bulbs/wiring
    Kitchen things
    Washer/dryers/vacuum
    Areas to organize
    Garage
Vehicle repair/maintenance
Pets
Health care
Hobbies
Books, records, CDs, DVDs
Errands
    Hardware store
    Drug store
    Supermarket
    Bank
    Cleaners
    Stationers
Community
    Neighborhood
    School
    Local government

List 5-2. Personal triggers

Awarenesses

To help you learn more about yourself and build a system that works for you, consider some of the awarenesses that my clients have observed while doing the "clearing the mind" exercise.

- I had a lot more personal items than I ever expected.

- My mind was random. I'd remember, small things, big things, personal things, business things, important, and unimportant things.

- I feel totally overwhelmed looking at this list!

- I like having it all written down in one place.

- The list is much bigger than I ever thought it would be.

- I feel guilty looking at what I haven't done that I need to do.

- I was storing more in my head than I realized.

- I feel much lighter getting all this stuff out of my head. It's a relief!

- I just got started and I have a lot more to go!

- I noticed a lot of little things that have been nagging at me.

- I remembered items that I had completely forgotten about.

As a result of this exercise, you will be feeling much lighter and relieved. You just freed up a whole bunch of "attention" units and centralized your list! However, you might also be feeling overwhelmed and wondering to yourself, "How will I ever get all of this done? I'm more stressed out now than before I started this exercise!" Don't be surprised. This is a common reaction!

Interestingly enough, you *didn't create more to do*. You may feel that way, but these items were already in your head *before* you started the exercise. By writing them down, you became more *conscious* of them, and it was a bit of a shock. Before, all your to-do items were unconscious and, as my mother used to say, "Ignorance is bliss!" Yup, ignorance *is* bliss, but the trouble with bliss is that you forget agreements, you can't buy soap in the shower, and you can't call Litware when you're in a meeting!

When you start being conscious of what you have to do, consistently recording your commitments in Outlook, your lists will get longer. You may not have been aware of how much you had to do because you tracked your tasks in your head. An important element in being organized is to getting comfortable having longer lists. This can take a little while to get used to, but the benefit of tracking your commitments in Outlook far outweighs the value of tracking them in your head.

You may not be aware of all the things you have to do because so much of it's in your head. After you put it in your system, the system helps you remember what you need to do and when you need to do it. The value of having a system like this soon overshadows your concerns about having longer lists. You'll end up feeling lighter, being more focused, and having the right data you need to effectively prioritize and plan your schedule.

Using Categories: (none) As a Collecting Point

Throughout the day, I use Categories: (none) to capture random ideas that pop into my head, action steps from meetings, and any other tasks that my mind is hanging onto. Categories: (none) is one of my five main Collecting Points. I have access to it both on my Pocket PC and my Tablet PC. Therefore, no matter where I am, I can capture information in my system instead of in my head. I make sure that I synchronize when I return to the office. This gives me a central Collecting Point that I can easily access. It sure feels good to get random information out of my head, and use my system to do the organizing for me.

When you're feeling snowed under, completing a mini "mind sweep" will help you feel better and clear your head. It's hard to make effective decisions when your mind is trying to get your attention. I recommend my clients do a mini "mind sweep" every week.

Recording Your Meaningful Objectives

Before moving on, I'd like to ensure that you've captured all of your Meaningful Objectives, both professional and personal. This is a critical step in setting up your Integrated Management System.

If you have "performance review objectives," add these to your Categories: (none) Collecting Point. You might need to summarize each individual objective so its description fits easily into the Subject line.

If you don't have performance review objectives, I'd highly recommend that you create them for yourself. Business objectives enable you to track and measure your progress. They assist you in choosing priorities, and they keep you focused on using your time effectively. I often say to my clients, "Your productivity is only as good as your objectives, so make sure they are clear and meaningful."

Take the time now to create your one-year objectives. Make sure that they're explicit so you can easily gauge whether you're achieving them. Also ensure that they're meaningful so you're inspired to work toward them. Objectives are commitments that you make with yourself and others. You're responsible for achieving them, so make sure they're realistic and that you have the time to complete them.

Here are examples of Carol Philips' annual business objectives:

- Generate at least $2.4 million in sales for the upcoming fiscal year
- Increase existing customer sales by 15 percent
- Increase sales staff longevity
- Stay within budget

If you want to improve your work/life balance, you must have personal, as well as business, objectives tracked in your system. When you've completed recording your business objectives, take some time to create your personal objectives. I want to encourage you to track these in Outlook. Together, they'll ensure that you're creating the right level of productivity and balance to support the lifestyle that you want to have.

Here are examples of Carol Philips' annual personal objectives:

- Finances—maximize retirement plan
- Health—run at least four times a week
- Home—renovate upstairs bathroom
- Spiritual development—meditate three times a week

Objectives are your North Star and guiding light. They are the foundation of your IMS and they're critical to increasing productivity.

Keeping Agreements and Eliminating the "I Can Do It All" Belief

After you've completed the "clearing the mind" exercise, you'll realize that some tasks are tasks you've procrastinated with. We all procrastinate and over-commit. A main purpose for setting up an IMS is to help you keep agreements and, if appropriate, renegotiate or disengage from them.

"Write it down. Written goals have a way of transforming wishes into wants, can'ts into cans, dreams into plans, and plans into reality. Don't just think it, ink it!"
— **Author unknown**

It's critical to centralize your agreements in one location so you can analyze whether or not you can realistically complete them. It's hard to complete an agreement that you can't remember.

In Figure 5-2, you'll see the ControlPanel, which provides the central location for your agreements. On the right are all of Carol's agreements, and on the left is her Calendar showing what time she has available. The ControlPanel enables you to see whether or not you have the time to complete your tasks. It gives you the information you need to make tough decisions about which agreements you'll keep, which agreements you need to renegotiate, and which agreements you need to disengage from. The process of using the ControlPanel makes you much more discerning about saying "yes" or "no" to future agreements. You are the only one who can support yourself in making these decisions. No one else will do it for you.

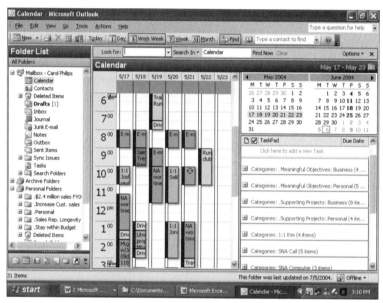

Figure 5-2 The ControlPanel provides a central location for all of your commitments and agreements.

After the "clearing the mind" exercise, you'll realize one of two things: you'll be pleasantly surprised that your tasks are doable, or you'll swallow hard and admit that they can't all get done. If the latter is the case, you'll need to renegotiate or disengage from them, which I'll cover in the sections below.

The truth is that you'll always have more to do than you can do, and *you'll never, ever, get it all done.* Realizing this will take a tremendous weight off your shoulders and, even more importantly, it'll help you decide which agreements you can keep.

Keeping Agreements

It's important to keep your agreements. I often say to clients, "Nothing lowers your self-esteem more than breaking your agreements, and nothing increases your self-esteem more than keeping your agreements."

As you can tell, I believe strongly in doing what you say you're going to do. Keeping your word sends a very strong message to your co-workers, family, and friends, and also to yourself. It inspires trust, respect, and integrity, and it says "you can count on me." It's also much easier to hold your family and friends accountable for their agreements when you hold yourself accountable for yours. At the end of the day, your word is really all you have.

I notice that some clients are better at keeping agreements with others than they are at keeping agreements with themselves. They seem to abandon their own personal commitments, making others their priority. They'll blow off their own exercise, commitments to being home at a certain hour, or their personal planning time. Of course, they have great justifications for their actions, but the bottom line is that they'd be better off not making commitments than breaking them. When you break agreements, people lose trust in you and, most importantly, you *erode personal trust in yourself.* Imagine how you would judge others if they were to consistently break agreements. Well, that's how you're judging yourself when you break the agreements you've made with yourself! How scary!

Remember, *nothing will lower your self-esteem more rapidly than breaking agreements.* I'm highlighting this statement because, later in the book, you'll look at how you process and organize your e-mail, and I'll suggest that you book a one-hour meeting with yourself each day to work through your messages. When you put this daily, concentrated, and uninterrupted time on your calendar, it's a commitment that you're making with yourself. You need to be clear that this is a commitment, and even though no one else will be meeting with you, your agreement is just as important as if they were. If you decide to schedule time on your calendar for exercise, that appointment should be as important as any other meeting in your day. When you get to the section on planning your calendar, this level of personal commitment will be essential to maintaining balance and making sure you get your work done at work.

> "He who controls others may be powerful but he who has mastered himself is mightier."
> **—Lao Tsu**

Renegotiating Agreements

After you have all of your commitments tracked in your system, your e-mail Inbox has been emptied, you've gotten through all of your voice mail, and your head is "clear," you'll have a very complete to-do list in the ControlPanel. When you review this list against your Calendar, you'll be able to see if you can, in fact, complete all of your agreements on time. It's incredibly empowering to have this information at your fingertips. You might come to the conclusion that you can't get everything done, so something has to give, and this is where *renegotiating* comes in.

Renegotiating involves contacting people who will be affected—the parties involved in your objectives—when you can't do what you've said you'd do. You promptly let them know that you won't be able to stick to your agreements, and offer them potential solutions. The solutions could take multiple forms, such as changing a deadline, hiring more people, disengaging from alternative agreements, or changing the scope of a project. The key is that when you determine, ahead of time, that you won't be able to keep your agreements, you let people know as soon as possible, so they have the opportunity to do something about it.

The situation we all dread is finding out *at the last minute* that a project won't get done. When this happens repeatedly, we lose respect for people. Renegotiation, however, allows you to maintain your credibility, integrity, and responsibility. When you let someone know, with enough warning, that you can't do what you said you'd do, you give that person the chance to evaluate the impact of the change and the time to go with alternative solutions. If you break an agreement without any advance warning, the person has no way to evaluate and reduce the impact of your change.

I really appreciate people who renegotiate with me. This lets me know that they care about their agreements, that they are sensitive to the impact they may have, and that they are being responsible. I'd prefer to know ahead of time, no matter how uncomfortable it'll be to hear the news!

By having a system that reflects all of your agreements, you can start to see what you can and can't do. This enables you to renegotiate in a very proactive way. It's extremely powerful, so keep writing down all your agreements in the Task list and keep reviewing the items you've put in your Integrated Management System.

Learning to Say "No"

In order to keep your word, stay balanced, and keep on track with your objectives, you'll have to say "no" to new opportunities that don't support your objectives. This is a paradigm shift—the more you say "no" to activities that don't move your objectives forward, the more you can say "yes" to activities that do. I've learned that there is tremendous power in saying "I will not be able to do that," as it enables you to maintain your focus on your objectives, and lets people know that they can rely on you to give straight, honest, and clear feedback. Remember, you have more to do than you can do, so you need to start saying "no" more frequently, if only to protect the current objectives you have.

As in renegotiation, a key to saying "no" is having the right information available to support your decisions in a central location, where you can see everything you've agreed to do. It's very hard to decline when you don't know what you've already agreed to.

Using the ControlPanel gives you very strong data to back up your decisions. You can say "no" with conviction because you have evidence that declining is necessary in order for you to be successful with your current objectives. When you truly acknowledge that by taking on more, you jeopardize what you've already agreed to do, it's a whole lot simpler to say "no" with confidence. You can have fun giving the "thumbs down."

I'm passionate about my objectives because they're meaningful to me; I truly want them to happen. I am equally passionate about protecting my time so I can accomplish my objectives. This makes it easier for me to stay focused and decline new incoming opportunities that are less critical. I take my time evaluating whether saying "no" is the correct course of action, and if I decide that it is, I'm very clear about it. No one wants to be left in limbo; they want to know if you can do something or not. You're better off saying "no" than letting down yourself and others.

When I'm asked to take on a new project or objective, I always go to my system *first* to see what the impact will be on my current work and home life. Here's how you can do the same: When your boss asks you to create a new proposal, you can say that you'll respond by the end of the day after you've reviewed your workload. At the end of the day, you can respond by saying, "I can do this by the end of February, however I'll need to put off the telecommunications proposal deadline until the first week of March. Is that OK with you?" This enables you to keep all of your agreements instead of burning yourself out to get everything done or missing other deadlines.

It also allows for a positive discussion with your boss about priorities so you can renegotiate what's on your plate and ensure that you're working on the most important activities.

I admire and respect my staff when I ask them to do something and they respond by saying, "I can't complete that unless I renegotiate my current timelines." I know my staff will take care of themselves, and I know that they'll do what they say they'll do. I also know that by saying "no," they are really saying, "I believe my objectives *are* important for me to focus on and they won't get done if I take on this project." It's hard to argue with that approach.

Saying "No" Without Justifying

Don't fall into the trap of feeling that you can't decline without sufficiently justifying why you're doing so. My clients often feel that they have to justify their "no's" and even apologize for them. Most of the time, people just want a "yes" or "no" so they can go about their day. If they want reasons, they'll ask for them. I often hear clients go into all kinds of justifications, wanting the other person to know why they need say "no," as though declining was a bad thing!

Saying "no" is a strategy that supports you in achieving your objectives on time, within budget, and at the appropriate level of quality. I know that in some companies, saying "no" is seen as uncooperative. Within the context of achieving your objectives, saying "no" can be a good thing no matter what the corporate culture is.

My clients have taught me that saying "no" in the appropriate circumstances keeps you focused on completing important objectives. In fact, in many instances, you must say "no" otherwise you'll never get meaningful work done. If you don't say "no," you'll be really, really busy, but really, really busy doesn't mean that you're working on your most important goals!

When I first started to say "no" without spouting out various reasons, I'd leave the conversation feeling guilty that I'd gotten away with something! After a while, though, it began to feel very good. I was standing up for myself and being true to myself and my priorities. Of course, people will sometimes ask for reasons and they'll deserve an explanation. But once you establish a pattern of accountability, you won't have to justify the decisions you've made. I soon discovered that people respected my word, and when I said "no," that was enough for them. I realized that I didn't trust myself as much as others trusted me and *that* was a great revelation!

It's important to use an IMS to centralize your tasks because this assists you in keeping your agreements and having the data you need to renegotiate or decline them. Do yourself a favor and get tasks out of your head and into your system. Then you can start to really manage your commitments and create balance in your life.

What Changes Will You Make?

Take a moment to contemplate the changes that you want to make as a result of this chapter: tracking your commitments and agreements in your Task list instead of your head, coming to grips with the reality that you'll always have more to do than you can do, and keeping your agreements or, when appropriate, renegotiating or disengaging from them.

In the Task list in Outlook, open the WEEKLY REVIEW task that you created in Chapter 4, and under the heading "Collecting," and enter the specific tasks that you want to do differently to support the completion of the Collecting Phase. It's very important to record the changes you want to make because this helps clarify what you're going to do.

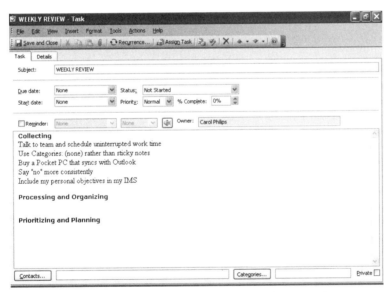

Figure 5-3　Keeping track of the changes you're going to make

For inspiration, here are some comments that my clients have written:

- Get tasks out of my head and type them into Categories: (none)

- When I am driving my car and I think of to-do's, call my voice mail and leave a message for myself

- Buy a PDA so I can type in actions when I am not at my computer

- Review my list against my calendar to see if I can get it all done

- Renegotiate agreements that I made that I know I can no longer do

- Disengage from agreements that I can't complete

After you've entered the changes you want to make in the task labeled "WEEKLY REVIEW," please close it into Categories: (none). You'll be referring to it again at the end of each of the Three Phases for Creating an Integrated Management System. Eventually it will get transferred to the Calendar as a recurring appointment to support you in completing your Weekly Review. I will detail the Weekly Review in Chapter 10, "Planning and Prioritizing."

Success Factors for the Collecting Phase

Congratulations! You're one-third of the way through setting up your Integrated Management System. Before you move on to the Processing and Organizing Phase, here's a summary of the key takeaways from these last two chapters.

- Be aware of the number of physical locations that you're using to collect your commitments and agreements. For most of us, this is quite an eye opener, and it demonstrates how overwhelming it can be to have multiple Collecting Points.

- Define the approved Collecting Points that you'll use, and eliminate the rest. By minimizing your Collecting Points to between five and eight, you'll find it easier to seamlessly capture data, find it quickly, and process it easily into your IMS.

- Use only approved Collecting Points to collect your information. This means that you have to identify specific behavior changes to ensure you keep using these points and not others.

- Use Categories: (none) as a Collecting Point. This is a quick and easy location that enables you to capture voice mail, ideas, and actions from meetings. It synchronizes with your Pocket PC, which enables it to be portable.

- Consistently "clear the mind" by tracking your agreements in your IMS. This will enable you to manage your agreements more carefully, be more present with others, and lighten up!

- Review the interruptions you've been unconsciously allowing. Set up an agenda with your team to reset expectations so you can reduce interruptions and get more of your real work done.

- Set up your IMS to support you in keeping your agreements, and renegotiating and declining them where appropriate.

You have now completed the Collecting Phase, the first of the Three Phases for Creating an Integrated Management System. As a result of reading this chapter, I hope that you truly recognize that you will always have more to do than you can do. Therefore the game is not *figuring out how to do it all.* Instead, the game is *choosing what you can do with the time you have, while maintaining balance.*

The next phase is the Processing and Organizing phase, in which you'll learn how to organize your mind sweep list into the Planning and Action Categories. This will give you a better idea of exactly what you have to do. The third phase, Prioritizing and Planning, will assist you in moving your actions successfully into the Calendar, giving you a better idea of exactly when you have to do it. This will be a super reality check in which you'll discover if you can do what you said you can do, and do it in balance. Keep in mind that this is a process that will transform your effectiveness and give you peace of mind.

Moving right along......

Part Three

The Processing and Organizing Phase

In this part

Chapter Six

Introducing the Planning and Action Categories

Now that you've completed the Collecting Phase, you'll take the next step in creating your Integrated Management System, which is to begin the Processing and Organizing Phase. In order for this to work, you'll need to set up specific categories in the Master Category List in Microsoft Outlook. These categories provide locations to process and organize the contents of your collecting points. I call these categories Planning and Action Categories, and you'll notice that they align with the Cycle of Productivity— *consistently completing Strategic Next Actions that link to Meaningful Objectives.* Figure 6-1 shows sample Planning and Action Categories set up by Carol Philips. I'll go into these categories in greater detail in Chapter 7.

Figure 6-1 Carol's Planning and Action Categories

Setting Up the Planning and Action Categories

The purpose of the Planning and Action Categories is to help you organize all of your tasks into one central location so you can easily manage and complete your agreements.

In the *Planning* categories, shown below, you'll be capturing your Meaningful Objectives, Supporting Projects, and 1:1 Meeting agendas. These categories will assist you in continually refocusing on your objectives and plans. This enables you to proactively plan, and prioritize your objectives.

In the *Action* categories, shown below, you'll capture Strategic Next Actions. These categories draw your attention to the most important actions that move you toward your objectives.

Planning categories:

- ■ .Meaningful Objectives: Business
- ■ .Meaningful Objectives: Personal
- ■ .Supporting Projects: Business
- ■ .Supporting Projects: Personal
- ■ 1:1 Meetings

Action categories:

- ■ SNA Call
- ■ SNA Computer
- ■ SNA Desk
- ■ SNA Errand
- ■ SNA Home
- ■ SNA Online
- ■ SNA Waiting For
- ■ Someday Maybe

You'll be using the Master Category List in Outlook to set up the Planning and Action Categories. This list enables you to access your categories from your Task list, and from the Contacts list and Calendar. To open the Master Category List so you can enter Planning and Action Categories, follow these steps:

1. Open the Task list.
2. If necessary, click the plus sign to the left of Categories: (none) to expand the category and see its tasks.
3. Right-click any task.
4. On the shortcut menu, click Categories to open the Categories dialog box.
5. In the Categories dialog box, click the Master Category List button. The Master Category List dialog box opens, and you'll see a list of default categories.

1. Click the plus button next to Categories: (none) to expand the category. The button becomes a minus button.

2. Right-click a task that's open and select Categories.

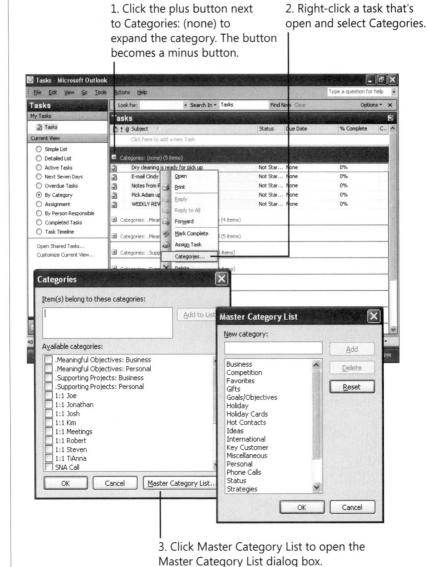

3. Click Master Category List to open the Master Category List dialog box.

Figure 6-2   Editing the Master Category List

Before you add the Planning and Action Categories to your Master Category List, delete any of the default categories that you don't consistently use. (A quick way to delete unused default categories is to click one of the categories, press and hold down the Ctrl key, and click additional categories. Release the Ctrl key, click the Delete button, and click OK.) If you're using categories you've already created, be sure to keep them. For those of you who are reticent about deleting the default categories, this will give you a little practice deleting items before you get to the e-mail section!

These Planning and Action Categories are critical to the success of your IMS. For now, I'd like you to use these specific categories exactly as they are presented in this chapter. Later in the book, you'll learn to customize them.

Enter the 13 Planning and Action Categories into your Master Category List, as shown in Figure 6-3, clicking Add after you type each category. Type these categories exactly as you see them in the list.

The first category is .*Meaningful Objectives: Business.* You'll notice that the category name includes a period in front of the words Meaningful Objectives. Be sure to include the period when you type the category name. Categories are listed alphabetically in your Task list, and the period brings this category to the top of the list. Meaningful Objectives are at the top because you want your objectives to drive everything you do.

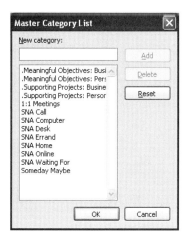

Figure 6-3   Entering the 13 Planning and Action Categories

After you've typed the 13 categories as you see them in the figure, click OK to return to the Categories dialog box. Click OK again to return to the Task list. At first, you won't see the changes you've made in the Task list because you must attach a category to a task before it will show up. You'll learn to do this in Chapter 7.

You'll notice that the Planning and Action Categories integrate with the Cycle of Productivity. The first step in the Cycle is creating your Meaningful Objectives, and the second step is creating Strategic Next Actions, as shown in Figure 6-4. If you consistently complete Strategic Next Actions that link to your Meaningful Objectives you will eventually achieve both your personal and professional goals. This is the foundation of your IMS and how the Planning and Action Categories link to this process.

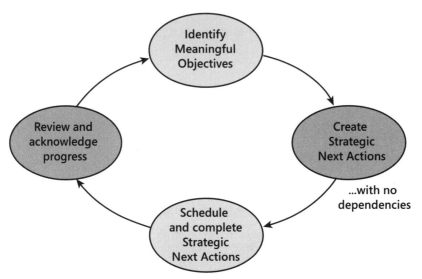

Figure 6-4 Cycle of Productivity

The next sections review how to use each of these categories.

Meaningful Objectives

- .Meaningful Objectives: Business
- .Meaningful Objectives: Personal

Meaningful Objectives, both business and personal, are alphabetized at the top of the list because all of your decisions are driven by these objectives. They are your North Star and guiding light. This category tracks business objectives that you're personally accountable for and that relate directly to your performance review. In addition, you can use this category to hold yourself accountable for any personal objectives you want to complete. In my case, this category inspires me to stay focused on both my business and personal objectives.

Supporting Projects

- .Supporting Projects: Business
- .Supporting Projects: Personal

A complex objective is easier to manage and track when you break it down into Supporting Projects. Supporting Projects are a component of your Meaningful Objectives. For example, the Meaningful Objective *publish a productivity book* could be split into a number of Supporting Projects such as:

- Complete a book proposal
- Select a literary agent
- Complete a vendor agreement
- Complete a book contract
- Write the book
- Edit the book
- Approve screen shots, quotes, and diagrams
- Approve cover inside and out

The Supporting Projects category enables you to track specific projects and their related action plans. This makes it easier for you to see each Supporting Project with its related Tasks and Subtasks in one place.

1:1 Meetings

- 1:1 Meetings

This category enables you to track key relationships in your business and personal life. If you delegate to key staff members, you probably organize monthly one-on-one meetings with them. This category enables you to track their objectives, and follow up on items and anything else you want to discuss with them at the meeting.

You can also use this category for one-on-one meetings with your manager to review how you're progressing with your objectives. This includes questions, coaching, escalations, and possibilities.

Here's an example of how Carol Philips uses her 1:1 categories at work and at home. She has six 1:1 categories altogether. Four organize her direct reports—Kim, Josh, Steven, and TiAnna. Figure 6-5 shows some of these 1:1 categories.

Figure 6-5   Carol's 1:1 categories

Carol's 1:1 categories are set up as follows:

- 1:1 Kim

- 1:1 Jonathan

- 1:1 Josh

- 1:1 Robert

- 1:1 Steven

- 1:1 TiAnna

Within each 1:1 category, you can use the Task list to track the following:

- Agenda items that you want to cover at the next 1:1 meeting

- Delegated tasks that you want to follow up on

- Meaningful Objectives that a person is accountable for

You can also use this category for 1:1 Meetings with anyone you have routine conversations with, such as outside vendors, clients, or cross-functional team members.

In addition to using categories in your business life, it's also effective to use them in your personal life. You can use the 1:1 category to track conversations with your spouse or any other personal relationship.

If you're involved in a community project, you probably have a point person you deal with. In this case, you'd create a specific category for that person so that all the items you want to discuss are recorded in one place.

It may sound clinical to include your spouse in your 1:1 category list. However, many of your personal objectives hinge on conversations with your spouse. How often do you talk to your partner about to-do's (kids, dogs, errands, garden, shopping, honey do's)? He doesn't remember what you say, and you don't remember what he says. Sound familiar?

As an example, I have a category for Stephen, my husband, which I use when I go to breakfast with him on Sunday mornings. This a great way to discuss all of our personal to-do's at one time. By the end of breakfast, we know who's going to do what for the week, and then we can enjoy the rest of our time together. By being organized, you can spend more quality time with the people you love!

Earlier, you created a category named 1:1 Meetings. Go ahead and delete this category, and set up the specific 1:1 categories that you want in the Master Category List, following the instructions given earlier. Remember that until you categorize a task under a 1:1 category, it won't show up in your category.

Strategic Next Actions

- SNA Computer
- SNA Online
- SNA Call
- SNA Desk
- SNA Errand
- SNA Waiting For
- SNA Home

Each category above records Strategic Next Actions that have no dependencies. You will notice that these categories are organized around particular locations where you need to accomplish specific tasks.

SNA Computer tracks actions that require you to be at your computer, but don't require you to be online. For example, if you have a task to "Edit the 2005 budget" and the budget document is in the My Documents folder in

Windows, you don't need to be connected to the Internet to edit this document. You can edit it while you're on a plane, in a hotel room, or wherever your computer is handy.

SNA Online tracks actions that require you to be online, such as, "Go to Amazon.com to buy a book for my father's birthday." These actions can't be accomplished unless you are on line.

SNA Call tracks actions that require you to use your phone; for example, "Call Helen and set up a staff meeting." If a phone is not handy, these actions can't happen.

SNA Desk tracks actions that require you to be at your desk, such as "Complete Credit Card application" This is a paper form filed in your desk drawer, so you must be at your desk to complete it.

SNA Errand tracks actions that require you to go somewhere to complete them, such as "Go to store to buy a new Pocket PC."

SNA Waiting For tracks actions that someone else must complete before you can move forward. For example, if you've ordered a book from Amazon.com for your father's birthday, you must wait for it to arrive so you can sign it and wrap it for him. This is a great category to track random items that you want to follow up on that don't relate to your 1:1 categories.

SNA Home tracks actions that you can only do at home, such as "Put up bike hooks in storage room." I already have the bike hooks and a drill, but installing the hooks is something I can do only when I'm at home.

Someday Maybe

- Someday Maybe

There's always too much for you to do, even though you may want to do it all. You must be realistic about what you can actually schedule onto your calendar. After you start planning and prioritizing agreements from your Task list onto the Calendar, you'll quickly see if you have time to complete them and, if not, whether you'll need to renegotiate or disengage from them. This category enables you to track those items you need to disengage from, such as "Sign up for Women's Business forum," and "Buy new smart-phone." It's also useful for actions you'd be excited about doing, but don't have the time to do, such as "Spend three weeks in Italy," or "Read the

Robert Jordan book series." The best part about the Someday Maybe category is that it unclogs your system from items you can't do, but it keeps track of them, in case you can do them later.

As you can see, all the Planning categories (Meaningful Objectives, Supporting Projects, and 1:1 Meetings) track very high-level thinking and planning. All of the Action categories (except Someday Maybe) track the Strategic Next Actions that you must complete to support the Planning categories.

The Planning categories are for thinking and planning. The Action categories are for doing. A phrase I use with clients is, "You don't 'do' objectives. You only 'do' Strategic Next Actions."

After you get used to working with your categories, you'll be able to customize them to better fit your own situation and circumstances.

Now that you've set up Planning and Action Categories, you can move on to the next chapter, "Processing and Organizing your Task List." Don't worry if the categories you've set up in this chapter don't yet make complete sense. You'll learn about using them in Chapter 7 in much more detail, so you'll have plenty of time to figure out how to employ them to your best advantage.

Chapter Seven

Processing and Organizing Your Task List

Technology has dramatically increased the volume of information we receive. Some of us get as many as 250 e-mails a day! As you know, if you don't process and organize this information effectively, it piles up and, before you know it, you've got 3,000 e-mail messages in your Inbox. With so much information arriving so quickly, it's harder and harder to stay focused and deal with it efficiently.

In this chapter, you'll learn how to *process and organize* your Categories: (none) Collecting Point into the Planning and Action Categories in your IMS. The result will be an empty Collecting Point and an extremely well-organized and prioritized to-do list. You're guaranteed to feel more relaxed, in control, and energized by the end of this chapter. I'll also review three models to help make this process easier: the Workflow Model, the Planning and Action Categories, and the Organizational Hierarchy Model.

You may find that learning the topics in this chapter is like learning how to ski. Ski school gives you skis, poles, boots, bindings, goggles and a hat, but you're not sure what to do with them all, and they feel clumsy and awkward at first. However, with enough practice, everything comes together, and the next thing you know, you're skiing down the mountain with a big smile on your face and a lot of hooting and hollering! The same will be true of using your IMS. It might seem a little awkward at first, but with consistent focus, it will all come together to increase your productivity and quality of life. I might even catch you doing a little hooting and hollering when you're done!

Introducing the Workflow Model

The Workflow Model in Figure 7-1 illustrates how to process and organize information. Processing involves making *effective decisions* for each and every item in your Categories: (none) list so you can move it to completion. Organizing involves deciding *where* you want to put the information, so you can transfer it from a Collecting Point into categories or folders you can easily access. In the Workflow Model, ovals represent the processing questions and rectangles represent the locations you can organize your information into.

The seven processing questions in the Workflow Model will help you make productive decisions, so you can move forward on your tasks instead of avoiding them and putting them back into your Collecting Points. As you know, it's all too easy to open an e-mail and then close it while saying, "Not sure what to do with it, it's too complicated, don't have time right now, I'll deal with it later!" Nothing happens except your Inbox eventually gets bigger. You're procrastinating! It may not feel like it, but you are. The processing questions you'll learn about are designed to help you make tough decisions. They'll assist you in moving your tasks forward so you can transfer them from your Collecting Points into your Action System which ensures they get followed up on and completed. These questions are simple but incredibly powerful, as you'll see.

You'll use the Planning and Action Categories to classify information so you can easily find it. These categories will help you organize and break down information from Meaningful Objectives to Supporting Projects, from Supporting Projects to Tasks and Subtasks, and from Tasks and Subtasks to Strategic Next Actions. These Categories are extremely powerful and can change the way you approach your work and life, making it easier for you to stay focused on your Meaningful Objectives and on the activities that truly matter to you and your family.

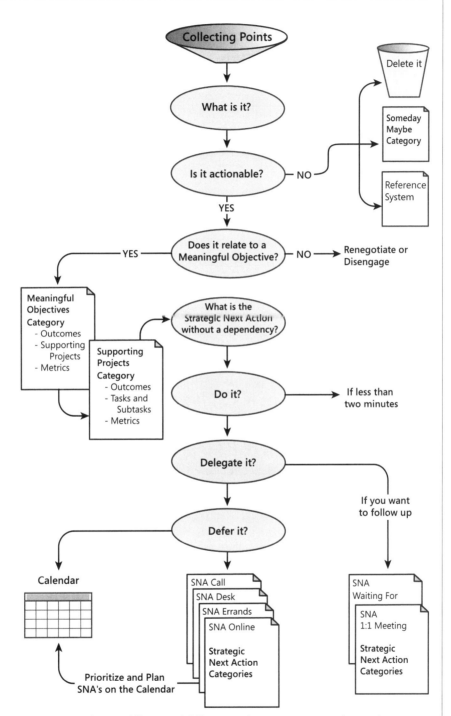

Figure 7-1 The Workflow Model illustrates how to process and organize your Collecting Points into your Integrated Management System.

Using the Workflow Model

To begin using the Workflow Model, look through your Categories: (none) list and pick out one of your Meaningful Objectives, either personal or business. You'll be working with this objective as you go through the Workflow Model so you can experience how the model works.

What Is It?

"What is it?" seems like a simple question, and it is, but it's also a revealing question! Sometimes what shows up in your Collecting Points is unclear, so you need to stop for a second and appraise it. I'm sure you've received e-mails and asked yourself, "What is this?!"

This first question is designed to help you pause and evaluate what's shown up. Is it reference or action material, personal or business, complex or simple? Is it an objective, or a project? A task or a next action? What the heck is it?

I've often captured actions in Categories: (None) and then, two days later, found that they're either not clear, need more thinking, or they turn out to be much bigger projects than I'd realized. Asking "What is it?" helps you evaluate what you're dealing with so you can decide how best to move it forward. *Don't be hasty with this question. Take a moment to reflect. The value's in the pausing.* This takes only a few seconds on the front end, but can save you hours on the back end.

Take the objective you've picked and ask "What is it?" Is it clear to you, do you really understand it? How big or small is it? Is it personal or business? Is it really a Meaningful Objective or could it be a Supporting Project?

When you're clear about what it is, you can move forward to the next question in the Workflow Model, "Is it actionable?"

Example　I was in a meeting at Microsoft when someone told me that I should submit a book proposal to Microsoft Press. I wrote it down in Categories: (none). Later, when I asked the question "What is it?" I realized that "Submit a book proposal to Microsoft Press" was part of a much bigger objective called "Write a book!" "Submit a book proposal" was a Supporting Project. I realized that if I decided to write a book, that objective would take me away from my normal, operational functions. I'd need to reorganize my current objectives and delegate parts of my job to make it happen. It was useful to take a few moments to pause and truly understand what I was really dealing with. I was dealing with an objective, not a simple task.

Is It Actionable?

We all want to please other people by saying, "Yes, I'll do that." I'm sure you've experienced that it's much easier to say "yes" than to say "no." However, right now, because your actions are scattered throughout your Collecting Points, you don't have a clear way to make realistic decisions about what you can and can't do other than by making your best guess. When your commitments are tracked in one location, it's easier to assess whether or not you can take on additional agreements or if you need to renegotiate or disengage from your current agreements in order to say "yes" to new ones.

Imagine that you've completed processing and organizing all of your Collecting Points so they're empty. Your agreements are now centrally located in your Task list in the Planning and Action Categories. Now, the question "Is it actionable?" has a lot more meaning because you can see all of your agreements in one location. This enables you to make well-informed decisions about accepting or declining new tasks.

Take the objective you've picked and ask, "Is this actionable?" Make sure, given all the commitments you have, that you can accomplish it and maintain balance at the same time. Because you don't yet have a complete list of commitments in one place, this question may not be easy to put into perspective. Just do the best you can. After your list is complete you can always go back and change some of your decisions.

When you come across a task that is not actionable, you have three choices, shown in Figure 7-1. You can delete it or, if the information relates to an objective or company policy, you can transfer it to your Reference System. If it's an action you're excited about doing, but can't do in the foreseeable future, you can track it in the Someday Maybe category.

Someday Maybe Category

I have clients who love the Someday Maybe category. It's their best friend because it helps them lighten their load and keeps them honest and realistic. Let's face it; you'll always have more to do than you can do. This category enables you to capture tasks that you want to do, but can't realistically complete given your current commitments and schedule. By putting a task in the Someday Maybe category, you disengage from the action, but it's not out of sight and out of mind. An example of this might be "go on an African Safari," or "hang new artwork in my office." With your current workload, you can't imagine completing these activities in the near future, but "Someday Maybe" you can. The Someday Maybe category doesn't work for everyone. Some of my clients want to eliminate a project or task entirely after they've decided to disengage from it. Storing it in another category simply doesn't work for them. However, for others, it's easier to disengage from commitments knowing that they can find them in their Someday Maybe category, if necessary. You need to decide what will work best for you. There's nothing wrong with trying it on for size and observing whether you use it or not. "The proof is in the pudding," as my mother used to say. She did make excellent English pudding, but that's another topic!

When you're clear that the objective you picked is actionable, you can move to the next question in the Workflow Model.

Example: Is it Actionable?   "Write a book" was my task, and when I asked the question, "Is this actionable?" the immediate answer was "No way! I don't have the time and energy given my current commitments." Accomplishing this task wasn't just about writing a book; it was about making the time to write the book. So was this item actionable? You betcha, but I was going to have to clear my plate before I could do it. I needed to disengage and renegotiate my work load to make room for this new objective to happen.

Does It Relate to a Meaningful Objective?

We're all trained to get things done, so we have a natural desire to "do." But are you spending your time doing the right things, or are you just doing things?

The purpose of asking, "Does it relate to a Meaningful Objective?" is to keep you on your toes and ensure that, as much as possible, every action you take relates to one of your Meaningful Objectives. If it doesn't, you need to question why you're working on it. Ask yourself whether you need to adjust an existing objective, add a new one, disengage from the activity altogether, or complete it because you said you would.

It's not easy to back out of an agreement you've already made. However, if you ask this question *before* you make your agreements, you can ensure that nothing hits your Task list that doesn't link to one of your Meaningful Objectives.

No matter who I work with, from the CEO on down, asking "Does it relate to a Meaningful Objective?" is a powerful filter that enables them to eliminate tasks and disengage from projects that don't support their objectives.

Example: Does it relate to a Meaningful Objective?   The task "Write a book" did not relate to one of my current objectives. However, I decided that it was important for me to do, so I chose to add it to my list of Meaningful Objectives, knowing I'd have to some serious renegotiation and delegation to make it happen.

Processing and Organizing Your Meaningful Objectives

In the Workflow Model in Figure 7-1, the question "Does it relate to a Meaningful Objective?" leads to an organizing category named "Meaningful Objectives." This is where you will plan and track your Meaningful Objectives by clarifying Outcomes, Supporting Projects, and Metrics.

My definition of a Meaningful Objective is *an ultimate aim or long-term result that links to corporate or personal mission and goals statements*. A Meaningful Objectives is something that you're personally accountable for achieving as opposed to a shared goal.

All of us have objectives, however they may not all be documented or clearly identified. This process will assist you in clarifying and recording them.

The six characteristics of a Meaningful Objective are:

1. Rolls up to a corporate or personal Mission and Goals statement

2. Has clearly defined Outcome(s)

3. Involves multiple Supporting Projects

4. Requires multiple resources

5. Takes place over time and has specific due dates

6. Includes corporate or personal Metrics

This is a good time to reevaluate if the Meaningful Objective you chose does indeed map to the six characteristics above. Often, people confuse objectives with projects. Objectives represent a higher level of activity and consist of multiple Supporting Projects. Supporting Projects are one step down from Meaningful Objectives and consist of Tasks and Subtasks. Make sure that you're dealing with a Meaningful Objective and not a Supporting Project.

"Work joyfully and peacefully knowing the right thoughts and right efforts inevitably bring the right results."
— **James Allen**

The Organizational Hierarchy Model, in Figure 7-2, may help clarify things. The hierarchy starts with Mission and Goals. These get broken down to Meaningful Objectives. Meaningful Objectives are divided into Supporting Projects, Supporting Projects are further broken down into Tasks and Subtasks, and then Tasks and Subtasks become Strategic Next Actions. The intention of this model is to demonstrate how Meaningful Objectives drive everything you do. Each level is separate and distinctly different, yet all levels are intrinsically connected.

Take a moment to evaluate if your objective is a Meaningful Objective or whether it's really a Supporting Project. Use the six characteristics of objectives as a reference point for your decision. If you decide your objective is actually a Supporting Project, pick another item in your Categories: (none) list—one that you feel confident is an objective—and work with it as an example from this point on.

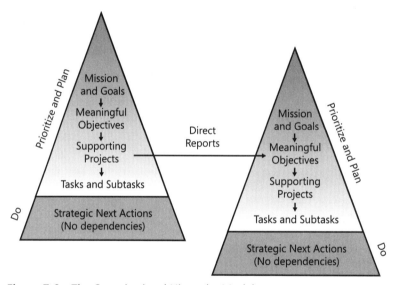

Figure 7-2   The Organizational Hierarchy Model

If you're not completely clear whether you're dealing with a Meaningful Objective or a Supporting Project, don't worry; just keep going through the Workflow Model. It'll become obvious before you finish this chapter.

Now that you've identified a Meaningful Objective, it's time to plan the Outcomes, Supporting Projects, and Metrics. Here are the specific steps to start this process.

1.   Double-click the objective task so it opens in its own dialog box.

2. Review its Subject line to ensure that it really states what your Meaningful Objective is. My original Subject line read "Submit book proposal to Microsoft Press." I changed this to read, "Publish a successful personal productivity book with Microsoft Press," as shown in Figure 7-3.

3. In the Notes section, enter three headings, all in capital letters: OUTCOME, SUPPORTING PROJECTS, and METRICS. (I'll define these elements in the following sections.)

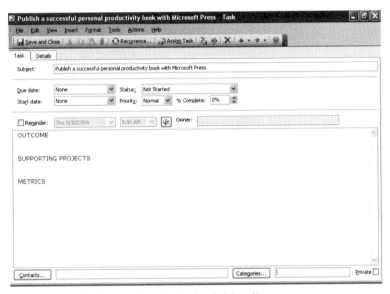

Figure 7-3 Clarify the objective in the Subject line.

Defining Your Outcomes

Outcomes define in more detail what you want to accomplish with your objective. They describe the end result, stating specifically what it'll look and feel like, and what will be different when the objective is completed. Outcomes include clear time frames and take into account the expectations of other interested parties who are impacted. They're specific enough so you can measure success by their completion, and they give you detailed information so the objective is clear enough to other people, and can drive their decisions.

"Crystallize your goals. Make a plan for achieving them, and set yourself a deadline. Then, with supreme confidence, determination and disregard for obstacles and other people's criticisms, carry out your plan."
—**Paul Meyer**

For my objective, I had two outcomes: a 250-page, black and white, paperback, productivity solutions book, published by Microsoft Press before the end of the year, and a book my management team members and I will be proud of. On a scale of 1 to 10, we want to rate the book at least a 9. See Figure 7-4.

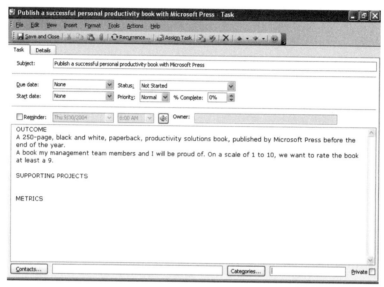

Figure 7-4   Clarify the outcome

Here are a few examples of objectives and their respective outcomes:

- **Objective**   Complete Finance department move to 1200 Speer Street.
- **Outcome**   By January 25th, we will have a new office space set up and 100 percent operational. All of our internal and external clients will have our new contact information.
- **Objective**   Increase revenue by $3 million.
- **Outcome**   Create new line of embroidered T-shirts to expand the product line into the collegiate market.

The key with outcomes is to be specific and to think through the various ways you can measure the objective. These measurements will be the guiding light for team members as they walk through the many decisions they'll have to make related to the objective. Clear measurements help people make clear decisions.

A client of mine, Don Hall, had been assigned a new project: to create a database program to collect evaluations from a new product his company was testing. He delegated the project to one of his key staff members and their team of 12. In the middle of creating the database, the team learned that they couldn't legally include the names of their beta testers. This didn't appear to be a problem, so they continued building the database. When Don heard about this two weeks later, he said, "That's the main reason for creating this database. Without the names, there's no point in doing it!"

This is a clear example of not setting and communicating clear outcomes! Ensuring that the team members collected the names of beta testers was not included in the objective, but it could have been in the outcomes. If the team had known this up front, they'd have made a different decision about continuing with the project. Outcomes give you reference points for making decisions. Without knowing what the outcomes are, your decisions are compromised.

Another client, Kelly Hogan, went on vacation with her husband to Hawaii while they were fairly new to their marriage and still learning about each other. As they finished different consulting engagements, Kelly arrived in Hawaii from the east coast; and her husband, Russell, arrived from the Midwest. As Russell unpacked his luggage, Kelly noticed tennis racquets, golf clubs, and scuba gear, and became a little nervous about the kind of vacation her husband had planned! She unpacked a couple of bathing suits, three books, earplugs, and her iPod. Kelly later told me "We didn't discuss our outcomes for the vacation! It seems as though he planned to be 'outdoor action man.' Chase it, hit it, stab it and whack it! I came to relax, sleep, read, watch movies and be a sloth by the pool!"

What they missed was a brief conversation about the kind of vacation they each envisioned. The objective was clear: go on vacation to Hawaii. However, they hadn't talked about how that would look and feel, and how they'd know if the vacation was successful.

Based on this information, I'd like you to buy a large 5-foot by 3-foot whiteboard and hang it in the kitchen so you can brainstorm together in your home. Only kidding!!!

You're probably not going to install a white board and write professional outcomes for your vacation, but you could talk about it over coffee! Chat about what the end results would be, what it would look and feel like, and how you'd know you had a great time together. Once you'd answered these questions, you'd have a better idea of what to expect.

Take a few moments now and enter the outcomes for your Meaningful Objective in the Notes section of your task under the heading

"OUTCOME." After you've completed this, you can check that your outcomes are SMART.

- S – Specific
- M – Measurable
- A – Achievable
- R – Relevant
- T – Time appropriate

Selecting a Due Date

Your next step is clarifying a due date for your objective and entering the date into the Due Date field. Be realistic when assigning dates. Check your schedule to ensure that the timeline will work given travel schedules, staff meetings, holidays, and other related appointments. When you're clear that your due date is practical, include it in the Due Date field, as shown in Figure 7-5. Most objectives—both personal and business—have due dates. If yours doesn't, take this opportunity to question once again whether it's truly an objective.

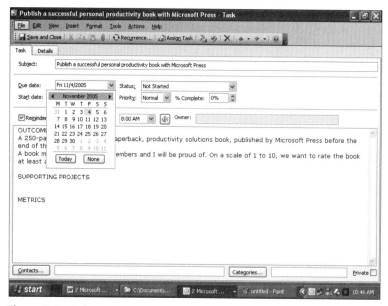

Figure 7-5   Select a due date.

Defining Your Supporting Projects

Planning is a process of breaking down an objective into sequentially smaller chunks so you can see everything that needs to be done to implement the objective successfully. Planning gives you a clear idea of the scope of the objective, how many resources are needed, and whether it can be done within the timeframe and budget allocated. It's a lot easier to manage an objective when you can break it down into smaller pieces. The larger the objective, the more chunks you need to break it down into.

The first level of "chunking" is Supporting Projects. These are large chunks that combine to make up your objective. In Figure 7-6, you'll see that I've chunked my Meaningful Objective into eight Supporting Projects. Each of these Supporting Projects is necessary for the objective to happen. Once I've typed them into the Task, I can arrange them in sequence so I can identify what has to be done first. Then I'm able to allocate due dates to ensure the objective is completed on time. Finally, I'm able to identify whether I can appropriately delegate any of these projects and, if so, enter the name of the person next to the project. This level of planning helps you identify how big or complex the objective is, how much time it will take, and what support you'll need.

"It does not take much strength to do things, but it requires great strength to decide on what to do."
—**Elbert Hubbard**

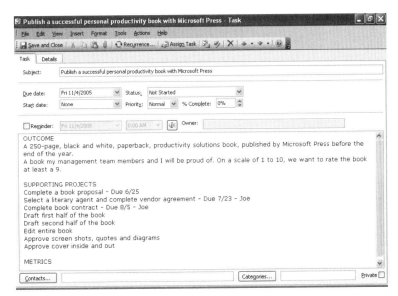

Figure 7-6　Clarify the Supporting Projects.

Take a moment and type in the Supporting Projects that will enable you to successfully complete your Meaningful Objective. When you've completed this, arrange them in sequence and then allocate due dates to ensure you can complete the objective on time. If you are able to delegate a Supporting Project, write the name of the person next to the project.

If you're having problems identifying Supporting Projects, here are several potential solutions:

- The objective you chose may be a project rather than an objective. Objectives are large, complex activities that affect multiple areas: customers, stake holders, department goals, corporate goals, or stock holders. If you can't find more than one or two Supporting Projects, you may have two projects instead of one objective. In the Organizational Hierarchy Model, the largest, most complex activities start at the top and then chunk down to Strategic Next Actions. You need to identify the level on the chart that you're starting at. Are you starting at the Meaningful Objectives level or the Supporting Projects level? The chart is designed to help you identify what size activity you are dealing with and where it sits in the model.

- You might need to do a mini "clearing the mind" exercise with regard to your objective. This often helps unblock your thinking. I suggest randomly typing in a list under the Supporting Projects heading of everything you can think of that needs to be done to complete the objective. When this list is in front of you and not hidden in your head, you can more easily identify the Supporting Projects.

Defining Your Metrics

The last step before moving on to tracking Supporting Projects is to define the Metrics that you'll use to measure your objectives. A Metric is a specific measurement that directly relates to your Meaningful Objective and allows you to evaluate progress.

It's critical to have reports or statistics that enable you to view the development of an objective. If your objective is truly meaningful then you'll want to know if you're making progress toward it. Metrics keep you honest and they're a great way for you and your team to view progress without going into all the details of a project plan.

Defining Metrics may not be necessary for all your personal objectives, but you'd be surprised at how useful it can be for many of them. You can track your financial goals, weight-loss goals, and athletic goals (for example, completing a marathon under three hours and fifty minutes is a specific Metric). You can even track renovating your house using budgets and timelines.

All of my business Metrics are stored on a company SharePoint site. I copy the links and paste them into my objective tasks under the heading "METRICS," so I can quickly access them when I review my objectives each week.

Specifically, I created an Excel spreadsheet to measure my objective "publish a successful personal productivity book with Microsoft Press." In the document, I outlined when chapters, screenshots, and diagrams were due for the first three rounds of book editing. This spreadsheet enabled me to see, in one view, where we were against our deadlines and publishing date. I posted this document on SharePoint for the team to review and copied the link into my objective task, as shown in Figure 7-7.

If you have a Metric document on a SharePoint or intranet site, go ahead and copy and paste the link into your objective task under the heading METRICS.

Alternatively, if you have a Metric document on your hard drive that links to your Meaningful Objective, insert that as a hyperlink under the METRICS heading.

To insert a hyperlink into a task, follow these steps:

1. Click the Insert button on the toolbar.

2. In the Insert File dialog box, browse through your documents to locate the file.

3. Select the file you want, and click the drop-down arrow on the Insert button.

4. Select Insert As Hyperlink.

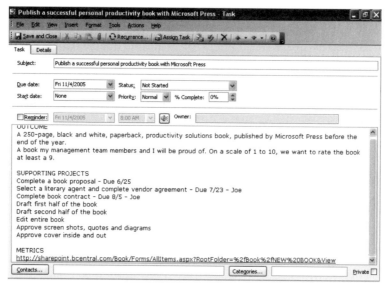

Figure 7-7 Insert a hyperlink into your objective task.

Selecting an Objective Category

Finally, you need to categorize your objective so it will appear on your Task list under one of your personal or business Meaningful Objective categories.

To select a category for an objective, follow these steps:

1. Open the task.

2. Click the Categories button near the lower-right corner of the task's dialog box.

3. In the Categories dialog box, shown in Figure 7-8, select the check box next to the .Meaningful Objectives: Business or .Meaningful Objectives: Personal category, and click OK.

4. Click the Save And Close button on the toolbar.

   If you don't see your specific objective under the Meaningful Objective category, click the plus sign next to the category to expand it.

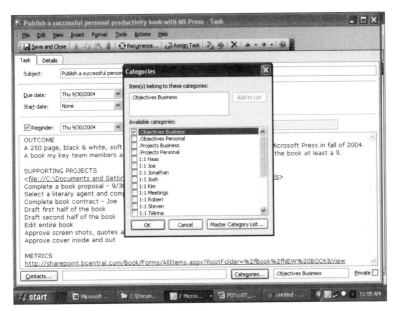

Figure 7-8   Selecting an objective category

After you've categorized a Meaningful Objective, it will instantly appear in its own category and will no longer be listed in the Categories: (none) Collecting Point. If you haven't used the Task list before, it can be very exciting to see the first signs of your system taking shape! Categorizing all your objectives will take some time, but when you're done, it will be hard to wipe the smile of your face! I can't tell you how happy my clients are when their Categories: (none) section is empty and their Planning and Action Categories are set up and working. Everyone loves this level of clarity and organization.

Processing and Organizing Your Supporting Projects

On the Workflow Model in Figure 7-1, the Meaningful Objectives category leads to the Supporting Projects category.

Our definition for a Supporting Project is: *a complex series of Tasks and Subtasks driven by a Meaningful Objective.*

The six characteristics of a Supporting Project are:

1.   Rolls up to an individual Meaningful Objective

2.   Has clearly defined Outcome(s)

3. Involves multiple Tasks and Subtasks

4. Require multiple resources

5. Takes place over time and has specific due dates

6. Includes corporate or personal Metrics

In this section, you'll organize and plan your Supporting Projects by clarifying Outcomes, Task and Subtasks, and Metrics. My Meaningful Objective, "Publish a successful personal productivity book with Microsoft Press," has eight Supporting Projects. Six of them I'm personally responsible for completing, and two of them I've delegated to direct reports. Each of the six projects I'm responsible for requires further planning on my part. The projects need breaking down into Tasks and Subtasks. To make it easier for me to view these six project plans, I took each of the Supporting Projects I'm responsible for and created six separate tasks, which I then categorized under the .Supporting Projects: Business category, as shown in Figure 7-9.

In this figure you'll see that my objective "Publish a successful personal productivity book with Microsoft Press" is categorized under .Meaningful Objectives: Business and the six Supporting Projects that I'm responsible for are separately categorized under .Supporting Projects: Business. (I'll discuss how to track the two Supporting Projects that I delegated in the section below, titled "Organizing and Tracking Your Delegated Items.")

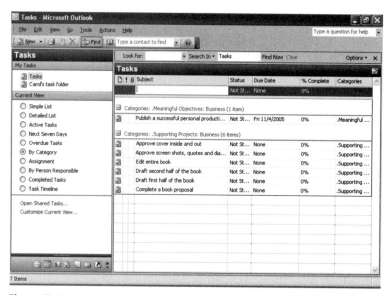

Figure 7-9   Categorizing Meaningful Objectives and Supporting Projects

The reason I separated these six Supporting Projects into their own project category was because each one of these projects required further planning in order for me to manage it successfully. Each one had a different due date and required my individual focus. Having them separated makes it easier to track and manage them. It also enables me to see how many projects I'm working on at any given time, which in turn supports me in being more discerning when taking on new projects.

Now that you've identified your Supporting Projects, it's time to plan the Outcomes, Tasks and Subtasks, and Metrics. Here are the specific steps to start this process.

- Creating and planning your Supporting Projects

    1. Open your Meaningful Objective task.

    2. Choose one of the Supporting Projects that you're responsible for, and right-click it.

    3. Select Copy from the shortcut menu, and close the task.

    4. Open a new task by using the "Click here to open a new Task" field.

    5. In the Subject line, right-click, and a shortcut menu will appear.

    6. Select Paste, which will paste the name of the Supporting Project you've chosen.

    7. In the Notes section of this task, type in three headings, all in capital letters, OUTCOME, TASKS AND SUBTASKS, and METRICS, as shown in Figure 7-10.

- Defining your Outcomes

    • Under the OUTCOMES heading, type one or more clear outcomes for this project.

- Selecting a due date

    • In the Due Date field, select a due date that maps to the due date of your objective so it can be completed successfully.

- Breaking down Supporting Projects and identifying Tasks and Subtasks

    1. Break down each project into tasks and, under the TASKS AND SUBTASKS heading, enter the tasks in a list.

    2. Under each task, enter subtasks, indented one level, as shown in Figure 7-10.

If you end up with more than 30 Tasks and Subtasks, you probably need to do your planning in Microsoft Project or in an Excel spreadsheet. You can then insert the document into your project task as a hyperlink, as shown earlier in Figure 7-7. Take a moment right now to complete entering the Tasks and Subtasks for the Supporting Project.

■ Identify your Metrics

The last step is defining the Metrics you want to use to measure this project.

1. If you have a Metric document already that measures this project, insert it as a hyperlink into the Supporting Project task under the title METRICS. If you don't have a Metric document for this project, take a moment to consider how you would measure the project and create a document to do that.

2. Save the document on your computer or on a SharePoint site and insert the link into your Supporting Project task under the title METRICS.

My first Supporting Project, "Complete book proposal," has a metric document in Excel. I listed all the "proposal sections" that needed to be completed, who had to get them done, and the dates these sections had to be finished. I stored this document on SharePoint so each team member could update the document. I then copied a link from SharePoint into the project task, as shown in Figure 7-10. This enabled me to quickly link to this document and view what was completed and what's left to be done.

■ Selecting a Supporting Project category

1. Click the Categories button.

2. Select either the .Supporting Projects: Business or .Supporting Projects: Personal category.

3. Click the Save And Close button on the toolbar.

By now, you will have one Meaningful Objective category with one objective task in it. Below that, you'll have one Supporting Project category with one Supporting Project task in it.

I'd like you to go back to your original Meaningful Objective and open it. If there are additional Supporting Projects in the Meaningful Objective task that you have not yet categorized and that you're responsible for, set up each of these as a new Supporting Project, categorized under the Supporting

Project category. Make sure you break down each Supporting Project into Outcomes, Tasks and Subtasks, and Metrics. Congratulations! You're now beginning to develop your own personal organizational hierarchy.

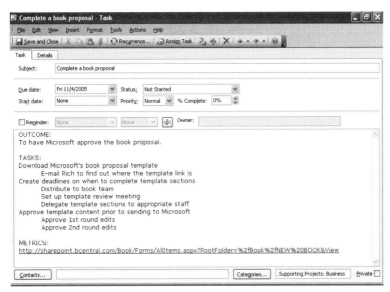

Figure 7-10   A completed Supporting Project, showing Outcomes, Tasks and Subtasks, Metrics, due date, and category

What's the Strategic Next Action Without a Dependency?

In the Workflow Model, the Supporting Project category (shown in Figure 7-1) leads to the processing question, "What's the Strategic Next Action without a dependency?" In this section you'll break down the Supporting Project Tasks and Subtasks into Strategic Next Actions. This is the last level of "chunking" you will do.

Before you create Strategic Next Actions, I want you to really understand what a next action *is*. My clients often confuse Strategic Next Actions with Tasks and Subtasks, and my experience has taught me to clarify the difference between the two. Defining Strategic Next Actions has the potential to save you an hour a day, reduce fires and crises, and assist you in making your life simpler and more graceful, so this concept is worth understanding.

"The secret of getting ahead is getting started. The secret of getting started is breaking your complex, overwhelming tasks into small manageable tasks, and then starting with the first one."
—**Mark Twain**

The Strategic Next Action Story

To help illuminate this, I'm going to tell you a story! I've picked an everyday example about light bulbs that's easy to relate to. However, I'm not really talking light bulbs here, I'm talking about any activity that you do at work and at home.

Many years ago, when I used paper to track my life, I lived in Malibu. A friend of mine, Kelly, used to stay in my guest room once a month to go to school. One weekend, she told me that one of the light bulbs in the guest bathroom had burned out. Because I wanted to be a good host, I wrote down in my paper system, "Change the light bulb."

Kelly came back a month later, and the light bulb was still burned out. Oops, I wasn't such a great host after all! I checked my paper organizer, and sure enough, there it was: "Change the light bulb." Hmmm... Why hadn't I done anything? I thought, "What do I need to change a light bulb?" Oh, that's right! I needed a light bulb! Silly me. I crossed off "Change the light bulb," and wrote down "Buy a light bulb!"

A month later, Kelly was back, and another bulb had burned out, so now she was in the dark! Oh no! I had a 911 situation on my hands. I looked at my list and "Buy light bulb for guest bathroom" was right there. I'd been to Home Depot two or three times since Kelly last visited, so how come I hadn't picked up a bulb? Hmm... I needed a "Things to buy at Home Depot" list! My memory just wasn't working well enough!

I quickly drove through the canyon to the hardware store. When I got there, guess what I saw. That's right; long light bulbs, short light bulbs, round lights bulbs, push-in light bulbs, and screw-in light bulbs. What kind of light bulb did I require? Oh, brother. I had no idea what kind of light bulb I was after. I really needed to write down the specific type of light bulb on my Home Depot list ahead of time to ensure I picked up the right one. Changing this light bulb was turning out to be a nightmare project!

I drove home as fast as I could, marched into the guest bathroom, and looked up. I had cathedral ceilings, so now I needed a ladder! This was getting frustrating as I had no ladder, but my neighbor, Wayne, did. I picked up the phone and asked him to drop it off for me. Later that day, he brought over the ladder and I was able to retrieve the light bulb and take it to the store. I bought five of the same light bulbs because this was definitely not going to happen again!

To review:

- Situation shows up–light bulb burns out in guest bathroom
  - ❑ Action: change light bulb
  - ❑ One month later...
  - ❑ Action: buy light bulb
  - ❑ One month later...
- Situation blows up–no lights in the guest room at all
  - ❑ Action: write a Home Depot list
  - ❑ Action: write down specifications on Home Depot list
  - ❑ Action: get a ladder
  - ❑ Action: call Wayne to get the ladder

What did you learn from reading this story? That's right; you need to think things through when they "show up," otherwise they'll "blow up" and take months to complete instead of days!

I didn't really take the time to think this one through. I reacted and wrote down "Change light bulb." The consequence of not pausing to think was that it took months to handle instead of days. This type of situation happens to us all the time–at work and at home–and it's a huge time waster!

Defining Your Strategic Next Actions

How many Strategic Next Actions are there on the list above? Take a look and give it your best guess.

Most of my clients say six. However, there's actually only one Strategic Next Action.

To make answering such a question a bit easier, here's the definition of a Strategic Next Action: *The next physically doable action with no dependencies.*

The best way to understand this is to appreciate what a dependency is. In order to change a light bulb, you need to buy a light bulb first, so changing the light bulb is *dependent* on buying one. A Strategic Next Action doesn't have any dependencies. Take another look at the list above and, with this definition in mind, identify the one Strategic Next Action on the list.

The answer is, "call Wayne to get the ladder." I knew Wayne's number and I had a phone, so there weren't any dependencies. All the other steps had dependencies. Changing the light bulb was dependent on buying one, buying one was dependent on having the specific type of light bulb tracked on the Home Depot list.

If I'd paused to really think this through, I'd have figured out that "Call Wayne to get the ladder" was my Strategic Next Action. I could've saved myself a whole bunch of time, and the situation would never have blown up!

All day, we write down actions that can't be done because they're loaded with dependencies. You can't complete a task that has a dependency. You can only complete a task without a dependency! This is an extremely significant concept to understand, and it's an important practice to help you move forward on your objectives. The time savings are extraordinary, and it makes life simpler and easier. I can't stress the benefit of this concept enough. You wouldn't believe the number of to-do lists I review in which only five percent of the items are actually Strategic Next Actions. Most of them are Tasks and Subtasks with multiple dependencies. These tasks become frustrating and hard to plan and they end up taking much longer than you think because of their unexpected dependencies. Having Strategic Next Actions takes away the unexpected and forces you to break down your tasks to the very next physically doable step without a dependency. Your tasks will be easier to schedule because you know how long they'll take, they have no unexpected steps, and you can complete them immediately.

Reducing Fires and Crises

In the story above, the light bulb problem became an issue because I didn't handle it when it *showed up*. If I'd paused to think and create a Strategic Next Action in the beginning, it would never have *blown up*, and I wouldn't have wasted my time going to the store without the specification I needed, not to mention taking three months to fix the situation!

We all procrastinate on tasks, opening an e-mail and thinking "It doesn't need to be done now. I'll do it next week. It's not important" and closing it back in the Inbox. However, three weeks later, the same e-mail becomes your next fire and crisis.

When you break down tasks into Strategic Next Actions, you'll end up reducing the number of mini-emergencies that you have because you're handling actions when they show up, not when they blow up. You'll save yourself a whole bunch of time, which will help you take back your life. Hey, an extra hour a day of puttering in your garden, riding your horse, playing golf, eating ice cream, or whatever else puts a smile on your face. That sure sounds good to me!

What I'd like is for you to shift your focus and do your thinking up front instead of after the fact. Changing the timing of your thinking gives you extraordinary rewards. Remember the quote in Chapter 1, "Small things done consistently in strategic places create major impact." Pausing to think and make a decision when an action shows up is a small shift in focus, but it's a profound shift. This concept in and of itself can change your life, and the results you accomplish.

Creating Your Strategic Next Actions

My definition for a Strategic Next Action is: *The next physically doable action with no dependencies.*

The four characteristics of a Strategic Next Action are:

1. Rolls up to one of your Supporting Projects or Meaningful Objectives

2. Has no dependencies

3. Starts with a verb

4. Is specific and measurable

For example, "Go to Home Depot and buy a 25-watt, three-way, round, push-in bulb" links to "maintain and improve my home."

"E-mail Joe and ask him to review the South Beach Development proposal by January 17th" links to "South Beach Development Project."

Give yourself time to think through your Strategic Next Actions. It's not as easy to create them as you might suppose. For example, "Buy a birthday present for my mom" seems like a clear Strategic Next Action. However, what are you going to buy your mom and where will you buy it? If you don't know *what* to buy her, you won't know *where* to buy it, so it'll end up sitting on your list until you make this decision. You could create an alternative Strategic Next Action that helps clarify what to buy her, "Call my dad to get recommendations on presents for mom." Another alternative is "Go to the Cherry Creek mall to find a birthday present for mom." In this scenario, you've decided to wing it and find something at the mall. You don't know what, but you trust that you'll find something! These scenarios are more specific than "Buy a birthday present for my mom," and they'll assist you in

"Handle it when it shows up not when it blows up!"
—**Sally McGhee**

completing a task successfully rather than having it sit on a to-do list for months.

Here are a few questions to help you test if your next action really is a Strategic Next Action:

- What do you need to *do* to complete it?
- What information do you need to *have* with you to complete it?
- Where do you need to *be* to complete it?
- How much *time* will it take to complete it?
- Does it *link* to an objective or project?

When you're happy with the Strategic Next Action you've decided upon, open a new task and type your Strategic Next Action into the Subject field. Make sure it starts with a verb, has no dependencies, is specific and measurable, and links to your Supporting Project or Meaningful Objective.

All it takes is a little bit of concentrated thinking on the front end to save you time and resources on the back end. It's work, but it's good work.

Do It?

On the Workflow Model in Figure 7-1, the question "What is the Strategic Next Action without a dependency?" leads to the question "Do it? – If less than two minutes"

If you can complete your Strategic Next Action in two minutes or less, there's no point in recording it in your IMS; it'll take you as long to complete it as it will to track it! The most effective thing to do here is *just do it*. After you've finished it, you can delete it from your list and celebrate a completed cycle of action. You'd be amazed at how many actions on your task list can be finished in less than two minutes.

Our statistics prove that, on average, 30% of your Task list can be done in less than two minutes. For example, order "My Father is My Teacher" from amazon.com for my dad's birthday, or e-mail Jennifer regarding next week's staff meeting agenda. Completing activities in less than two minutes is a great way to build energy and move forward on your objectives.

If you can complete your Strategic Next Action in less than two minutes, *just do it!* (Nike has the right approach!)

Delegate It?

If you can't do a Strategic Next Action in less than two minutes, the next question on the Workflow Model is can you "Delegate it?" This is another potent filter question that everyone who has the opportunity to delegate can ask more consciously throughout the day.

My clients move so fast that they literally forget to use the "delegate" option. You must remember that you've been given the privilege of having other people work with you. You're paid a certain salary because much is expected of you, so don't spend your time doing things that other people can do, and can probably do better than you! My clients say, "I don't have the time to train other people; I can do it faster myself!" I say, "Great! If you keep up that approach, you'll never move forward. You'll be stuck doing the same old thing and so will the people around you! I suggest that you consider changing your approach so you can change your results. You're fortunate to have staff. Take the time to train them so they can improve what they're doing. Ultimately, this will support you in improving what you're doing. The only person in the way might be you!

If you can delegate a task by e-mail or over the phone, go ahead and get it done right now, it will probably only take you two minutes to complete. I'll talk about how to track and follow up delegated items in the section below, "Processing and Organizing Your Delegated Items."

Defer it?

If you can't do a Strategic Next Action in less than two minutes, and you can't delegate it, the next question on the Workflow Model in Figure 7-1 is can you "Defer it?" Defer means that you are the only person who can complete the Strategic Next Action, and it will take you longer than two minutes to complete. You'll categorize your deferred next actions into one of the six SNA categories. These categories are designed around the locations where you physically need to be located to complete the actions. This is different from the categories that most people use to organize their action lists but I've discovered that clients must be in the right location to complete an action, so it's simpler to organize them in this way. The Strategic Next Action categories are listed below, with an example of how to use each category.

SNA Computer Category

Example: Review next year's budget to evaluate how to cut out $100,000. You need your computer to complete this Strategic Next Action, but you don't need to be online. Next year's budget is in your My Documents folder so you can complete this action anywhere, as long as you can turn on your computer; on the train, on the way home, on an airplane, in a hotel room, or at home.

SNA Online Category

Example: Order leadership book from Amazon.com to send to Jane. Your client contact information is in your Contacts folder, so all you need is to be online to complete this next action.

SNA Call Category

Example: Call Brian Johnson to book a client dinner with him and his wife–September 9th, 7 PM. Brian's phone number is programmed into your phone, so all you need is the phone to make the call.

SNA Desk Category

Example: Complete credit card application. This form is filed at your desk, so you can't complete this task unless you're at your desk.

SNA Errand Category

Example: Go to Cherry Creek Mall to buy your mom a present. This requires that you get into your car to drive to the mall to complete the action.

This category is very useful in your personal life. For example, if you shop at Costco for your once-a-month supplies, you can create a task under SNA Errand that is titled "Costco." Inside of the task you can list all the household items you want to purchase. After you synchronize with your PDA and laptop, the next time you're at Costco you can view your SNA Errand list on your PDA to direct your shopping. You can use this method for any errands that are important to you, such as setting up a task for Blockbuster with your favorite DVD's listed or Barnes & Noble with a list of the books you want to purchase.

SNA Home Category

Example: Paint the garage door. You have the paint, drop cloth, and brush, so all you need is to be at home to complete the Strategic Next Action.

Categorizing your Strategic Next Action in a SNA Category

If you haven't completed your Strategic Next Action in less than two minutes or delegated it, take a moment to choose a SNA category for your action, select a due date if appropriate, and then save and close the task.

Now, go to the Supporting Projects category and refer to the Supporting Projects you've created. Make sure that each of them has at least one Strategic Next Action that's categorized in an SNA category. This will make certain that you keep moving forward towards completing your Supporting Project.

My Strategic Next Action was a deferred action that only I could do and it took more than two minutes. I needed to "Create an Excel spreadsheet to track deadline dates." I organized this in the SNA Computer Category, as shown in Figure 7-11.

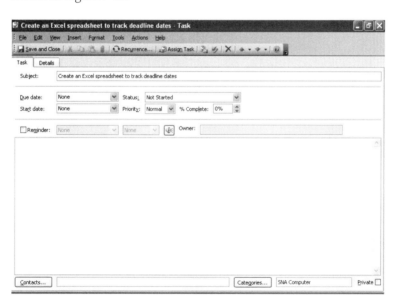

Figure 7-11   Clarify the Strategic Next Action

Imagine you've processed all of your actions in the Task list using the Workflow Model. Everything you can *delete* is deleted. Everything you can *do in less than two minutes* has been done, and everything you can *delegate* has been delegated. At this point, all that is left are your Strategic Next Actions that take more than two minutes and only you can complete them. All of these SNA's directly relate to your Meaningful Objectives and are the most strategic actions for you to focus on to move toward your goals. This is a powerful list to have at your fingertips.

Congratulations! You've just completed your first experience of processing and organizing one of your Meaningful Objectives from the Categories: (none) Collecting Point into the Planning and Action Categories using the Workflow Model. Later in this chapter, you'll complete processing your Categories: (none) Collecting Point. However, we have two more categories to cover and a few questions to answer to help this process go more smoothly.

Processing and Organizing Delegated Items

In the Workflow Model, the question "Delegate it?" leads to two different organizing categories, SNA Waiting For and 1:1 Meeting. I'll describe how to use each of these categories in the section below.

1:1 Meeting Categories

1:1 Meetings are recurring meetings that take place with key business or personal contacts. This category supports you in preparing for your 1:1 Meetings, as well as tracking and following up on Meaningful Objectives, Supporting Projects, and delegated items. Using the 1:1 Meetings category is another way to transfer what's on your mind and put it in your system so it's no longer in your head!

Most managers set up regular one-on-one meetings once a month with their direct reports and their boss so they can discuss progress related to their objectives. If you're not meeting regularly with your key staff members and boss, I highly recommend scheduling these appointments on your calendar. A face-to-face meeting is a good time to connect in person, and it gives you an excellent idea of how things are going at all levels—objectives, projects, challenges, and work/life balance. During a 1:1 meeting, you simply review that person's 1:1 Meeting category for an instant reminder of the items you want to discuss. It's an effortless way to manage these appointments, and it enables you to take your attention off remembering tasks and put it on the important aspects of running a team, being a leader, and developing skills and strategy.

In Chapter 6, you set up your specific 1:1 Meeting categories in your Master Category List. (These categories won't show up in your Task List until you attach a category to the task.) We're now going to add some tasks to your 1:1 Meeting categories. Go to your Meaningful Objectives task and identify the Supporting Projects you've delegated to your direct reports. Each Supporting Project that you've delegated will become one of your direct reports' Meaningful Objectives. I recommend that you copy and paste the Supporting Project from your objective task directly into a new task, and categorize it using the appropriate direct report's 1:1 Meeting category. This reminds you of what they're working on, and how it rolls up into your objectives. It also creates a very clear hierarchy so that all the objectives of direct reports support your objectives.

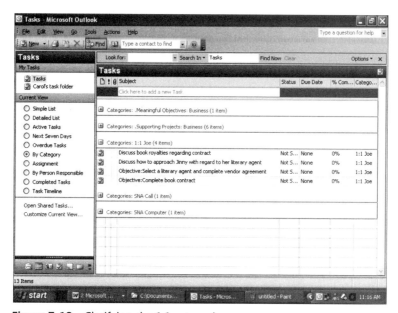

Figure 7-12   Clarifying the 1:1 categories

In Figure 7-12, you'll see a category for one of my direct reports named Joe. Under the 1:1 Joe category, I've listed the two Supporting Projects that I delegated to him and two items that I want to discuss. My two Supporting Projects became his two Meaningful Objectives.

When adding items to your 1:1 categories, you must be cognizant of timing. Anything you track using this category will not be discussed until your next meeting. If the discussion must happen prior to your scheduled

1:1 meeting, you need to use alternative methods of tracking it, such as Strategic Next Action e-mail, a Strategic Next Action call, or telepathy. Ha! Just checking to see if you're still with me!

You can also use the 1:1 Meeting category for personal use; for your spouse, partner, children, and community service contacts. My husband has his own 1:1 Meeting category! This might sound a little clinical at first, however it's actually helped our relationship. In the old days, I'd remember everything I wanted to talk to him about in my head. When we were skiing—riding on a chair lift and enjoying a wonderful moment—I'd remember that we needed to talk about our flights to London to meet my parents. This was not the right time for the discussion as we couldn't do much about it on the chair lift without our calendars, and it was interrupting a unique moment together. The alternative was that I'd forget to talk about it altogether, and then it would backfire on me. Now, I simply set up a breakfast with him and handle everything at once so it gets done, and then we can go have fun and don't worry about discussing to-do's.

SNA Waiting For Category

The purpose of the SNA Waiting For category is to track items that you're waiting for from a person outside of your team. This is a person with whom you don't have regular contact, so you can't justify setting up that person's own 1:1 Meeting category. Here's an example of such a task: "Eric—update the sales metrics on SharePoint by the end of April." When you want to track an item that you've delegated to an individual outside of your direct reports, this category is appropriate. By putting the person's name at the beginning of the Subject line, you can clarify to whom you've delegated the action.

The Waiting For category is also a good place to track miscellaneous Waiting For items. Example: "Waiting for Amazon.com to send leadership book." You're waiting for someone else to complete an action so you can move forward on your project. In this case, you're waiting for confirmation from Amazon.com that the book has been sent.

If your Strategic Next Action is a Waiting For action go ahead and categorize your task in the Waiting For Category.

Completing the Workflow Diagram

In the Workflow Model, after you've categorized your Strategic Next Action into a SNA category, the last step is prioritizing when you're going to do it on your calendar. At this point, because you haven't completed emptying your Collection Points, you'll be prioritizing in a vacuum. After you've emptied all of your commitments into the Planning and Action Categories, you will be able to see all the SNA's that you have to complete. At that point you can prioritize them and move them to your calendar. You will be doing this in Chapter 10, in the Prioritizing and Planning Phase.

Frequently Asked Questions

Before you start processing and organizing the rest of your Categories: (none) Collecting Point, here are the most frequently asked questions I receive from clients. The answers will make emptying your Collecting Point simpler.

Why separate Strategic Next Actions from Supporting Projects and Meaningful Objectives?

The intuitive way to organize Strategic Next Actions is to link them directly to your project or objective. *However, the intuitive way to organize is not always the most productive way to organize!* At first, you might feel a little awkward separating Strategic Next Actions from Supporting Projects, but remember the skiing metaphor. You're going to have to trust the process, and it won't be long before you're hooting and hollering down the mountain!

Your objective and project categories, by design, consist of Supporting Projects and Tasks and Subtasks, all of which have dependencies. This means you can't complete anything in these categories. You can *review, prioritize and plan* within them, but you can't *do* them! You can only *do* Strategic Next Actions, which is why we're separating next actions into their very own categories. This enables you to focus on them and ensure progress toward your goals. If actions are hidden in a project or objectives category, you can't view them easily, and you can't drag and drop them onto the Outlook Calendar to schedule them.

If you use a PDA that synchronizes with Outlook, you have immediate access to your Task list and can view your Strategic Next Action categories. This means that when you're in the airport with an hour to spare, you can pull up your SNA Calls category and get to work on the phone. However, if they're hidden in 19 different project tasks, you might not make the effort to find them.

"You don't *do* projects. You review, prioritize, and plan, projects. You *do* next actions."
— **Sally McGhee**

You may have inadvertently created Strategic Next Actions in your Supporting Projects when you were breaking them down to Tasks and Subtasks. If you did, you can cut and paste these items into new tasks and save them in the appropriate Strategic Next Action categories. In this way, you can make certain that all your Strategic Next Actions without dependencies are in your Strategic Next Actions categories and your tasks with dependencies are in your Planning categories.

Planning categories consist of Meaningful Objectives, Supporting Projects, and 1:1 Meetings; and the Action categories consist of Strategic Next Actions. You'll be using your Planning categories to plan and prioritize, and you'll be using your Action categories to take action and get things done. It's actually very simple when you recognize this distinction.

Splitting up Strategic Next Actions into their own SNA categories might feel strange at first, but it's ultimately a very effective process. The answer is to train yourself to *trust in your system*, which might take two or three months to do. So just be patient, and it'll all fit into place and I guarantee you'll be smiling!

Can I still associate my SNA's with my Supporting Projects?

If you feel uncomfortable that your Strategic Next Actions are separated from your Supporting Projects, you may want to connect them by including the project name at the beginning of the Subject line of the SNA task. For example, "Publish book–Create an Excel Spreadsheet to track deadline dates" creates a link between the objective and the Strategic Next Action. In this way, you can also search your Task list for project-related Strategic Next Actions, which is nifty.

Some of my clients are so comfortable with their systems that they don't need this additional step. When they read a Strategic Next Action, it's obvious to them what project it links to. It's up to you what level of detail to include to make your Integrated Management System work for you.

How do I insert e-mail messages and documents into tasks?

Sometimes it's necessary to include supporting documentation in order to complete a task. Therefore, it's important to be able to insert e-mails or files into your Tasks.

Example: "Call Litware regarding licensing contract." The contract is attached to an e-mail message in your Inbox. By inserting the e-mail into your SNA Call task, you'll have the contract handy when you're ready to make the call to Litware. You can just as easily insert files or e-mail messages into Tasks, Calendar appointments, and contacts. It's a clever little trick that Outlook provides us!

In order to insert an e-mail message into a task, follow these steps:

1. Open the task that you want to insert the e-mail into.

2. Click Insert on the menu bar, and select Item.

3. In the Insert Item dialog box, make sure Inbox is selected.

4. Select the e-mail message that you want to insert.

5. Decide whether you want to insert its contents (choose Text Only) or add it as an attachment (choose Attachment), and click OK.

To insert a document into a task, follow these steps:

1. Open the task that you want to insert the document into.

2. Click Insert on the menu bar, and select File.

3. In the Insert File dialog box, browse for and select the document to attach, and click Insert.

Does every task require a due date?

Not every task needs a due date. It's easy to assign dates, and it's just as easy to ignore them! Sometimes, my clients insist on deadlines, saying "If I don't give it a due date, it won't get done." However, when I ask, "Do you keep all the due dates you set?" the answer is always "No!" Therefore, giving tasks due dates doesn't necessarily ensure that they'll get done!

After all your Collecting Points are empty and your Planning and Action Categories are complete, you'll have a much better idea of what you've agreed to do. At that point, you can prioritize your list and establish realistic due dates, otherwise you're prioritizing in a vacuum. When you make a due date, you're making an agreement with yourself. So be discerning when you choose one, and be sure you can keep it. Check your calendar to make certain you have the time given meetings, vacations, travel, and personal events. Check completion dates on your projects and objectives to make sure your due dates are supporting those deadlines. And finally, check that

you can maintain a work/life balance as well as keep your due dates.
As you can see, selecting a due date takes some homework, but once again, taking the time on the front end will save time and disappointment on the back end.

When you're more discriminating about specifying due dates, you'll find it easier to keep them, and you'll begin to recognize how to manage your life so you can live in balance as well as honor your agreements. Productivity is an art, and requires a change in lifestyle.

Can I have more than one Strategic Next Action per project?

Yes, you can have more than one Strategic Next Action per project, as long as they have no dependencies. In fact, you can have as many actions as you like. However, I don't normally encounter more than two or three Strategic Next Actions per project at one time. You will find that 95 percent of your project plans consist of Tasks and Subtasks with dependencies. These dependencies are only unlocked when you complete the appropriate Strategic Next Action. In other words, "change the light bulb" was dependent on buying the light bulb. Therefore "change the light bulb" was a task and "buy the light bulb" was a Strategic Next Action. Once I bought the light bulb, that unlocked the task "change the light bulb" and turned it into a Strategic Next Action. That's why 95 percent of your project plans have dependencies and there are only a few Strategic Next Actions. I'm having you pay special attention to identifying and completing Strategic Next Actions because they're the key that unlock your Tasks and Subtasks, that unlock your Supporting Projects, and finally unlock your Objectives.

When do I transfer a Strategic Next Action into the Calendar?

Up to this point, you've tracked all deferred Strategic Next Actions in your SNA Categories in the Task list. When you get to the Planning and Prioritizing Phase, you'll review all of your Strategic Next Actions, prioritizing them and deciding which ones to schedule on your calendar. If you were to transfer them into your calendar now you'd be prioritizing in a vacuum because you don't yet have a completed task list. Once your task list is complete, you'll be able to make effective decisions about prioritizing the items to schedule on your calendar.

After your Integrated Management System is set up, it will be easier to identify what actions you want to schedule on the calendar rather than tracking them on the Task list. You'll learn about this process in detail when you learn about the Planning and Prioritizing Phase.

Can I choose multiple categories?

After three to six months of using your IMS, you'll have more tasks in your Task list, and duplicating them in multiple categories will create confusion and triple or quadruple the size of your lists.

Clients sometimes want to put Strategic Next Actions into multiple categories because they have choices about what actions to take. They could either make a call or send an e-mail. My suggestion is to make a decision about which one category to put it in, and stick with it. This will create less confusion and reduce the size of your list. Once again, place your decision making on the front end and don't postpone the decision for a future time.

How do I track both personal and work items?

Some personal items you'll need to do at work, such as "Schedule doctor's appointment," and "Schedule car maintenance." To help you feel more comfortable about using tasks to track your personal actions, you can mark a task as private. That way nobody can view the task, even if they have access to your Task list. If you open a task you will see a Private check box at the lower right-hand corner of the Task dialog box.

There are several solutions to tracking both personal and business tasks in one system:

- You can continue the concept of individual categories for personal and business objectives to your SNA categories; for example, SNA Call: Personal, SNA Call: Business. The down side to this approach is that you end up with a lot more categories to manage and they become more awkward to review on a PDA. The upside, of course, is that your personal and business items are clearly separated.

- You can create an SNA Personal category and track all personal Strategic Next Actions there; such as phone calls, errands, and computer items. Compared to the previous option, this reduces the number of categories you have and makes them more manageable. If you decide to run some errands, you'll need to view both the SNA Errands and SNA Personal categories to decide which tasks you can do within the time you have and the location you're in.

■ You can keep your categories as they are, and include personal items within your existing categories. When you're at the airport and decide to make some phone calls, you can view the SNA Calls category and choose whether you want to do personal or business calls.

As always, this is a personal preference and you need to decide what you think will work best for you.

Each week, you'll be doing a Weekly Review—prioritizing your Strategic Next Actions and transferring the week's actions from the Strategic Next Action categories onto your Outlook Calendar. The ultimate destination for a Strategic Next Action is the Calendar, so it's not so critical what categories you choose for your personal items. It's all about what works best for you.

Reviewing the Workflow Model

You are now ready to complete processing and organizing your Categories: (none) Collecting Point. This will take about an hour. I suggest that you find a time and location where you can have uninterrupted time and be quiet. Do not answer the phone, read e-mail, or take interruptions. Seriously, you need uninterrupted time. Give yourself that gift!

The Processing Guidelines

Start with the first item on the top of your Categories: (none) list and work your way down. No need to jump around. You'll complete the entire list anyway so everything will get processed. It's an extremely good discipline to go from top down. See if you can do this!

Once you start to process an item, don't close it back into Categories: (none). Make sure that you go completely through the Workflow Model. No procrastinating!

I've listed three tasks that were in my Categories: (none) Collecting Point. I'll take these through the Workflow Model so you can get an even better understanding of how the system works.

■ Categories: (none)

❑ Buy dog food

❑ Launch new Web site and corporate identity

❑ Write a proposal for Terry Adams at Proseware

Example: Buy Dog Food

- What is it? I need to buy more dog food for Maya. We're about to run out.

- Is it actionable? Yes, otherwise she'll be eating scrambled eggs and toast for breakfast with me and Stephen!

- Does it relate to a Meaningful Objective? Yes, I have an objective related to family and friends and she is part of that objective, which is already listed in my .Meaningful Objectives: Personal category.

- If so, define my Objective Outcome, Supporting Projects, due date, Metrics, and Category. This has already been done

- Does it have any Supporting Projects? No, it doesn't.

- If so, define Project Outcome, Tasks and Subtasks, due dates, Metrics, and Category. Doesn't apply.

- What is the Strategic Next Action? Go to Wild Oats food store and buy Maya two bags of Pinnacle dog food.

- Can I do it in less than two minutes? No

- Can I delegate it? No

- Can I defer it? Yes, I put it under SNA Errands with a due date of next Wednesday

Example: Launch new Web site and corporate identity

- What is it? Our company recently launched a new Web site and corporate identity. We want to let all our customers know so they can see it. This involves creating a letter and sending it out to our customers.

- Is it actionable? Yes, the Web site has been completed for a month so the letter needs to go out soon, and it's a great marketing opportunity.

- Does it relate to a Meaningful Objective? Yes, it relates to an objective that is recorded in .Meaningful Objectives: Business, "Create and implement a new Web site and corporate image."

- If so, define Objective Outcomes, Supporting Projects, due date, Metrics, Category. This has already been done

- Does it have any Supporting Projects? Yes, one of the Supporting Projects is to launch the new Web and corporate identity.

- If so, define Project Outcomes, Tasks and Subtasks, due date, Metrics, and category. I created a new project: Launch Web site and corporate identity. I defined the Outcomes and Tasks and Subtasks, and I selected a due date. No metrics were necessary and I categorized it as a .Supporting Projects: Business project.

- What is the Strategic Next Action? Talk to my assistant and ask her to write the copy for the newsletter regarding the Web site and corporate identity launch.

- Can I do it in less than two minutes? No

- Can I delegate it? Yes, I tracked this under my 1:1 Jennifer category so it was ready for our next meeting, which was in two days.

- Can I defer it? Not applicable

Example: Write Terry Adams, of Proseware, a Proposal

- What is it? I just opened Proseware as a new account and the chairman of the board wants me to work with him and his team.

- Is it actionable? Yes, in fact, this is how I spend 25 percent of my time.

- Does it relate to a Meaningful Objective? Yes, it relates to an overall revenue goal and a product goal to work with senior executives. Already listed in .Meaningful Objectives: Business

- If so, define Objective Outcomes, Supporting Projects, due dates, Metrics, and category. Already done.

- Does it have any Supporting Projects? Yes, this account becomes one of my projects.

- If so, define Project Outcome, Tasks and Subtasks, due date, Metrics, and category. I created a .Supporting Projects: Business category for Proseware and completed the Outcomes and plans.

- What's the Strategic Next Action? Type proposal to Terry Adams detailing work to be delivered.

- Can I do it in less than two minutes? No

- Can I delegate it? No

- Can I defer it? Yes, I recorded it under SNA Computer with a due date of Friday.

Completing Processing and Organizing the Task list

I highly recommend that you don't read on until you've emptied your Categories: (none) Collecting Point. This will give you the experience of how to process and organize information effectively. You'll empty a

Collecting Point, which is a real motivator, and you'll have set up your IMS so you can use it moving forward. This is the most exciting part. It feels good when all of your tasks are categorized in the Planning and Action Categories. Remember, Categories: (none) is only one of your Collecting Points. You still have e-mail, voice mail, notepads and paper to empty! So take the opportunity to completely empty this Collecting Point first!

Awarenesses

I'd like you to notice the value you got from this exercise and what you did to produce that value. If you know what's working, you can keep doing it and, therefore, keep getting the value.

Here are some of the statements my clients have made.

"Having all my objectives in one category so I can access them easily was useful!"

"Driving all my decisions from objectives will help me stay on track."

"Once I started breaking down my tasks, I realized I had a lot more projects than I thought."

"Keeping all of my Tasks and Subtasks in a Project category reduced my original Task list. Now, I just need to focus on my Strategic Next Actions to move them forward, which is less overwhelming."

"Chunking down to Strategic Next Actions is extremely useful, and it creates a more powerful to-do list."

"I never knew how to use categories in the Task list before...Categories rock!"

"I like having my personal and business items all in one place."

"Synchronizing this list with my Blackberry will help me when I am traveling."

"I feel more relaxed and in control of my life, knowing my commitments are organized in one place."

Customizing Your SNA Categories to Your Role and Functions

Another awareness clients have when they get more comfortable with processing information in their IMS's is how to customize their categories to their specific role and functions. When I work with clients individually, I have the opportunity to do a lot more customization, which offers further value. The Planning and Action Categorizes that you've created are cross-functional categories; most people work with objectives, projects, e-mail, and errands. However, you might have a specific role—HR, Financial, Sales, Customer Service, or Legal. Roles like these can generate a need for greater customization of categories. You can customize your work around these roles to provide greater application and value. For example, you may want to consider tailoring some of your Strategic Next Action categories around the repetitive functions that your role requires. For example:

- **Executive Administrator**   SNA Calendaring
- **HR**   SNA Resume Reviews
- **Accounting**   SNA Invoice Requests

Rather than figuring out what customized categories you think you might need, you can allow your tasks to drive these decisions, which makes the process much easier. For example: Imagine you work in the financial department of an organization as a bookkeeper. A request comes in for you to create a customer invoice. Take a moment and ask yourself, "How many of these customer invoice requests do I get a day? Am I repeating the same sequence of actions to complete them?"

If you're receiving two or three a day and you follow the same steps to complete them, this would justify creating a "SNA Invoices to be processed" category. You would then be able to schedule one hour on your calendar and work on all of them at the same time. It's much easier to work on similar tasks at one time rather than spreading them out throughout the day.

This level of customization is very specific to the role and functions you perform, so I won't be able to go into much detail in this book because there are too may different ways to customize, and my choice might not apply to you. However, my company specializes in role-related training, so if you're interested, give us a call. Our contact data is in the back of the book.

What Changes Will You Make?

Take a moment to think about the changes you want to make as a result of this chapter, such as setting up Planning and Action Categories in the Task list, creating Strategic Next Actions without dependencies, using 1:1 Categories, and following the Workflow Model to process and organize information.

In the Task list in Outlook, open the WEEKLY REVIEW task that you created in Chapter 4, and under the heading "Processing and Organizing" enter the specific actions that you want to do to support the completion of the Processing and Organizing Phase. You'll refer to this task in the Prioritizing and Planning chapter, so it'll be extremely useful to capture all of your thoughts now so you can review them later.

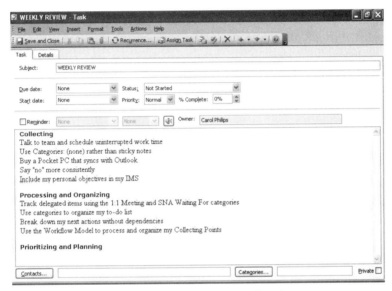

Figure 7-13   Keeping track of the changes you'll make.

Here's what some of my clients have to say:

- Use the categories in the Task list to help me organize my to-do list.

- Use the 1:1 categories to track my direct report's objective and delegated items.

- Have my objectives tracked right in front of me so I can see them daily.

- Create Strategic Next Actions without dependencies so I know I can take action immediately.

- Link Metrics into objective and project tasks so they are immediately available.

- Track Tasks and Subtasks inside of the project task so everything is in one place.

- Organize Strategic Next Action categories by location.

Success Factors for Processing and Organizing the Task List

Before you move on to processing e-mail, here's a summary of the key topics in this chapter

- Schedule uninterrupted time to process and organize your Collecting Points. Schedule a daily, recurring appointment for one hour to do this.

- Use the Workflow Model to clarify your commitments and communications. This diagram makes it a lot easier to get through the Processing and Organizing Phase simply.

- Process tasks one item at a time, starting at the top. This ensures you empty the Collecting Point and get into good habits.

- Use the Planning and Action Categories to organize your actions into the Task list.

- Remember, Meaningful Objectives and Supporting Projects are Planning Categories. They're loaded with dependencies, and they're not Strategic Next Actions.

- Strategic Next Actions are Action categories and do not have dependencies.

- Organize all of your tasks in the Task list so that your list is centrally located, accessible, and flexible.

- Identify personal behavior changes so you can successfully maintain your system going forward.

Congratulations! You've set up 50 percent of your Integrated Management System, and you're probably much clearer about what you're doing and how it's going to help you take back your life and create more productive time.

Chapter Eight

Setting Up Your Reference System

How would you like to have an additional five weeks each year to do whatever you want? According to our company's statistics, people spend 60 minutes a day, on average, finding and filing information. After they set up an effective Reference System, that number can be reduced to 10 minutes a day. That's a 50-minute savings every day of the week. Almost five weeks a year! Now *that's* something worth working towards! In this chapter, you'll discover the value of setting up a Reference System where you can find and file everything easily. Yes, it's possible, and it works!

How Well Does Your Reference System Work?

I've worked with clients who are clueless when it comes to setting up an effective Reference System, and I've worked with other clients who do a fantastic job. To determine which camp you're in, ask yourself, "Is my Reference System really working for me? Am I able to find everything I need, when I need it?" If you're happy with your system, there's no point in revamping something that's working. However, if you conclude that your system is not working, then this chapter will be incredibly useful and may result in big time savings and a huge reduction in frustration.

The Difference Between Action and Reference

The key distinction between a Reference System and an Action System is that the Reference System stores *reference information* and the Action System stores *action information*. I know this sounds simple but you wouldn't believe the number of clients who get this confused.

Action information is data you must have to complete an action, such as, "Call Jeremy to go over the sales proposal." It's essential that you have the sales proposal with you when you make the call; therefore, this classifies as *action* information. "Call the landscaper to review the quote for the dog run." You must have the dog run quote to make the call, therefore the quote is also *action information*. In both these examples, the proposal and the quote would be stored and tracked in your Action System. Your Action system includes the Outlook Task list and Calendar.

Reference information is not required to complete an immediate action. It's material you may want to access later, so it's stored in your Reference System.

David Hamilton is a Financial Director who creates annual budgets for six of his company's departments. After these budgets are distributed, he doesn't need them anymore, so he stores them in his My Documents folder, in a top-level folder named "Finances," and within a subfolder named "Departmental Budgets." Inevitably, he'll get asked questions that will require him to refer to these documents, and he also uses them at the end of the year to create the following year's budgets. There are no immediate action items related to this information, which is why he stores it in his Reference System.

Karen Berg, a mother at home, loves to cook. She collects recipes from friends that arrive in e-mail. She stores them in her Personal Folders list, under a top-level folder named "Personal," and within a subfolder named "Cooking." Karen doesn't use these recipes daily; she only goes to this folder when she needs a particular recipe, so keeping the recipes in her Reference System works well for her.

When you can discern the difference between *action* information and *reference* information, you'll be able to set up your Reference System with greater confidence.

Getting Started

By becoming more aware of your current system, you'll be able to determine if it is working for you or not.

Here are five questions that'll help you increase your awareness:

- How many locations are you currently using to store reference information?
- What type of data are you storing in what type of system?
- What Folder Hierarchy are you using to store files, and is it working?
- Do you use the same Folder Hierarchy across all reference locations?
- What percentage of the data that you're storing are you using?

I'll review each of these questions in detail in this chapter. You'll find out where you're storing your reference data and evaluate if these locations are working for you. You'll set up a Folder Hierarchy that can be used across multiple reference locations, and you'll evaluate what you've been storing and decide if you need to continue to store the same quantity and quality of data.

Identifying Your Current Reference Locations

Your first step in setting up a Reference System is to identify where you're storing reference information so you can evaluate if these locations are working for you. As with setting up a Collection System, it's important to know how many buckets you're using.

When I ask clients how many reference locations they have, they reply "Two or three; e-mail, My Documents, and paper notepads." On closer scrutiny, it can be as many as 16-20! This is a huge discrepancy!

Where Do You Really Store Your Reference Information?

It's important to know exactly how many locations you're using so you can evaluate whether or not each one is working for you. I'd like you to take a moment and scan through you life—from home to work—and identify as many places you can think of where you're storing reference information. Use the list below to write them down. If you have a file cabinet at home and one at work, that counts as two separate locations on your list, so be aware of having duplicate systems for personal and for business. If you run out of steam, Table 8-1 shows a list of potential reference points to help jog your memory.

"In your thirst for knowledge, be sure not to drown in all the information."
—**Anthony J. D'Angelo**

1. _____   11. _____

2. _____   12. _____

3. _____   13. _____

4. _____   14. _____

5. _____   15. _____

6. _____   16. _____

7. _____   17. _____

8. _____   18. _____

9. _____   19. _____

10. _____   20. _____

Table 8-1 Potential Reference Locations

Sticky notes on your monitor	Papers on desks at home and/or work
Business cards in your wallet	File folders on your Windows desktop
Inbox	My Documents
SharePoint	PDA
Personal Folders	Multiple notepads
Word documents	Paper filing system at home and work
Paper address book at home	Briefcase
Kitchen drawer	Refrigerator magnet
Archive boxes in the garage	Kitchen counter
OneNote	PDA Notes application
PC Notes application	Paper pictures
Digital Pictures	Digital music
CDs and Tapes	Stacks of magazines

Seeing how many places you're storing information and how spread out your system is can be very revealing! When our clients realize how extensive their systems are, they immediately want to consolidate and simplify.

The Six Reference Locations I Recommend

In this section, I'll review six different reference locations that you can include as part of your Reference System.

The ControlPanel, in Figure 8-1, shows a Folder List on the left, and the Start menu button on the bottom left. These two features give you access to your Reference System. Your Reference System can potentially contain six subsystems, each tracking a specific type of reference information. The six locations are:

- Folder List – tracking e-mails
- Contacts – tracking contacts
- My Documents – tracking documents
- SharePoint – tracking shared documents
- OneNote – tracking notes
- Filing Cabinet – tracking paper

Each of these systems, except for the paper system, can all be accessed from either the Folder List or the Start button in the ControlPanel.

In Carol's Personal Folders list, shown in Figure 8-1, you can see her Contacts and Personal Folders on the left. If she were to click the Start button, she'd see her My Documents folder, SharePoint program (discussed in detail later in this chapter), and OneNote program. This view is extremely useful to Carol and gives central access to her Reference System.

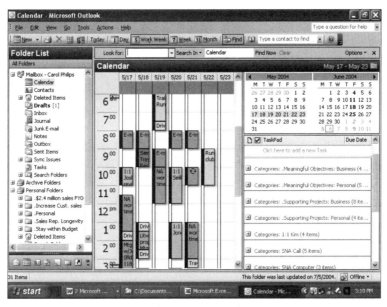

Figure 8-1   The ControlPanel shows your Reference System.

Folder List: E-mail Reference System

The Folder List is the ideal location to store e-mails. It's easy to drag and drop messages from your Inbox directly into this folder. Later in this chapter, you'll decide which folder in the Folder List you want to use to set up your e-mail Reference System; the Mailbox, the Archive Folders, or the Personal Folders. You will learn how to create an appropriate *Folder Hierarchy* to make finding and filing e-mails easier. You'll also learn where to store attachments to e-mails and how to reduce the number of e-mails you store. This is one of the easiest Reference Systems to work with, and you can get tremendous value from it when it's set up and running smoothly.

Contacts Folder: Contact Reference System

The Contacts folder is the ideal location for personal and frequently used business contacts. Most PDA's and Smartphones will synchronize with your Contacts, enabling you to access them 24/7.

If you're connected to a server on a corporate network, you'll see two Contacts folders in the Folder List; one is for global Contacts, which is shared by all employees in your company; the other folder is only in your PC, so you alone can see it. If you're not connected to a server, you'll have only one Contacts folder, which is located on your PC.

Later in this chapter, I'll review how to set up categories within Contacts to help you find and file your contacts more easily, and I'll provide some useful tips on information to include in Contacts.

My Documents Reference System

Your My Documents folder is the ideal location for storing documents: Excel spreadsheets, PowerPoint presentations, Word documents, PDF files, and pictures and music files. Later in this chapter, I'll review why you also want to store attachments to e-mails in My Documents, and how to create a useful Folder Hierarchy that'll make it easier to file and find documents.

SharePoint Reference System

Microsoft Windows SharePoint Services is an online site where your team can communicate, share documents, and collaborate on projects together. SharePoint is an ideal location to include in your Reference System because it allows you and others in a team to share and edit documents so easily. Later in this chapter, I'll review how to access SharePoint from the Start menu, and how to create a useful Folder Hierarchy within SharePoint to make it easier for your team to file and find documents.

OneNote Reference System

OneNote is a note-taking program that's designed to run on a desktop, laptop, or Tablet PC. It's the ideal location to capture notes and thoughts while you're in meetings. Later in this chapter, I'll review how to access OneNote from the Start menu, and how to create a useful Folder Hierarchy in OneNote that'll make it easier for you to file and find notes.

If you have a Tablet PC, OneNote allows you to store both typed and hand-written notes, enabling you to eliminate your paper notepads completely.

Paper Reference System

A file cabinet is the best location to file papers, though you wouldn't know it from the stacks of paper in most people's offices. The folders in a file cabinet are the only folders that you can't access from your Outlook Reference system. My file cabinet is the "ever-shrinking cabinet," and I hope that within two years, I'll no longer need it! Later in this chapter, I'll review how to create a Folder Hierarchy that makes it easier to file and find papers.

Deciding Which Locations to Use

Setting up your Reference System is much like setting up your Collection System. You to need to analyze where you're capturing data and decide which of those buckets you want to eliminate, which you'll keep and combine, and what new systems you want to create.

Write down a list of the reference locations you want to use going forward. I recommend listing no more than six.

1. _____   4. _____

2. _____   5. _____

3. _____   6. _____

Now compare your original list of locations with this new list. If your original list matches the new list, you're on track with the locations you're using, and your only improvement might be to set up a Folder Hierarchy. If they don't match, you need to identify the locations to eliminate or combine, and the new locations to set up. I suggest you capture these actions in the Task list, in the task you labeled Weekly Review; you can type it right under the Processing and Organizing heading.

Setting Up Your E-Mail Reference System

You're now going to set up your e-mail Reference System in the Folder List. This is extremely important to do because in the next chapter you'll be organizing your Inbox and filing all your reference e-mail messages. To be able to file them easily you'll want your new e-mail Reference System set up.

Which Folder Do I Use in the Folder List?

The Folder List contains three possible locations in which to set up the e-mail Reference System: your personal Mailbox, Personal Folders in your computer, and Archive.

Which folder you use depends on how much time you want to spend synchronizing your local folders with the server, how accessible you want your data to be, and the policies in your company about where to store personal and business e-mails.

Unless you have a valid rationale for using your Mailbox or Archive folder, such as if you're using two different computers and need to access these folders from both, I strongly recommend using the Personal Folder list to set up your e-mail Reference System, for these reasons:

- You have access to the information 24/7, which is extremely useful when traveling.

- You're not using valuable e-mail storage space, which can be an issue for some people.

- You don't need to endure long dial-up connections for synchronization when you're on the road. This will be a relief for "road warriors."

- Most companies allow personal e-mails to be stored as long as they're on your hard disk and not the company server.

My computer is automatically backed up once a week, so I'm extremely confident about using my hard disk to store my e-mail Reference System. However, if your company doesn't back up your hard disk, and doesn't allow you to use a third-party vendor to back up your hard disk (for IT reasons), then you should reconsider where to store both business and personal e-mails.

If you have no issues with synchronization, e-mail storage space, and 24/7 access, then using your Mailbox or Archive folder works just fine. Some of my clients like to use the Archive folder instead of the Mailbox folder because it's stored as a .pst file, which gives them unlimited storage. However, this file is connected to the server, so you won't have 24/7 access when you travel, and you'll have to endure synchronization dial-up connections.

Take a moment and decide which of these three locations you want to use for your e-mail Reference System. When you've decided where to set up your e-mail Reference System, your next task will be to create your Folder Hierarchy.

Creating a Folder Hierarchy that Works

A critical element to successful reference storage is creating the right kind of Folder Hierarchy. There's millions of ways to store reference data, but you need to find a Folder Hierarchy that fits your needs and reflects your work and home life.

Most people drive the creation of their Folder Hierarchy from the information they *receive*. When an e-mail comes in that they want to keep, they create a new folder for it. This type of filtering system is very broad. Every time a client says, "Yes, I want to keep this," a new folder gets created. This can lead to a cumbersome and confusing Folder Hierarchy that has too many folders.

I recommend creating your Folder Hierarchy *first*, before you file any e-mail. This is the complete opposite of what most people do. By creating a Folder Hierarchy and then putting data in it that fits the hierarchy, you're creating a natural filtering system. This filtering system forces you to be more discerning about what data you keep. Some of my clients are in desperate need of such a filtering system, coping with hundreds of file folders and finding this approach burdensome and frustrating.

To start this off, here's a challenge: create only 15 or fewer top-level file folders in your Folder Hierarchy. Multiple studies about Reference Systems have indicated that finding and filing information is easier when you have 15 or less top-level folders. However, you can have as many subfolders as you want! The question then becomes how do you label these top-level folders?

Organizing Your Top-Level Folders by Meaningful Objectives

There are many ways to create a Folder Hierarchy, and I've used hundreds of them over the years. However, everything in your IMS has been built around Meaningful Objectives—the Cycle of Productivity, the Workflow Model, and the Planning and Action Categories. Because everything else is driven by objectives, I'd be remiss if I didn't suggest you do the same thing here! The best filtering system in the world will be your Meaningful Objectives and your Supporting Projects. Remember, they're your North Star and guiding light.

"Goals provide the energy source that powers our lives. One of the best ways we can get the most from the energy we have is to focus it. That is what goals can do for us; concentrate our energy."
—Denis Waitley

A Folder Hierarchy based on your objectives supports a very clear focus and enables you to be more discerning about the information you keep and the information you delete. When you try to file an e-mail that doesn't relate to one of your objectives, you'll need to ask the question, "Why am I filing something that doesn't relate to one of my objectives?" By focusing primarily on your goals you can dramatically reduce the amount of information you're filing, and by duplicating this taxonomy across all your reference locations, you'll discover that finding and filing will become second nature. It also reinforces your focus on your supporting projects.

In Figure 8-2, you'll see Carol's E-mail Reference System in the Folder list under Personal Folders. Carol has five top-level folders, and under each of these folders are a number of subfolders. You'll notice that the names of the top-level folders mirror Carol's business Meaningful Objectives on her Task list, and her subfolders mirror her Supporting Projects.

One of Carol's top-level folders is titled "Personal," and the subfolders under this folder mimic her personal objectives.

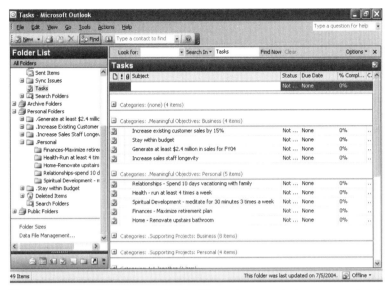

Figure 8-2 Carol's Reference Folder Hierarchy maps to her personal and business objectives.

I think you'll be surprised by the benefits of setting up your Folder Hierarchy by Meaningful Objectives and Supporting Projects. In a world full of distractions, it's essential to keep redirecting your thinking to what's important. Once all of your Reference Systems are set up with this Folder Hierarchy, you'll be reminded of your objectives and projects every time you go to find or file something. This is very powerful and helps you consistently redirect your attention. This kind of Folder Hierarchy has integrity and truly helps you focus on your most important activities.

Organizing Your Folders by Function and Role

If your objective and project folders really represent what you're doing, you won't need additional folders for functions or roles. Sometimes, the fact that you need these additional folders is an indication that your objectives are not clear and could use a little adjustment. However, I've come across examples in which a few additional function and role folders came in handy. For example, you might need to store information related to company policies, such as parking regulations, retirement plans, cafeteria coupons, and company gym use. These can be filed in a "Company Policies" folder, or in a folder that indicates to you that it stores general information about corporate guidelines.

Reference Systems can be highly customized so it would be impossible to review every approach to setting them up. Instead, I'll describe the system we recommend the most. Our company specializes in customized coaching in this area. Contact us if you are interested.

Setting Up the System

Plan on reserving one to two hours to complete setting up your new e-mail Reference System. How long it will take depends on the size and quantity of your existing e-mail Reference System. Generally speaking, the process will take anywhere from 30 minutes to two hours, depending on the number of files you have.

I recommend that you set up your top-level folders first. Each top level folder will represent one of your Meaningful Objectives. If you have eight objectives, you'd have eight top-level folders. I suggest you use the same nomenclature for each of these objectives that you used in the Meaningful Objectives category on your Task list. I would then set up subfolders under each objective folder to represent your Supporting Projects, using the same nomenclature used in your Supporting Projects category. For example, if your first objective has four Supporting Projects, you'd have one top-level objective folder with four subfolders representing the Supporting Projects.

If you have a large number of e-mail reference files, I'd suggest creating your new objective folders using a "." (period) at the beginning of the file name. This will sort your folders to the top of the folder tree. Typing folder names in all capital letters will enable you to distinguish your new folders from the old ones. After you've created your Folder Hierarchy by objectives and Supporting Projects, you can then drag and drop your old files into the new folders.

Eventually, you'll want to go into each of your personal folders and give them a good pruning. This is always an extraordinary eye opener! My clients typically find that they're not using 50 percent of what they're filing.

To create a new folder, follow these steps:

1. Select the folder that will contain the new folder.

2. On the menu bar select File, New, Folder

3. In the Create New Folder dialog box, enter the name of the new folder, and click OK.

Using a File Hierarchy Consistently Across Systems

As I mentioned earlier in this chapter, you have several locations you can choose to store information: Personal Folders, Contacts, My Documents, SharePoint, OneNote, and paper files. Now that you have a Folder Hierarchy set up, you can take this very same folder structure and use it across all of your systems. You can literally take the same taxonomy you used for your Folder List and set up the exact same top-level and sublevel folders in My Documents, OneNote, and SharePoint. (Contacts will be a little different, as you'll learn later in this chapter.) You won't believe how simple that makes filing and finding! You're creating a path that will become automatic so using it will become habit and you won't have to think twice.

Tips for Using Reference Folders

Before you move on to setting up the five remaining reference locations, I want to cover a few tips that I think will be helpful.

Stop Using Your Inbox as a Reference System!

Some of my clients use their Inbox as their e-mail Reference System because using Personal Folders wasn't effective. With the sophisticated sort functions available in Outlook today, this works for some people. However, I always recommend moving your reference e-mails out of the Inbox so you can have the *pleasure* of an empty Inbox.

I recommend creating a folder named "E-Mail Reference" and moving all of your e-mails into it. When I mention this, clients typically have a hernia. "You've got to be kidding!" I show them their e-mail and their Folder List and politely say, "See that vertical line in the middle that separates your e-mail and your folders? All I'm asking you to do is move your e-mail from the right side of the line to the left side of the line." From the look on their faces, you'd think I'd asked them to delete all their e-mails! Obviously, that line is a powerful boundary!

Remember, your Inbox is part of your Collecting System. It's not part of your Reference System. To keep the integrity of your IMS, I urge you to use your Personal Folders as part of your Reference System and leave the Inbox as part of your Collecting System. You can sort just as easily in the Personal Folder list as you can in the Inbox, and if you store your e-mails in an Archive .pst folder, you can dramatically reduce storage issues in your main e-mail file.

I have clients who resist moving e-mails out of the Inbox because leaving them in the Inbox has become a habit. They say that an empty Inbox wouldn't motivate them. But you can't pull the wool over my eyes! I've never worked with a client, ever, who on emptying his Inbox, didn't have a humongous smile on his face and an expression that said, "I didn't realize how good I'd feel. I haven't had an empty Inbox since the day I started, ten years a go!" *The problem is that we forget how good it feels to have an empty Inbox.* Use your e-mail as a Collecting Point and store reference information in the Reference System. You'll feel better!

Store Documents in My Documents

Many of my clients store e-mail messages that have large documents attached in their e-mail Reference System. I suggest you save these documents *separately* in your My Documents Reference System. When you save documents in e-mail, they increase the size of your e-mail file enormously and your Search function only searches your e-mail Subject lines and messages, not your documents. If you store documents in My Documents, your search functions are phenomenal and storage is much less of an issue.

There are a few exceptions to this rule, however. When keeping a document with an e-mail is important, save the document both in My Documents and also in your e-mail Reference System with the message. That way, it's in two places so you can be confident that you'll find it either way.

Determine What to Keep and What to Delete

This topic is really for "keepers" who are reading this chapter. My company's statistics show that, on average, people working in companies save 20 to 30 percent of their e-mails a day. That's a lot of e-mail, and for those of you who are "keepers," this percentage is much higher.

Here are some questions to help you discern what to keep and what to delete:

- Does this e-mail information relate to an objective I'm currently working on?

- Can I find this information somewhere else, such as on a Web site, on an intranet, or from a colleague?

- Will I refer back to this information in the next three months?

- I am required to keep it? Is it legal, HR, or financial?

The cry of a keeper is, "But you never know when I might need it." I ask that when you answer the questions above, you remove this sentence from your mind. Answer the questions logically rather than from your emotions or your fear! I know this is hard to do when your habits are so strong, but if you always do what you've always done...you know the rest by now!

It's so easy to store data today, dragging and dropping it into your folders in nanoseconds! However, it's not so easy to go through your folders and clean them out. That takes hours! If you take the time to pause and ask the four questions above, you'll be making decisions on the front end so you won't have to make them on the back end, when it'll take a lot more time! Don't be afraid to make best friends with your Delete key, and make it OK that you're no longer the person to whom everyone comes to find the e-mails they deleted! You weren't hired as a librarian.

Take the Time to Set Up Your Folder List

The most time-consuming element of setting up your IMS is creating your Collecting System, Action System, and Reference System. When you have these set up, you're golden!

Of course, all of us have time, but the truth is we just don't *want* to spend our time organizing Reference Systems. For most of us, this task is really low on the priority list, not to mention dull, boring, monotonous, and for some people, just plain confusing. However, when you can save 50 minutes a day by having a system that works, there's really no excuse! The value's too great so take the time to set up your Reference System properly. In the end, you'll be happy you did.

Keep Your Folder List Current

Changes will happen in your world. You'll complete objectives, take on new ones, your direct reports will change, reorganizations will happen, you might move, or you'll have a new baby. As these events happen, you'll need to adjust your Meaningful Objectives, which will then need to be reflected in your Reference System. At the same time, you'll want to delete or archive completed objectives and Supporting Projects so they're not clogging up your system. It's important to keep this connection between your current reality and your folder structure; otherwise you'll end up carrying around unrelated files for years, which will distract you from your focus on objectives.

I worked with a Senior VP who had thousands of reference e-mails that were completely out of date. After we created a new Folder Hierarchy based on his objectives, very few of these old messages fit in. He was a "keeper" so I knew I needed to tread carefully! I asked him when he'd last looked at these old messages and he said "Well, probably not for years, but, but, but, but…" I asked if they supported his current objectives in any way, and he said "No, but, but, but, but…" My final question was, "So why are you keeping this information if you're not looking at it and it doesn't support your current objectives?" He was like a deer in the headlights! He said, "Well, I suppose for sentimental reasons." I said "That's OK. At least you now know why you've been keeping it. If you want to create some kind of "Personal Archive" folder for your "special memories," that's fine. He looked at me and said, "You know, I don't want to be responsible for taking care of any more stuff. I want to lighten my load and simplify, not make it more complex. I've already done that!" He deleted all those old messages, right then and there, on the spot! He was brave! I spoke to him again recently and he was thrilled with his new Reference System. He said, "The biggest reward is being able to find data quickly, and it makes me feel so organized."

When you get used to having a Reference System, you'll find it pretty easy to maintain. My personal objectives have stayed consistent for many years so they've only required minor tweaking.

Keep Your System Simple

Some of my clients have hundreds of file folders that they use to store e-mails. I watch them take considerable time trying to find and file information, all the while convincing me that their system is working!

Of course, we're all very attached to our systems; that's a given! However, when clients start to become more aware of how long they're actually taking to file and find information, they become more open to alternatives.

The key is to keep your Folder Hierarchy simple so you can file in your sleep. Hundreds of file folders means hundreds of decisions about filing and finding, and lots of time dragging and dropping between long lists of folders. It's so much simpler to minimize the number of your top-level folders and, if necessary increase the number of your second-level folders. I've consistently found that less is more when it comes to filing.

Some of my clients have an extremely simple Folder Hierarchy. They have four folders—Q1-04, Q2-04, Q3-04, Q4-04—to represent the four quarters of the year. E-mail search functions are so good that they don't need anything more complex. This is extremely simple, and if it works for you, keep doing it. There's nothing wrong with easy!

The most uncomplicated system I've seen consisted of a single folder titled "Reference." My client stored e-mail in it and used the Search function to find e-mails. There is beauty in simplicity; however, for some of us that structure is too simple and would prove to be complicated.

Now back to setting up your five, remaining Reference Systems.

Using My Documents

I highly recommend that you take the time to set up your new Folder Hierarchy in My Documents. As with the Folder List, you can set up new folders using capital letters to distinguish them from your old folders. Then, you can drag and drop your old files into the new Folder Hierarchy. At the same time, you can do a little cleaning house, deleting the items that don't fit into your objectives or supporting projects. In Figure 8-3, you'll see Carol Philips's My Documents folder using the same Folder Hierarchy she used in her Personal Folders. Both sets of folders map to the objectives in her Task list. This is extremely simple and extremely powerful.

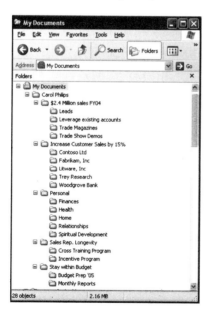

Figure 8-3 Carol Philips' My Documents Folder Hierarchy maps to her personal and business objectives.

Using the Contacts Folder

Clients have gained tremendous value from using the standard Contacts list in Outlook. In this section, you'll learn about alternative ways to use Contacts and Categories.

Carol has two Contacts folders in her Folder List: Contacts under the Mailbox heading, which is located on her hard disk, and Contacts under the Public Folders heading, which is located on the server. She uses the Contacts list on her hard disk to store her personal information and her frequently used business contacts. She uses the Contacts list in the Public Folders to share business contacts. Carol can access this list only when she's connected to the server, so she keeps her frequently used business contacts in the Contacts folder on her hard disk. That way she can access it when she's no longer connected to the server.

If you have a PDA or a Smart Phone you can synchronize your Contacts list with these devices. This enables you to have immediate access to all of your personal and frequently used contacts 24/7, which is extremely helpful.

I've found that most companies will allow you to keep track of personal contacts in your Contacts list on your hard disk. I recommend that you check to ensure that you're complying with corporate policies.

Taking Advantage of Your Contacts Reference System

There are lots of ways to benefit from having additional information in your Contacts list. Here are a few examples from clients:

- Keeping directions in Contacts. When you're driving to a business or friend's house you can use your PDA to view directions.

- Posting birthdays in Contacts so they appear on the Calendar. By opening a contact, clicking the Details tab, and entering a date in the birthday field, you can have a reminder appear on the Calendar for that day.

- Including clothes sizes for family and friends. When you're shopping and see a potential wardrobe gift, you'll have the data handy.

- Tracking client/vendor conversations if you don't use a customer relationship database. I have clients type their notes directly into their contact when they're on a call with a client. When they call the client again, their comments from the previous call are handy in the contact.

- Remembering vaccinations for children and pets.

- Recording equipment warranty expiration dates, and contact information, such as a Help Line number.

Recently, my husband and I got a dog. I immediately created a new contact to track her birth date, vaccinations, and other relevant data. This proved to be incredibly useful when I found myself at the vet's office. The doctor asked questions about vaccines and I was dumb founded until I remembered my Contacts in my Pocket PC! Organization strikes again! It took me two minutes to track this data in my Contacts, and saved me much more by having it immediately available for the veterinarian.

I never have to worry about birthday reminders because once I enter them into my Contacts list, they automatically show up on my Calendar. And having directions in my Contacts helps me get to my appointments on time. I synchronize my laptop with my PDA so when I'm in the car, my PDA helps me get where I'm going. I'm directionally challenged so having directions handy is beneficial to me.

Take the time to set up and keep your Reference System current and it'll save you precious time and improve your quality of life.

Using Categories in Contacts

By grouping contacts into categories, you'll be able to find specific contacts more easily and access your contacts by groups for mailing purposes. In Figure 8-4, you'll see contacts grouped by categories.

As an example of how useful grouping contacts can be, imagine you need to call a contractor for some home maintenance and you can't remember his name. Rather than scan your entire Contacts list, you can look in the "Home" category.

I have a client who has an "Entertainment" category in which he tracks favorite restaurants and theatres in the cities he travels to. This makes booking reservations much easier. Another client uses a "Friends & Family" category to help her create her Christmas cards and gift list each year. The category reminds her of whom she wants to send cards and gifts to. She also uses this list to print out Christmas card envelopes.

There are lots of good reasons to view contacts by categories. However, in order for this view to work effectively, you must categorize each contact you create. If you don't do this consistently, your system will break down. Be careful. Only use categories if they add value, otherwise they'll become one more thing for you to do.

To view contacts as address cards, click Address Cards.

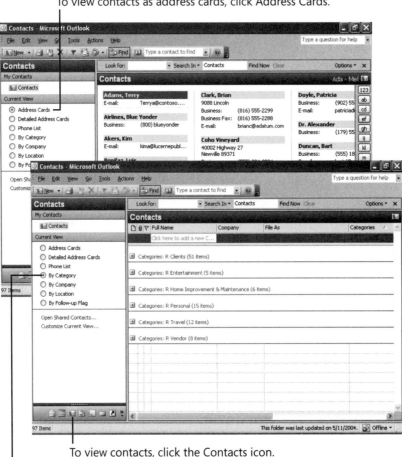

To view contacts, click the Contacts icon.

To view contacts by category, click By Category.

Figure 8-4 Viewing contacts by categories

To view your contacts by categories, click By Category in the Navigation Pane to the left of the Contacts list.

Shared Contacts Lists

When you're sharing a Contacts list, you need to set up guidelines about how to sort the contacts. Do you file them by last name, first name, or company name? Will you use categories and, if so, which ones? You need to be consistent with how you organize Contacts so you can be consistent with how you find them!

Using SharePoint

Many companies now use SharePoint sites to help intact work teams share documents. We organize our internal company SharePoint site by department, and then by Meaningful Objectives and Supporting Projects. This allows us to continue using a consistent Folder Hierarchy across all our Reference Systems. Because of this scheme we can all find data, and we're consistently focused on our objectives.

Using OneNote

OneNote is a great location to store all of your meeting notes. Some of my clients use this exclusively for all of their note taking and they've completely let go of paper. As with your other reference locations, you can create the same Folder Hierarchy within OneNote for storing notes. OneNote also has a feature that enables you to transfer actions directly to your Outlook Task list. This makes it possible for you to keep your notes in your Reference System and your actions in your Action System. Wow! You gotta love that!

Using Paper

I have only one file drawer of paper remaining and it relates to a limited number of my objectives because I am becoming increasingly more electronic. I use Pendaflex hanging files to represent my top-level objective folders and Manila folders in those to represent my Supporting Projects. I'm praying for the day when I can empty my file cabinet completely so I have one less reference location to manage and maintain each year.

What Changes Will You Make?

In your Outlook Task list, open the task named "Weekly Review." This is the location you created to capture all the behaviors you'll do differently as a result of the Three Phases for Setting Up an Integrated Management System. Under the heading "Processing and Organizing," list the changes that you want to make to set up your Reference System effectively.

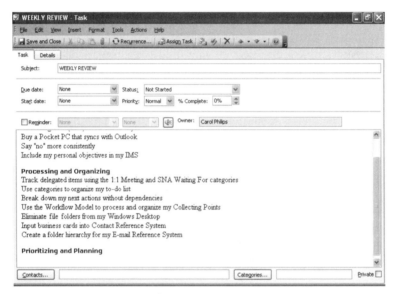

Figure 8-5 Keeping track of the changes you'll make.

Here are a few examples from clients:

- Set up Personal folders so I can stop using my Inbox as a Reference System, and start using my Personal Folders instead.

- Reduce my 45 top-level folders to 17, so it's easier to file and find!

- Synchronize my Folder Hierarchy from my Personal Folders to My Documents.

- Set up SharePoint for my team so we can share documents using the same Folder Hierarchy.

- Enter my names and address's into Contacts, so I have one central place for them instead of multiple buckets.

- Find out if I can integrate my personal contacts into my Contacts file on my hard disk.

- Keep action information with actions in the Action System and reference information in the Reference System.

- Categorize my contacts to make it easier for me to find them.

Success Factors for Creating an Effective Reference System

With an effective Reference System you can find and file critical data easily and dramatically reduce the amount of time you spend doing so. It's well worth putting the time and effort in on the front end because you'll have extraordinary time savings on the back end.

As you set up your Reference System, remember these key items:

- Define the difference between action and reference information so you know what data to store in which system.

- Decide what locations you're going to use to store information and minimize the list to six systems, if you can.

- Create a clear Folder Hierarchy based on objectives, functions, and roles so you're driving your IMS from this focus.

- Use 15 or fewer top-level folders so you can simplify your system.

- Mirror your file hierarchy across systems to create a consistent taxonomy that makes it easily to find and file data.

Now, the moment you've all been waiting for: Processing and organizing e-mail. Hold onto your hats, and prepare to get friendly with the Delete key!

Chapter Nine

Processing and Organizing Your E-Mail

E-mail is one of the biggest challenges facing our organizations today. My clients often comment, "We get too much of it, we can't keep up with it, but we can't stop doing it. We're addicted!" Many companies are now questioning the value of e-mail and how to bring it back into balance. An IT director I spoke to recently commented, "E-mail has become unproductive. We're overusing the Cc line, sending messages that aren't valuable, and spending too much time with our heads stuck in the Inbox." It sure seems like e-mail is a big problem. However, is e-mail really the problem or is it how we approach e-mail?

Technology has eliminated many personal boundaries, and some of my clients have allowed e-mail to drive their behavior instead of the other way around. As in dealing with interruptions, if you don't set conscious boundaries for yourself, the world will set them up for you. I'm sure you've experienced working on e-mail at home, late at night, early in the mornings, during meetings, and while on telephone conference calls. Some of my clients have Blackberries and even process their e-mail while driving the car or standing in line at the grocery store!

E-mail is not the issue. The issue is how we approach using it. The first step to controlling your e-mail is to identify the changes you need to make to manage it more effectively, and that's what this chapter is all about.

I'll discuss how to process and organize your e-mail so you can empty it successfully into your Integrated Management System. (Yup, I did use the word empty!) When you've learned how to do this, you'll find that it can relieve a tremendous amount of stress and help you make better choices about what your priorities are and how to get them done.

I'll review how to use the E-mail PASS Model, which includes learning to create meaningful e-mail, to correctly use the To, Cc, and Subject lines, and to ask certain questions before clicking Send. I'll also review the Workflow Model and the Four D's for Decision Making, which will enable you to effectively process and organize your Inbox. And finally, I'll review how to establish e-mail guidelines within your team to improve e-mail communication and management.

If you have hundreds of e-mails in your Inbox, there's hope in sight. The search for the empty Inbox is close at hand, and there's gold at the end of the rainbow! Many of our clients go to bed at night with an empty Inbox! (If your Inbox is already clear, read on, because I'll be introducing some very nifty Outlook tips and tricks that I think you'll definitely find valuable.)

E-Mail Is a Communication Tool

I think we have all forgotten that e-mail is primarily a communication tool. The purpose of communication is to exchange information so that it's clearly understood. Therefore, one of the main functions involved in processing and organizing your e-mail is communicating effectively. Communication is an art we can practice and improve. If your messages are not clear, your recipients will not be clear, and effective action will not take place. I'm certain you've gotten e-mails and said to yourself "What is this, what does it mean, and why did I get it?" Think about the number of times you've sent an e-mail that came back with questions because you didn't write the message clearly enough to begin with.

Introducing the E-mail PASS Model

The E-mail PASS Model is designed to help you think about your e-mail communications before you send them. This results in clearly defined messages that produce effective action with the minimal number of communication cycles. By writing effective messages you can actually reduce the number of e-mails you receive in a day. That was my motivation to take another look at how I was constructing my e-mail messages.

The E-mail PASS Model consists of three sections:

- Creating meaningful e-mail using the PASS Model questions
- Using the To, Cc, and Subject lines appropriately
- Asking three questions before clicking Send

Creating Meaningful E-Mail Using the PASS Model Questions

The E-mail PASS Model consists of four questions, I'll review them one at a time, and you can type in your responses as you go. Review your e-mail for a moment and pick out a message that you need to respond to. Choose one that appears to be complex and that would take more than two minutes to write. Choose a really meaty, chewy example so you can experience the value of this model.

The four E-Mail PASS Model questions are:

- P—What's the Purpose of your communication and does it relate to a Meaningful Objective?

- A—What Action is involved and does it have a due date?

- S—What Supporting documentation do you need to include?

- S Have you effectively summarized your communication in the Subject line?

What Is the Purpose of Your Communication?

To help you clarify the purpose of your communication, first identify the Meaningful Objective the e-mail relates to. If it doesn't relate to one of your objectives, you'll need to renegotiate it or disengage from it. If this is the case, go ahead and pick another e-mail to work with.

Next, ask yourself "What's the outcome you want to produce as a result of this message?" Describe in detail what you want to have happen. When it's obvious, start your reply and take a few moments to write your communication. Notice that I haven't asked you to complete the To line, the Cc line, or the Subject line. Write the communication first.

Susan Smith, an IT program manager, received an e-mail from her boss asking her to update him on the Microsoft Outlook Migration project. She realized she didn't know the status of the project and needed to get accurate data. She started to type a quick e-mail to Jennifer, her assistant, to find out what was going on. I interrupted her and said, "Step away from the keyboard!" Susan looked at me a bit surprised. In her mind she was mumbling, "Hey, this is a simple enough e-mail. I can do this on my own, thank you very much!"

"If any man wishes to write a clear style let him first be clear in his thoughts."
—Johann Wolfgang VonGoethe

I asked her two questions, "What objective did it relate to?" and "What was the outcome she really wanted?" As Susan stopped to think about the communication, she realized that what she really needed was to receive a reoccurring, monthly project status report. This would enable her to monitor what was going on, and if the report was posted on SharePoint, she and her boss could assess it whenever they needed it. Her eyes lit up! This was a much better solution. She smiled and said, "OK, perhaps I need to think through these communications a bit more!"

What Action Is Involved and Does It Have a Due Date?

What type of action do you want the recipient or recipients to take as a result of your communication? By clearly stating the action, you have a better chance of it's getting done.

Listed below are the four most common e-mail actions that I recommend.

- **Action** The recipient has to take a physical action step—Order an extension cable. Write a Review. Read a document. Book a meeting.

- **Respond** The recipient needs to only respond to your communication. There's no action to complete. "Let me know if you can attend the staff meeting at 9 AM on Friday."

- **Read** The recipient needs to only read the information. There is no need to take an action or respond. "Read sales plan before our next STP meeting."

- **FYI Only** The recipient needs to file the information for future reference. There is no need to take action, to read, or to respond. "Enclosed is your approved expense report for your records."

The reason to identify the type of action you're asking the recipient to perform is to eliminate any confusion or guessing about your expectations. In many cases, the benefit is as much for you as it is for them! In Susan's example she realized, with a little thought, that asking one of her direct reports to post a regular status report on SharePoint was a much more effective action than asking her assistant to find out what was going on with the project. If she hadn't thought this through, she wouldn't have reached that conclusion. Think about your communication and clearly identify the action you want the recipient to perform.

Susan decided that her action was to delegate her task to Joe Henry, one of her direct reports. She asked him to create the report for the Microsoft

Outlook Migration project and post it each month to SharePoint, enabling her and her boss to easily access it.

Next, identify if your requested action needs a due date. Be careful not to assume that all tasks require due dates, as not all of your actions will need them. Revisit the deadline of the related objective first, and evaluate if the action needs to happen by a specific date to ensure that the objective stays on track. Check the Calendar to ensure that the timeline will work given staff meetings, vacations, and other appointments. When you're clear that your due date is realistic, go ahead and add it to your message.

Clarifying dates can help recipients prioritize their tasks more effectively. If everything you delegated was absent of a timeline you'd be relying on the recipient's best judgment to know what your priorities were. That's not a fair request to make of everyone. Most people need clear direction.

Be discerning in how you use timelines, and make sure they mean something. It's easy to use due dates and it's just as easy to overuse them. If you don't hold people accountable to your timelines, they'll eventually come to the conclusion that your timelines don't mean anything. One day, when you give a date that really matters and your team don't respond, you'll wonder why. Don't give out timelines unless you're willing to follow up on them.

You can't expect others to keep their due dates if you don't keep yours. Remember, "what's good for the goose is good for the gander." When you demonstrate being accountable to timelines, then other people around you will aspire to do the same.

Finally, be sensitive when giving out timelines to recipients that don't work for you. It's important to mention a timeline so everyone is aware of the impact if a task misses a deadline. However, you can't reinforce a due date outside of your own team unless you're working on a project with mutual benefit to both parties.

Take a moment now to review your e-mail, clarify the action, and select a due date if it's appropriate.

Example Susan wanted Joe Henry to create a Microsoft Outlook Migration project monthly status report. She wanted it posted to Share-Point by the fifth of each month and to have the first report completed in April. This would enable her to get back to her boss on time and would give her regular data so she could ensure that the project stayed on track.

What Supporting Documentation Do You Need to Include?

Next, identify the supporting information that the recipient requires to successfully complete the action. This will reduce the likelihood of your message coming back to you with questions, creating additional e-mail.

Recently, I asked my Operations Manager to create a cash flow analysis report. I attached an example of the report I wanted her to complete. This enabled her to accomplish my request without further e-mails inquiring about layout, data to include, comparisons, and time frames. Once again, moving your thinking to the front end saves you time and effort on the back end.

If you want to include supporting documentation in your e-mail you can either type it in the body of the communication, attach a file (Excel, PDF, Word, PowerPoint, and so on) or insert an item (Inbox, Contacts, reference or e-mail files). To attach a file or an item, open a new e-mail, click Insert on the menu bar, and make one of the following choices on the submenu:

- **File** to insert a file from your computer
- **Item** to insert an item from your Folders List in Microsoft Outlook

---

Example   Susan inserted a "monthly status report" template so Joe could view a sample of what she was looking for, and told him which Share-Point site to post it on. Figure 9-1 shows Susan's e-mail message. This type of information reduced all kinds of guessing on Joe's part, making it easier for him to duplicate the report and post it where Susan could find it.

Have You Effectively Summarized Your E-Mail in the Subject Line?

After you've completed writing your e-mail communication, you can then summarize your message using the Subject line. In the old days, I often fell into the trap of trying to construct my Subject line first because it seemed the intuitive thing to do. However, I always ended up changing it after I completed writing my e-mail. It took me a while to break that habit. I suggest you construct your communication first and then tackle the Subject line.

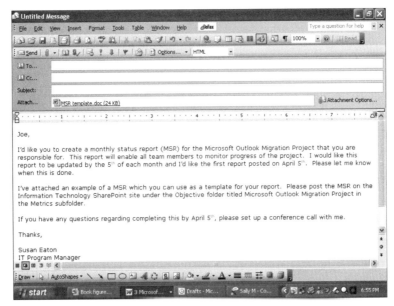

Figure 9-1 Susan's e-mail message clarifying purpose, action, and supporting documentation

There are three elements that make a good Subject line:

1. Clarify the Meaningful Objective or Supporting Project that the e-mail relates to.

2. Clarify the action requested.

3. Identify a due date, if there is one.

An example Subject line might be "Microsoft Outlook Migration project. Create a monthly status report (MSR) posted on SharePoint, by April 5th."

There are four different types of action that you can use in your Subject lines.

■ **Action Requested**   The recipient has to complete an action before they can respond. Example: AR: Outlook Migration: post monthly status report to SharePoint starting April 5th.

■ **Response Requested**   The recipient needs only to respond. No action is required. Example: RR: When do you need the PowerPoint slides for your October 1 vendor meeting?

■ **Read Only**   The recipient is required to read the document. Example: RO: Performance Review enclosed for your Holly Henson meeting on Friday August 10th.

■ **FYI only**   The recipient doesn't need to read the document they need to file or delete it. Example: FYI: Updated P&L report for your Q1 records.

Imagine if you could sort your Subject lines by action—Action Requested (AR), Response Requested (RR), and Read Only (RO)—or if you could sort them by objectives or due dates. Clear subject lines speed up your ability to process and organize your e-mail effectively. The objective lets you know immediately what it relates to. The action lets you know what your responsibility is. The due date enables you to look at your Calendar and Task list to see if it is possible. Taking the time to create clear subject lines makes e-mail communication more effective and increases the chance that your e-mail will be responded to.

Another helpful tip is to use "EOM" at the end of your Subject line when you can complete your message in the Subject line. EOM stands for End Of Message. With this technique, you'll have no need to open the e-mail and enter a full message. By using EOM, you're informing the recipient that the message in the subject line is complete and he doesn't need to open the e-mail. This is a courtesy and it saves time for the recipients.

For example: "AR: Honeywell Delivery. Book one hour follow-up meeting with Henry Jefferson to review progress by June 15th. EOM"

Just as it's easy to overuse due dates, it's easy to overuse Subject lines so they become meaningless instead of meaningful. One client of mine so overused the "Action Requested" Subject line that it now holds no value and people disregard it. Be discerning about how you use the Subject line, reinforce its value by reminding people when they are using it appropriately and reminding them when they're using it inappropriately.

You also have to be sensitive when using Subject line acronyms (AR, RR) with people outside of your team. They won't understand what you mean. In this case, your best solution is to avoid using acronyms altogether and stick with the basic three Subject line elements: Objective, Action Requested, and Due Date. This type of Subject line is clear and universally understood.

The Purpose of the To Line

The To line and the Subject line are intrinsically linked. The Subject line clarifies the action that the recipients on the To line have to take. Therefore, be aware of who you're placing on the To line and ensure that they are responsible for the action in the Subject line.

Here are two simple and useful questions to help you filter To line recipients.

- Does this e-mail communication relate to the recipient's objectives?
- Is this recipient responsible for the action in the subject line?

If the Subject line requests an action, each individual on the To line is responsible for taking that action. Some people send e-mails with four or five people in the To line in the hopes that one of them will respond. Each person receiving the e-mail assumes that someone else on the To line will reply, and no one ends up responding. Be thoughtful and respectful when you assign recipients to the To line. People will observe your thoughtfulness and the results will be more effective.

If the action in the Subject line relates to multiple recipients who need to take different actions, clarify this in the body of the e-mail so everyone is clear exactly what's needed. Figure 9-2 provides an example of a message with multiple recipients who must take different actions.

Example   Susan put Joe on the To line because he was responsible for creating the status report. She also put her assistant, Jennifer, on the To line because she wanted her to download a document and send it to her. Susan clarified Jennifer's action in the body of the e-mail, as shown in Figure 9-2.

The Purpose of the Cc Line

The Cc line dominates our e-mail boxes and is an endless source of frustration and unproductive behavior, although it really doesn't have to be. The Cc line is only a courtesy copy, which means it needs to be read or filed, and no action or response is required. The Cc line is linked to the Subject line only by the objective and not by the action. Therefore, a useful question to help you filter your Cc line recipients is, "Will this e-mail impact the recipient's objectives?"

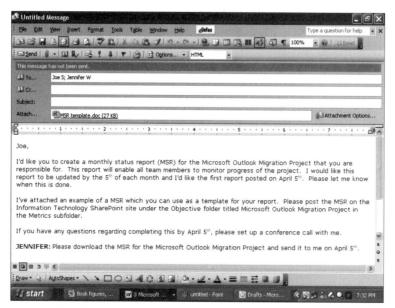

Figure 9-2   E-mail message demonstrating multiple recipients taking different actions

If you ask this question whenever you're about to type a person's name in the Cc line, you'll end up sending considerably less e-mail. I consistently question my clients' use of the Cc line, and eight times out of 10, they don't need to use it. Take the time to pause and ask the question, "Does this communication impact the recipient's objectives?" If it doesn't, or you don't know what the recipient's objectives are, refrain from including the recipient on the Cc line. Believe me, you're not helping people by sending them information that doesn't impact their objectives. You're just giving them more work to do and more distractions to overcome. Don't be part of the e-mail problem. Be part of the solution by demonstrating effective use of the Cc line.

Take a moment and complete your e-mail message, assigning the appropriate To and Cc lines.

The Purpose of the Bcc Line

Protecting a distribution list and keeping individuals from receiving a Reply or Reply All are good reasons to use the Bcc line. When placing individuals on the Bcc line to protect them from Reply and Reply All, make a note in the body of the e-mail that they have been Bcc'd so others don't forward information to them unnecessarily.

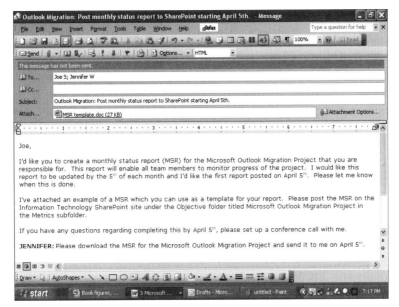

Figure 9-3 Susan's e-mail message demonstrating the E-mail PASS Model questions

Does Your E-Mail Message PASS?

The three final questions to ask before sending your e-mail message are:

■ Does your e-mail PASS?

■ Have you written the e-mail so it will not come back to you with questions?

■ Do you need to track this e-mail in one of your 1:1 Meeting or SNA Waiting For categories?

This is your last chance *before* clicking Send to ensure that your message is clear and will produce the results you intend.

Does Your E-Mail Message PASS?

The PASS test is your final check to ensure that your e-mail will be clearly understood.

To take the test, ask these questions:

■ Have you communicated your *purpose* and made sure that it relates to an objective?

- Have you communicated the *action* requested?

- Did you include the appropriate *supporting documentation*?

- Have you *summarized your Subject line* effectively?

- Did you use the To, Cc, and Bcc line appropriately?

Have You Written the E-Mail so It Won't Come Back to You with Questions?

When I ask clients this question, they inevitably go back and edit their message to make it clearer. This is not only polite and respectful, but it also reduces e-mails. When your communications are clear, people can move forward with requests instead of e-mailing you back and forth to gain clarity.

Don't underestimate this question. Just recently I worked with a CIO and asked him this question repeatedly. He was a fast-thinking person who was having trouble understanding why I wanted him to slow down and put so much thought into his messages. At the end of the day, he received several responses from his e-mails with questions asking for more information and clarity. He raised one eyebrow and said, "Wow! You weren't kidding. I really do need to be clear to ensure I don't get e-mail responses asking questions! I suppose I better change my standard for what clear means."

Writing e-mail messages so recipients understand what you mean and don't need to ask questions is not as easy as people think. It takes pausing, and collecting your thoughts. To do this you need a quiet uninterrupted environment because processing e-mail during meetings, when you're talking on the phone, driving in the car, or late at night doesn't support this process. Writing clearly is a skill and it takes practice.

Do You Need to Track this E-Mail in One of Your 1:1 Meeting or SNA Waiting For Categories?

The third question reminds you to track delegated items if it's appropriate. The simplest way to do this is to add yourself to the Cc line of the e-mail. When the e-mail comes back in your Inbox, you can transfer it into your Task list and categorize it into one of your 1:1 Meeting categories or your SNA Waiting For category.

To transfer an e-mail into the 1:1 Meeting or SNA Waiting For categories, follow these steps:

1. Right-click and drag the e-mail to the Task icon in the Folder List.

2. From the shortcut menu, choose Move Here As Task With Attachment.

   In the Task window, the e-mail Subject line appears in the Task Subject line, and the e-mail is inserted into the task as an envelope icon.

3. Click Categories in the lower-right corner of the message window, and select the appropriate SNA category.

4. Click OK, and click Save And Close to close the task.

Figure 9-4   Transferring e-mails into the 1:1 Meeting or SNA Waiting For Categories

I only recommend tracking a delegated item if you need to track the completion of the action to support one of your Meaningful Objectives or Supporting Projects, question a person's ability to complete the item on time, or train a new team member to be accountable. You don't want to police people by tracking everything you delegate just because you can! It's important to trust the people you're working with, and only track a delegated task if you have a specific reason to do so.

Clients often ask me, "Why do I need to Cc myself? Why not drag and drop the message from the Sent Items folder?" Imagine that you've sent your e-mail, and you're about to go to the Sent Items folder to drag and drop it into your SNA Waiting For category when the phone rings. You answer the call and get involved in a conversation and completely forget to drag and drop the mail from the Sent Items folder. The only way to ensure you don't forget these e-mails is to Cc yourself *before* you send e-mail. This way the messages will come back into your Inbox to remind you to file them. Once again, a little bit of effort on the front end saves work on the back end.

Now you're ready to send your e-mail!

It took longer to write your e-mail using the E-mail PASS Model, but when you write clear, purposeful e-mail, you'll end up reducing the amount of mail you receive and the amount of mail you send. You'll reduce cycles of communication, and make progress toward your objectives. When it comes to processing e-mail, slowing down does, in fact, help you speed up!

Unfortunately, some people have allowed the speed of technology to dictate the pace at which they work. But just because technology moves fast doesn't mean that you have to. Your best results will come from pausing and giving yourself time to think.

The more you practice and demonstrate writing clear, meaningful e-mail messages, the more those around you will take note. Demonstration is one of the most powerful instigators of change. When you're consistent in your behaviors, others will start to do the same. It's inspiring to work with people who go the extra mile and demonstrate excellence. This is another example of how "small things done consistently in strategic places create major impact!"

Using the Workflow Model to Process and Organize E-Mail

Now that you've learned how to create meaningful e-mail using the E-mail PASS Model, you're ready to go to work on Processing and Organizing your e-mail using the Workflow Model. Most of you probably scan your e-mail throughout the day, jumping around your Inbox and opening and closing messages without taking any action. The more you do this, the quicker it is for your Inbox to grow in size. For some people, the Inbox grows to as many as 7,000 e-mail messages. To get through large volumes of e-mail, you need a system for managing them. The Workflow Model will help you process and organize your mail with a systematic approach so you don't scan it and leave it in the Inbox.

Reviewing e-mails during meetings, in between meetings, and while you're on the phone, is not a productive way to process mail. You need quiet time during which you can concentrate, pause and think clearly. Therefore, the first step in processing and organizing e-mail effectively is to schedule at least one hour of uninterrupted time each day to process and organize your e-mail.

The second step is to sort your e-mail into the order in which you want to process it, organizing it by date, subject, or person. You will be processing your e-mail one at a time, starting at the top of the list. This means that after you open an e-mail, you will decide what the action is, and transfer it out of the Inbox. You're not allowed to close it back in the Inbox! Some people are "jumpers," processing e-mail by jumping around from one message to another. However, during this exercise, I want you to refrain from jumping, and work *one e-mail at a time in sequence.* Don't move to the second e-mail until the first is processed.

Now, you're ready to start working through the Workflow Model. Double-click your first e-mail message, and let's get cracking.

"The shortest way to do many things is to do only one thing at a time."
—**Sydney Smiles**

What Is It?

Is the e-mail you've selected reference or action, big or small, a Meaningful Objective or Supporting Project, personal or business? When you're clear what the e-mail is, move onto the next question in the Workflow Model.

Is It Actionable?

Given everything else on your plate right now, is it appropriate for you to take on this action? If not, you have three options:

1. File it in your new, improved E-Mail Reference System.

2. File it in your SNA Someday Maybe category (I will discuss how to do this in the sections below).

3. Swiftly delete it, never to be seen again!

All of these options remove the e-mail from your Inbox. If you want to take action on this e-mail, move on to the next question.

Does It Relate to a Meaningful Objective?

Ensure that the action it requires maps to one of your personal or business objectives. If it doesn't map to one of your objectives, question why you want to take an action on it. Just because a message shows up in your Inbox doesn't mean you need to act on it. Be discerning about what you put your energy into. At the end of the day, you're measured on your objectives (at work) so it's important to stay focused on them and not get distracted into other areas. This is also true of your personal life. Because you're not measured on your objectives, it's easy to abandon the goals you've created and get lost in distractions. Asking whether the message relates to a Meaningful Objective helps you pause and question how you're using your time and energy.

Example   Todd Elton, a Director of Sales and Marketing, wasn't increasing revenue as quickly as he wanted to. I sat down with his boss and we clarified the three most important objectives that Todd needed to focus on to increase revenue. I then had Todd list all of the activities he was working on and we checked each activity against his top objectives. It was a tough process for Todd because a good number of them did not link to his top three objectives. They did relate to overall Sales and Marketing, but not to the three most important objectives that would support him in increasing revenue. Todd realized how important it was to be clear on his objectives and ensure that all his actions directly supported them.

If your e-mail communication does map to one of your objectives, move on to the next question.

What Is the Strategic Next Action Without a Dependency?

Take a few moments to clarify what your Strategic Next Action step is. Start the step with a verb followed by a physically doable instruction that has no dependencies. Make sure there really are no dependencies, so you can complete the step immediately. You can't put off this decision and close the e-mail back in the Inbox. You must create an SNA in order to move forward. After you've created your SNA, you're ready to move onto the next section of the Workflow Model.

The Four D's for Decision Making

After you've mastered the Workflow Model, you can process and organize your e-mail simply by following the Four D's for Decision Making. This model is simpler to use and helps with large volumes of e-mail that require rapid decisions.

The 4 D's are:

- Delete it.
- Do it if it takes less than two minutes.
- Delegate it and, if appropriate, track it in your 1:1 Meeting or SNA Waiting For category
- Defer it to one of your SNA categories in the Task list or transfer it to a specific time on your calendar

Delete It

The Workflow Model covers this question by asking "Is this actionable?" However, when using the Four D's for Decision Making separately from the Workflow Model, this question is first.

Deleting e-mail is not easy for all of us and it has a lot to do with past experience. Some people are extremely uncomfortable letting go of infor mation, and for good reason. Remember your very first job. You were incredibly nervous and wanted to do everything right. It was your fourth day and your boss asked you for a document you didn't have. You'd deleted it two days earlier! He was unhappy you couldn't produce the document and made a big, huge fuss about it. You felt disappointed and beat yourself up for deleting it. After this experience, you decided never to delete anything ever again, to ensure you didn't have to repeat the experience.

However, not all people are the same. If you delete a document, it doesn't necessarily mean it's going to come back to bite you! What happened 10 years ago may not happen today. So ask yourself, in all honesty, how many times have you referenced the e-mails you've saved? I'd guess maybe 10 percent of the time! The truth is that you really don't get paid to file, you get paid to complete Meaningful Objectives successfully, so be watchful of how much e-mail you file, how much you use it, and how long it takes you to find it.

Did you know that, on average, clients delete 50 percent of their e-mail? (Deep breaths now, in and out!) For those of you who are uncomfortable deleting e-mail, there are four questions below that will help you determine what to keep and what to delete. If your answer to any of these questions is "no," I strongly suggest that you delete the message. (Keep breathing!)

- Does this e-mail information relate to a Meaningful Objective I'm currently working on?

- Can I find this information somewhere else? On a Web site, on an intranet, or from a colleague?

- Will I refer back to this information in the next three months?

- Am I required to keep it? Is it legal, HR, or financial?

I am sure you've lost your entire Inbox in the past due to a crash or virus. Remember what happened? Most of my clients say, "Nothing! I was so surprised. I just got on with business as usual." So don't be afraid to step outside of your comfort zone, let go of the "keeper" role and see what happens. I think you will be pleasantly surprised.

Do It

A "do it" action is a Strategic Next Action that you can personally complete in less than two minutes. On average, clients complete 30 percent of what's in their Inbox in less than two minutes. It's motivating to complete this many cycles of action, and it proves how much you can get done in less than two-minute cycles.

Here's an example of a "do it in less than two minutes." In an e-mail, my assistant asked me to send her an updated schedule for the book-editing project. I had the updated schedule in my Reference System in My Documents. There was no point in typing this action into my task list; it would have taken longer to do that than it would have to send the schedule to her.

If it takes less than two minutes, just get it done and get it out of your Inbox. If it takes three minutes, that's fine, too. You don't have to be too rigid about the time limit. The key is to complete an action if you can complete it faster than you can track it.

I used to work with a stopwatch, timing clients while they processed their e-mail. It was inspiring to me how much they'd get done in two minutes or less. Often, clients would try and convince me that a reply would take longer, so I'd say, "Let's time it and see." Voila! It was almost always completed in less than two minutes.

You can also scan an e-mail in less than two minutes to decide if you really need to read it. Clients say to me, "Oh, I need to defer this e-mail. It will take me 15 minutes to read!" I always suggest scanning it in two minutes or less to decide if they need to spend 15 minutes reading it. Often, the scanning was enough to decide that they did not need to read it. We all underestimate what we can do in less than two minutes.

If you can complete your SNA in less than two minutes, do it now. If not, move to the next question in the Four D's for Decision Making.

Delegate It

A "delegate it" action is a Strategic Next Action that you can delegate to someone else. Often, we forget to ask ourselves whether we can delegate an action. We're moving so fast that it doesn't occur to us. Just recently, I worked with a client and asked this question four times in 30 minutes. Each time, the client was able to delegate the item and was thrilled to have one less thing to do.

I received an e-mail from one of my most important clients, Scott Feely, who works for Adventure Works. He requested that I create a sales proposal for a leadership meeting he was having, and he detailed exactly what he wanted in the body of his e-mail. I recognized that I could delegate this to Eric, our Sales Director. In less than two minutes I wrote an e-mail to Eric delegating the task. I decided to track the action to ensure Scott got the proposal, so I included myself on the Cc line. When the e-mail arrived in my Inbox, I transferred it into my 1:1 Eric category on the Task list. This is a very nifty technique that enables you to record items you've delegated so that you can easily follow up with them in your 1:1 Meetings.

The Subject line I created for the e-mail message was "AR: Adventure Works: Write up a North American Leadership Proposal and send to Scott Feely. Due April 4th." This heading clearly stated what Eric had to do. When you move an e-mail from your Inbox to a 1:1 Meeting category, the Subject line stays the same. The next time I reviewed my 1:1 Eric category, this Subject line would immediately let me know what it was I wanted to follow up on.

If your Subject line isn't useful, you'll want to modify it. A comprehensible Subject line is important because in your 1:1 meetings you'll want to avoid having to open and read an e-mail to clarify its discussion point. You want the Subject line to do that for you. This kind of preparation on the front end will save you time on the back end. Are you tired of hearing that message yet?

If your Strategic Next Action is a delegated item that you want to track in your 1:1 Meeting or Waiting For category, go ahead and send that e-mail and Cc yourself. When the e-mail arrives in your Inbox, transfer it to the appropriate category. Ensure that your Subject line reflects the item you want to follow up on. See Figure 9-4 as a reference for transferring e-mail into your Task list categories.

If you cannot delegate this e-mail move to the next question.

Defer It

A "deferred action" is a Strategic Next Action that you can't complete in less than two minutes, and that you can't delegate. Therefore, the only option left is for you to personally complete it. This is where the buck stops and the real work begins, especially if you're an individual contributor who has no staff to delegate to.

The number of deferred next actions you have depends upon your role and your seniority in the company. My executive clients delegate most of their tasks, which means they end up with very few deferred items. However, individual contributors, with no one to delegate to, end up with a considerable list of deferred next actions. The good news about deferred items, however, is that they've gone through a tough prioritizing process to get on to your list, so they're important tasks to record and complete. You filtered out all the activities that did not relate to your objectives, items that could be deleted, items that could be completed in less than two minutes, and items that could be delegated. The end result of this process is a list of deferred items that only you can complete and that will take more than two minutes.

Our statistics prove that, on average, 50 percent of most people's e-mail can be deleted, 30 percent can be completed in less than two minutes or delegated, and 20 percent can be deferred. That means that out of 100 e-mails you receive, only 20 of them end up being deferred items in your SNA categories.

Here's an example of a deferred Strategic Next Action. I received an e-mail from John Wittry, our Web site project manager, asking me to spend 20 minutes reviewing our new site for my edits and corrections, which were due by April 15th. I couldn't delete the task, do it in less than two minutes, or delegate it. I personally had to do it, so I transferred the e-mail into my SNA Online category, with a due date of April 15th. In this case, the e-mail Subject line that John wrote related to the action I had to take, so I didn't change the Subject line.

If your e-mail is a deferred action, transfer it into the appropriate Strategic Next Action category on your Task list. When it's transferred, check that your Subject line details the Strategic Next Action, and select a due date, if it's appropriate.

You've now successfully completed processing one of your e-mail messages through the Four D's for Decision Making model. I hear you saying. "That took a while!" You're right. However, when you get the hang of this model, you can move through it quickly and process at least 60 e-mail messages an hour. By pausing to ask the Four D's questions you're making effective decisions and moving e-mail out of your Inbox.

Before you continue processing and organizing your Inbox, you need to know about two other features that will help you empty it: Inserting e-mails into existing Calendar appointments and inserting e-mails into existing tasks in the Task List.

Inserting an E-Mail into a Calendar Appointment

Let's say that you receive an e-mail outlining the agenda for your Friday staff meeting. You need the agenda for the meeting so you decide to insert the e-mail into the Friday staff meeting appointment, as shown in Figure 9-5. When the staff meeting starts, you can open the appointment and double-click the e-mail icon, and your agenda will be there. It takes less than two minutes to complete this transfer.

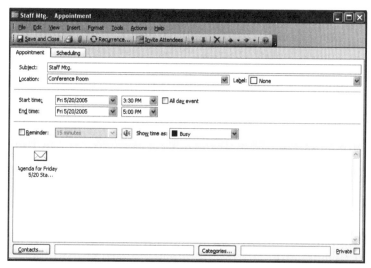

Figure 9-5 Inserting an e-mail or text into an existing Calendar appointment

To insert an e-mail or its text into an existing Calendar appointment, follow these steps:

1. Double-click an existing calendar appointment.

2. Choose Insert from the menu bar, and select Item.

3. In the Look In text box, select Inbox.

4. Locate the e-mail that you want to insert, and click it once to select it.

5. In the Insert As dialog box, choose either Text Only or Attachment.

6. Click OK.

When you insert an e-mail message into an existing appointment, you can insert the text only or you can insert the full e-mail, which will appear as an icon in the appointment. When you include the full e-mail in an appointment, you can open the e-mail and respond to it or just view the information in it. When you insert the text of the e-mail, you can't respond to the e-mail but you can see its text. When you synchronize with a PDA, this e-mail text will show up in the appointment, but the inserted e-mail will not. Based on how you are going to view this information you need to discern whether you'll insert text or the e-mail itself.

In the example above, if I inserted the Friday staff meeting agenda as text, I could then use my PDA to view the agenda, which is pretty cool.

When I go on trips, I insert travel data as text into my travel appointments, such as air, hotel and car rental confirmations. It's much easier to view my PDA when I'm on the road than it is to use my laptop. This information is extremely helpful, and having it readily available saves time and makes me look good! It's very important to look good and have the latest equipment! Only kidding!

Inserting an E-Mail into a Task

Imagine that you have a Strategic Next Action in your Task list under SNA Calls. The task reminds you to "Call Henry Skelton about the latest Boeing sales proposal." You are waiting for the updated proposal from one of your staff members. When it arrives in your e-mail, you insert it into the task named "Call Henry Skelton about latest Boeing proposal," as shown in Figure 9-6. When you make the call you will have the proposal right where you need it.

Figure 9-6   Inserting an e-mail or text into an existing task on the Task list

To insert an e-mail or its text into an existing task, follow these steps:

1. Click the Task icon in the Folder List and double-click an existing task.

2. Click Insert on the menu bar, and select Item.

3. In the Look In box, select Inbox.

4. Locate the e-mail you want to insert, and click it once to highlight it.

5. In the Insert As dialog box, select either Text Only or Attachment.

6. Click OK.

Again, you have a choice about how to insert e-mail. If the proposal is an attached document in your e-mail, the attachment goes with a task when you insert the e-mail. If you don't need the e-mail and only need the attached document, you can first save the document in your My Documents Reference System and then insert the document into the task. This way, you have it in two places. When you delete the task, you sill have access to the document in your My Documents Reference System.

Processing and Organizing Your E-mail for 30 Minutes

OK, you're now ready to process your e-mail using the Four D's for Decision Making. You'll do this for 30 minutes because I want you to discover exactly how many messages you can process in that time frame. For example, if you receive 60 e-mails a day and can process 30 e-mails in 30 minutes, you can assume you'll process your e-mail in one hour a day. That's important information to know!

You'll also learn that using the Four D's For Decision Making is invigorating as you make a decision for each message and move it out of your Inbox. If your Inbox is particularly full, don't worry, you'll work on emptying your Inbox later in this chapter, but for now I want you to experience processing e-mail for just 30 minutes.

Get an alarm clock and set the timer for 30 minutes or use your computer's clock. Sort your e-mail in the view you want to work with by sender, by date, or by Subject line. Work one e-mail at a time until the alarm clock goes off or 30 minutes has elapsed on your computer's clock.

A few guidelines before you start. When you open an e-mail, do not leave it in the Inbox, make sure you take action and move through the Four D's for Decision Making. Watch yourself when you want to avoid dealing with a message. Push through your reluctance and keep focused on making decisions and transferring mail out of the Inbox. I've never found an e-mail that couldn't be deleted, done, delegated, or deferred. Somewhere, there's always an answer for every message, but you might need to dig for it. Don't get caught up in responding to an e-mail if it takes more than two to three minutes. See if you can delegate it or, if not, defer it to one of your SNA categories. No jumping around now, one e-mail at a time, starting from the top. Away you go!

Awarenesses

After 30 minutes is up, take the total number of e-mails you started with, deduct the current number, and subtract the number of new e-mails that came in over the last 30 minutes. This will give you the total number of e-mails you processed in 30 minutes. It's extremely useful to see how many you can handle in that short a time period, and observe what it's like to make effective decisions on each and every e-mail you touch. Hey, I bet you were surprised by how many you processed and organized in 30 minutes.

So what were your awarenesses while doing this?

Here's what our clients have to say:

- It's much easier than I thought to complete e-mails in less than two minutes.
- I deleted at least half of them!
- I'm concerned about moving everything onto my Task list.
- I like being able to track delegated items in my 1:1 Meeting categories.
- I got a lot done in a concentrated period of time!
- It worked to force myself to make decisions for each and every e-mail.
- It was easy to transfer reference material into my new Reference System.
- I like writing clearer Subject lines.
- I used the Cc line a lot less!
- Deferring e-mails to my Task list was useful.
- I still have 2,000 e-mail messages to go, and at 60 an hour, that's 16 hours!
- I was surprised how many e-mails I receive that don't relate to my objectives!
- It takes discipline to make decisions about what to do with each and every e-mail in my Inbox.
- Most of what was in my Inbox was reference material that I hadn't filed.

Now that you know how many e-mails you can process in 30 minutes, I want you to apply that to the number of e-mails you actually receive a day and calculate how much time you'll need per day to process your e-mail. Make sure you answer this question accurately and avoid guessing on the basis of the number of e-mails that are currently in your Inbox. If you have 500 or more messages in your Inbox, it can feel like you're receiving hundreds a day. However, you may actually be receiving only 50 a day, so don't go by the total volume. Find out how many you actually receive a day.

When you know what your daily volume is, you can calculate how much time you'll need to schedule to process your e-mail each day. You might be pleasantly surprised at this number. If you receive 60 messages a day and you're able to process 60 e-mails an hour, you'll be able to complete your e-mail in one hour each day. The empty Inbox is in sight! All you need to do is book an hour of uninterrupted time each day and follow the Four D's discipline. This habit will keep your e-mail under control and your Inbox empty. If you have a higher daily e-mail volume, you'll learn, later in this chapter, how to reduce the number of incoming messages.

By now, I hope you're realizing that by changing your approach to how you process and organize your e-mail you can change your relationship with it. You can gain control of your e-mail and have it be a productivity tool that serves you. Education is a powerful tool, especially when clients are motivated to change.

Frequently Asked Questions

Before you continue processing and organizing the rest of your Inbox, I'd like to address some of the most frequently asked questions I receive from clients. I believe that these answers will help you approach your e-mail more effectively and they'll make it easier for you to empty your Inbox. We're going for the empty Inbox here. I want you to imagine being at zero e-mail. Visualize a completely white screen. Your Inbox is so empty that it echoes!

When's The Best Time to Process E-Mail?

Before I answer this question I want to clarify the difference between "processing" your e-mail and "monitoring" your e-mail. Processing requires uninterrupted time, allowing you to make effective decisions and create meaningful e-mail. Monitoring e-mail is reactive, allowing you to scan your mail for emergency situations, and communications from senior staff. You might also monitor your e-mail because you need a distraction. There's nothing wrong with that as long as you know what it is you're doing, and don't get addicted to it! (When you've set aside time to process and organize your e-mail, you can still monitor it during the day. Just be clear that monitoring and processing are not the same activity.)

I recommend that you create recurring appointments in the Calendar to process and organize your mail. Estimate how much time you'll need based on the figures you calculated earlier. I schedule an hour a day for e-mail processing because I receive 50 to 60 messages each day. Then, evaluate the best time of day to schedule uninterrupted e-mail processing time. Consider when your prime meeting times are so your e-mail appointment won't compete with other activities. This will take some thought if you have a busy schedule.

I process e-mail from 8 to 9 AM because my meetings generally start at 9 or 9:30. I have the energy at 9 AM to make 60 decisions, and I'm relaxed enough to pause and think about what I am doing.

Look through your calendar and find a good time for you to set up a reoccurring appointment for yourself. Make these appointments important so you don't give them away for other meetings. Be ruthless because that's what you'll need to do to make e-mail work and inspire those around you to do the same.

If you work with a team of people in close physical proximity, ask them to avoid interrupting you during your e-mail processing time. Let them know that if they interrupt you, they'll get a gentle reminder to come back later. You have to be prepared to reinforce your request or people won't take you seriously.

If you're a customer service agent, dealing with electronic customer requests, an hour a day of e-mail time will not work for you. You'll need to be working in your e-mail for most of the day, excluding breaks. Specific roles require more customized e-mail solutions.

What's an Appropriate Amount of E-Mail to Receive?

The volume of e-mail you receive depends on your role and function, but in general, from 50 to 120 messages a day is a good range. Anything more becomes unmanageable because it takes too long to process each day.

Some of my clients receive up to 300 messages a day, and although they want to receive less, they spend most of their time justifying to me why the need to get 300 messages. This is understandable, given how much time they've invested in dealing with this kind of volume. I have to gently remind them, "If you always do what you've always done, you'll always get what you've always got." Therefore, you have to do something different for change to take place, and in order to do something different, you have to let go of something you're currently doing. Deep down, they know they'll need to let go of this in order to be open to the possibility of receiving less.

As you know, success in a company isn't based on the volume of e-mail you can handle each day. It's based, instead, on your ability to achieve your objectives within budget, timelines, and resources. You have other activities you have to do besides e-mail, so you need to monitor how much time you spend processing messages. If you receive 40 to 60 e-mails a day, it will take you an hour to process your messages, which is very doable. Receiving 60 to 120 messages is still doable, but more time consuming, taking you up to two hours a day to complete. I would always err on the side of less is more when it comes to e-mail. Anything you can do to reduce volume will be productive.

How Do I Reduce the Volume of E-Mail I Receive?

Daily mail volume is not difficult to reduce when you're willing to make behavioral changes. Here are a few changes you might consider.

- Send less e-mail.
- Write clear e-mails so they don't come back with questions.
- Use the Cc line only when it impacts the recipients' objectives.
- Unsubscribe from newsletters and subscriptions.
- Meet with your team to discuss when to Cc.
- Clarify roles so you're not getting mail that someone else really needs to get.
- Resist getting involved in e-mail threads that don't impact your objectives.
- Post information on an internal Web site, so employees pull the information from a site instead of the company pushing it through mail.
- Establish e-mail protocol so team members know when to use e-mail rather than instant messaging, land line phone calls, or cell phone calls.

There are hundreds of ways to reduce mail. You must first have a very clear intention to reduce it, and then you'll start to find solutions that'll help you. Without an openness to change, it won't happen. So be open to the possibility. Reducing your e-mail volume will only increase your productivity.

Can I Customize My Own Subject Lines?

Of course you can, and you can request others to customize their Subject lines, too. Imagine that you're in the Finance Department of a company, for example, and you ordinarily receive three to five invoice requests each day. Because it's easier to process these requests in a single batch rather than one-by-one, you can ask internal customers to start the Subject line of an invoice request with the words, "Invoice Request." This would enable you to quickly transfer these messages into an SNA Invoice Request category to be processed once a week at a specific time. The same applies to any repetitive task, such as "Resumes to be reviewed," "Calendar appointments to be booked," or "Expenses to be approved."

Another form of customization is using different e-mail addresses to capture repetitive tasks. For example, if you spend eight hours every Thursday handling accounting tasks, you could set up an alternative e-mail address named "accounting@cpandl.com." Your internal clients would send all accounting requests to that address. On Thursday, you'd simply download the *accounting@cpandl.com* e-mail and handle the requests. In emergencies, clients could use your regular address, which you download daily. Any kind of customization that helps you use your time more effectively is useful.

Didn't I Only Move E-Mail from the Inbox to the Task List?

Yup, it sure seems like you did nothing more than move e-mails from one location to another! But be careful not to underestimate the value of what you've done. You didn't just move an e-mail; you processed and organized it using the Four D's for Decision Making. The end result of this process is an extremely well-prioritized Task list. You determined whether the e-mail related to one of your Meaningful Objectives. You created a Strategic Next Action without a dependency. You confirmed that you couldn't do the task in less than two minutes and that you couldn't delegate it, so you decided you had to defer it. You transferred it into a specific SNA category with a clear Subject line and included a due date and supporting documentation (if it was needed). I wouldn't say you only moved it from the Inbox to the Task list. Far from it!

Acknowledge what you did. You created a centralized, easily accessible Task list, which is prioritized and directly maps to your objectives. You still have one step to go, of course, which is to schedule these tasks onto the Calendar, as you'll see in Chapter 10.

How Will I Remember to View the Task List?

Most of my clients have depended on their Inbox and their memories to track their action steps. Therefore, using the Task list to centralize their actions feels uncomfortable, and some clients have never used the Task list so they're especially anxious about remembering to look at it. Their concern is valid, much like their putting car keys in a new location at home.

Will they remember where they put them? If you put your car keys in the same place each time, it won't take long to remember where they are. In fact within two or three days, you become dependent on the new location, and you'll say, "Don't move my keys!"

In the Prioritizing and Planning Phase, you'll be setting up a recurring Weekly Review appointment on your Calendar. You'll use this appointment to prioritize and plan your tasks from the Task list onto your Calendar. You'll have plenty of time each week to work with your Task list, and it won't be long before it becomes a habit, and your Task list becomes your best friend.

When Do I Put E-Mails Onto the Calendar Versus the Task List?

So far, I've asked you to transfer all of your deferred Strategic Next Actions onto the Task list because until you've captured all of your agreements from all of your collection points, you're prioritizing in a vacuum! After your Task list is complete, you can decide whether to transfer a task onto the Calendar or onto the Task list. The Calendar is the last place a task goes. When it's scheduled on a date in the Calendar, you're making an agreement to do it on that day. Use the Calendar with great respect. It's not a place to put a task that you think you only may get done. It's a place to schedule a task because you've promised to do it on a particular day.

If you receive an e-mail that turns out to be a Strategic Next Action that can be deferred, but must be completed on a particular day, simply transfer it from the Inbox directly to your Calendar for that day.

To transfer an e-mail onto the calendar, follow the steps in the section, "Inserting an E-Mail into an Existing Calendar Appointment," earlier in this chapter.

The Tasks on your Task list do not have to be done immediately. You're waiting to transfer them onto the Calendar as they come due. More on this concept in Chapter 10.

Can I Use the E-Mail Ding?

Clients ask me if it's OK to use the Outlook feature that enables them to see or hear new e-mail messages as they arrive. I highly recommend that you don't use these features except in an exceptional circumstance, or if your role requires it. Being notified when an e-mail comes in is an interruption and a distraction. You need to stop what you're doing, scan the e-mail, and decide whether you'll take action on it right away. Taking action distracts you from what you're doing. If you don't take action, you're still reminded that the e-mail needs attention, and you'll track it in your head as well as tracking it in your e-mail. All my clients want to reduce this level of interruption and distraction so why create more? Turn off the ding.

If you process and organize your e-mail once a day and successfully reduce your messages to zero, there's no purpose in reviewing each e-mail as it arrives other than to distract you. You've spent a full day in meetings without access to your computer, so you can certainly go eight hours without looking at mail! If you have no valid reason for the ding, eliminate it and create more uninterrupted time for yourself. You'll scan e-mail anyway, so you don't need each and every e-mail that arrives to remind you! This is your chance to drive technology instead of having it drive you.

Emptying the Inbox and Getting to Zero

If you still have e-mail in your Inbox, let's see what you can do to get it to zero. (If your Inbox is empty, then skip ahead to the section, "Establishing Effective E-Mail Guidelines," in this chapter.)

I encourage you to take the time right now to get your e-mail message count to zero. You can do it! I've worked with people who have as many as 7,000 messages in their Inbox and they got to zero, so I know you can.

Here are three steps you can follow to help you eliminate e-mail.

1. Identify the "shelf life" of your e-mail. It can be anywhere from one week to two months or more, depending on your role. (Legal and financial roles have strict rules with regard to how to keep e-mail.) After a certain point, e-mail is no longer meaningful so there's no point in keeping it unless it's helpful to have as reference information. Sort your Inbox by the oldest e-mail first and then eliminate all of the out-of-date e-mail. This can dramatically reduce your volume.

   Erasing lots of e-mail can be scary, but ask yourself "What am I willing to let go of to get what I want?" Remember Linda in Chapter 1? She eliminated 1,991 messages in one press of the Delete key! If this makes you very nervous, create a new Archive folder. Use the date range of filed e-mail for your folder title. Drag and drop the old e-mail into the folder. You can always go back to it later. Meanwhile, it's not cluttering up your Inbox.

"We're drowning in information and starving for knowledge."
—**Rutherford Rogers**

211

2. When you've eliminated the "outdated shelf life" e-mail, go through what's left and delete Calendar notices, Inbox full notices, e-mails from anyone who's left the company or moved to a different department, and project-related e-mails for projects that are now complete. Do whatever you can do to quickly eliminate unwanted e-mails.

3. Identify how much e-mail you have left and calculate how long it will take you to empty your Inbox. If you have 400 messages and you can process 60 an hour, then it will take you 6.6 hours to get to zero. However, you need to ask yourself whether that time would be worth it? What could you do in six hours that would add more value than processing e-mails? After you've answered these questions, you can choose to work through your messages or delete and archive even more e-mail, leaving only the last week's worth of messages to process.

If you have hundreds or thousands of messages in your Inbox, processing the 60 new messages for the day won't help you get to zero. You'll need to eliminate the buildup to really get on top of your e-mail. When you get to zero, you'll be motivated to stay there because there's nothing like a blank e-mail screen to ease your mind and put a smile on your face! Go for it!

Establishing Effective E-Mail Guidelines

Establishing effective e-mail guidelines helps to improve the communication among your team members, reduce volume, and clarify response times. It also affects employees' work/life balance when they learn to process their e-mail at work instead of at home.

Most teams haven't set conscious expectations about e-mail. They're living with the expectations that the company culture set for them, which are usually unconscious and unsupportive. An expectation, for example, might be "respond in less than three minutes," "do e-mail on the weekends or at 4 in the morning," "take care of your e-mail during meetings, or do whatever it takes to stay on top of your e-mail." I'm over-dramatizing, but I'm certain you know what I mean. To learn more about setting and changing expectations, see "Changing the E-Mail Culture," in Chapter 4.

Creating e-mail guidelines will help you reset the standards by which e-mail is managed. It's important to customize these guidelines to fit specific target audiences. Information Technology staff, for example, carry pagers so they can be highly responsive to server issues. Program Managers, however, don't need to respond to communications as quickly. When creating e-mail guidelines, be sensitive to your audience.

We've seen great success when teams establish e-mail protocols, especially when they customize these protocols. Everyone wants e-mail to improve, so any education that you can offer will make a difference. Some of our clients have built these guidelines into their performance review so employees are measured by how well they stick to the e-mail protocol. E-mail is a serious issue in companies today and employers realize it's going to take dramatic action for some employees to make dramatic changes.

To help you set up and clarify e-mail guidelines for your team, here are the two steps involved.

1. Get on the agenda at a staff meeting to talk about establishing and reinforcing e-mail guidelines with your team. It's important for the team to create these guidelines together to ensure that they buy in to them and are motivated to change their behaviors.

2. Identify a point person to track the decisions and distribute a document that reflects the agreed-upon guidelines.

When you discuss e-mail guidelines with your team, consider the seven topics that follow.

Writing Effective E-Mail Messages

Recommend the E-mail PASS Model because it creates a simple, systematic approach to clarifying e-mail communications, and it includes how to appropriately label Subject lines and use the To, Cc, and Bcc lines. This model is a good baseline for you to work from.

Formatting E-Mail Messages

Suggest maximizing the readability of e-mail by proposing these rules:

- Paragraphs need to be short—no more than five or six lines.

- Limit e-mail text to a single page. If you have more text, either reduce the message or attach a Word document.

- Use fonts no smaller than 10 points or larger than 12 points (except for headlines or embedded details)

- Use white space to separate paragraphs and areas of detail.

- Use bold and underlined text, but not to excess.

- Use bullets to break down the key points in e-mail and to highlight action to be taken.

- Write clearly and avoid run-on sentences.

- Avoid jargon or acronyms, particularly when you're sending e-mail to a large audience.

- Use the spelling checker, but recognize that using the spelling checker isn't a substitute for careful editing.

- Re-read messages one last time before clicking Send.

Preparing E-Mail Signature Lines

Recommend the following information be included in e-mail signatures, which are designed to display complete contact data:

- Name

- Title

- Phone number(s)

- Organization

- Web site address

- Expected response time for e-mail based on your preference

Answering E-Mail Within a Response Time

Establish when the team is required to respond to e-mail. This helps your staff move away from processing e-mails all day long within three minutes, to processing messages once or twice a day. Suggest the following guidelines:

- All e-mail will be responded to within 24 hours.

- If you can't give a complete response within 24 hours, let the recipient know when you can complete the response.

- Use the Out Of Office (OOO) function when you can't respond to e-mail within the 24-hour response time.

- When using the OOO function, let recipients know when you will respond to e-mail or whom else they can contact to get a response.

- Monitoring e-mail is OK.

A full 24 hours seems like a long time when you've been answering in less than three minutes. However, if you receive an e-mail at 5 PM at night, you probably won't answer it until 9 AM the next morning. That's a 16-hour response time, not a three-minute response time. The point of a response time is to clarify the expectation upfront so your staff can meet it effectively. Some roles require longer response times due to extensive travel, or shorter times due to customer service issues. Talk through each situation until you come up with an appropriate solution.

Responding to E-Mail Effectively

Consider these guidelines for responding effectively to e-mail because responding is as important as writing your initial e-mail.

- Consider whether a reply is actually warranted. Ask whether it would add value to the communication.

- Reply only to those individual who need to know.

- When responding to e-mails, follow the same guidelines on the proper use of the To, Cc, and Subject lines.

- Change the Subject line on a thread only when the subject matter of the e-mail is changing, and recognize that this will impact Subject line sorting.

- Reply All should be used only after serious consideration and understanding that it proliferates e-mail.

- When removing individuals from a thread, consider placing their names on the "Bcc" line and indicate who is being removed in the first line of the new message.

- Send confirmation e-mails only to the sender and only when requested by the sender.

- E-mails should not be forwarded to "hand off ownership." Establish a clear understanding of roles and responsibilities in person or on the phone before forwarding an e-mail.

- Read (and re-read) responses to identify and remove emotion before sending e-mail.

- Work out disagreements one-on-one, or by phone. E-mail can escalate conflict.

Scheduling E-Mail Processing Time

Suggest these guidelines for e-mail processing time so everyone is clear that
this time is important, and so everyone will avoid scheduling over it on each
other's Calendars, unless absolutely necessary

- Schedule a reoccurring one-hour meeting to process e-mail.
- Schedule e-mail processing time outside of busy meeting times.
  For example, 8 to 9 AM or 4:30 to 5:30 PM.
- Mark your e-mail processing time as busy on your calendar.
- Respect others' e-mail processing time and avoid interruptions.

E-mail guidelines are critical to the efficiency of your team and organization.
Let's face it, technology arrived without clear guidelines for how to apply it
productively. As a result, we've allowed technology to drive our behaviors
rather than making sure our behaviors drive technology. With the information in this chapter, you can use technology the way it was intended, to
increase the efficiency and quality of life of you and your team. E-mail is
not the problem. The problem is the lack of education regarding how to
use e-mail effectively. When you change your approach, you can change
your results.

What Changes Will You Make?

Take a moment to reflect on what changes you'll make as a result of the
topics in this chapter:

- Using the E-mail PASS Model to write more meaningful e-mail
- Properly using the To, Cc, Bcc, and Subject lines
- Using the Four D's
- Reducing volume
- Scheduling e-mail processing time
- Establishing e-mail guidelines

Now go to your Task list and open the task you created in Chapter 4, labeled
WEEKLY REVIEW. Under the Processing and Organizing heading, record
the specific changes you want to make, as shown in Figure 9-7.

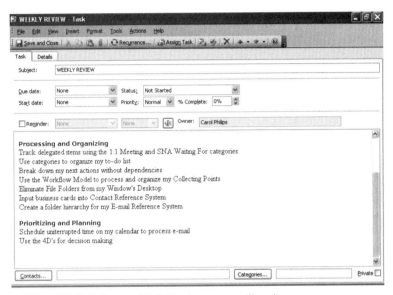

Figure 9-7 Keeping track of the changes you'll make

After you've recorded these changes, close the Task back into Categories: (none). You'll refer to it again at the end of the Prioritizing and Planning Phase.

For inspiration, here are few examples of what my clients have written:

- Use the Delete key!
- Handle e-mail in less than two minutes.
- Schedule uninterrupted time to process e-mail.
- Be way more careful about how I use the Cc line.
- Meet with my team to clarify e-mail standards and reinforce them.
- Save attachments into My Documents instead of my Personal Folders E-mail Reference System.
- If I can do it in less than two minutes, do it.
- Scan long messages in less than two minutes to establish if I really need to read them.
- Never close an e-mail back in the Inbox. Make a decision and do something with it.
- Talk to my team about how we Cc so I can reduce my e-mail volume.

"Start with doing what's necessary; then do what's possible, and suddenly, you are doing the impossible."
—**Saint Francis of Assisi**

- Use the drag-and-drop feature to defer tasks into the SNA categories.

- Don't save e-mails that don't relate to my objectives.

Success Factors for Processing and Organizing E-Mail

Here are success factors that you should keep in mind when you process and organize e-mail.

- Use the E-mail PASS Model to help you create meaningful e-mail so recipients understand your communication and its purpose. By writing clear e-mails, you can effectively move toward your objectives and reduce e-mail volume.

- Use the To, Cc, and Bcc line effectively to reduce e-mail and increase the effectiveness of your communications.

- Use the Subject line to help recipients anticipate the purpose of your e-mail even before they read your message.

- When you open an e-mail, make a decision using the Four D's for Decision Making: delete it, do it in less than two minutes, delegate it, or defer it to a SNA category. Never close an e-mail back in the Inbox!

- Schedule uninterrupted time to process and organize your e-mail each day so you can empty the Inbox. If you can process 60 e-mails in an hour and you receive 50, it'll take you less than an hour to process your e-mail for the day.

- Clarify e-mail guidelines with your team so you can reset their expectations and help your team increase productivity and work/life balance.

Each person can choose to become part of the e-mail solution. The results are so huge that it's impossible to ignore them and hard not to be motivated by them. Our statistics prove that departments can reduce the total number of e-mails in employees' Inboxes by as much as 81 percent, reduce daily e-mail volume by as much as 26 percent, and increase work/life balance by as much as 25 percent. Education works, so take the time to change your approach and work with your team to help them do the same. Everyone will benefit and you'll inspire change throughout your company.

On to the final chapter, "Prioritizing and Planning."

Part Four

The Prioritizing and Planning Phase

In this part

Chapter Ten

Prioritizing and Planning

Most of us are living in an illusion that we'll get everything done one day. That day won't happen. The truth is that you'll always have more to do than you have time for. Therefore, you must prioritize what you're going to do, and put it on your calendar to make sure it can be done. In this chapter, I'll introduce the concept of using your Calendar as a valuable prioritization tool, ensuring you keep your agreements.

Most of us currently use the Calendar to track meetings. I want to encourage you to use the Calendar to also track daily, reoccurring activities, such as e-mail processing, travel, and Strategic Next Action (SNA) time.

When you put a task on the Calendar, it brings the task into reality. Our statistics prove that there's a 75 percent greater chance that you'll complete a task if it's on your Calendar rather than your Task list. Therefore, it's essential to use the Calendar to prioritize and plan all of your activities.

The Prioritizing and Planning Phase has two purposes. The first is to ensure that your Calendar accurately represents the time required to complete your Meaningful Objectives while maintaining work/life balance. The second is to update your ControlPanel so you can effectively prioritize and plan your decisions. In order to do this, you'll learn how to create a BaselineCalendar, schedule your SNA's onto the Calendar, handle meeting requests, and complete a Weekly Review. This is the last of the three phases for creating an Integrated Management System and it will help you maintain an experience of control, focus, and balance.

Are You Managing to a Calendar or a To-Do List?

The most important aspect of the Prioritizing and Planning Phase is coming to grips with the reality of using your Calendar to accomplish your goals while maintaining work/life balance. Remember, you have only 24 hours in a day. No matter how well you manage them, you can't make them 25. Conversely, they won't become 23 if you mismanage them. However, most of my clients don't manage to a daily calendar. They manage to a to-do list. "I'll get this list done today. I'm not sure when, but I'll get it done." This leads to very long days, broken agreements, and the experience of being stressed and overwhelmed. As a result, clients protest, "I just don't have enough time to get it all done!"

One of the reasons clients aren't getting everything done is because they're not booking their daily activities on their Calendar. Consequently, actions like processing e-mail and completing Strategic Next Actions happen after hours or they get squeezed around meetings (and sometimes happen during meetings!). The problem isn't lack of time; it's planning more into your day than your calendar will allow. Therefore, the solution is scheduling your actions on the Calendar so you know how long they'll take. I often say to clients *"You can't do everything, but you can do anything, as long as it fits into your calendar."* In other words, it's not about managing time. It's about *managing what you agree to do, so you can get it done within the time you have.* It's about self-management, not time management.

I was working with a group of executives, and we started our seminar at 9 AM. Eileen, one of the participants, had been up since 4 AM doing her e-mail! I asked everyone in the room, "How many of you book daily appointments on your Calendar to process e-mail?" No one raised a hand. Then I asked, "When do you do your e-mail?" Eileen exclaimed, "4 AM!" Other comments were, "At home in the evenings or early in the mornings." I then asked the group, "How many of you plan 'Strategic Next Action' work time on your Calendar?" Again, no one raised a hand. I asked, "When do you do your Strategic Next Actions?" The response was "In-between meetings, on the fly, after work, or maybe not at all." If you aren't planning your day, you can be sure someone else will plan it for you, and their plans aren't likely to reflect your priorities or objectives.

I asked Eileen why she did her e-mail at 4 AM, and she replied, "I don't have time during the day." I said, "I'd like you to consider that you do have time. The problem is that you don't book the time on your Calendar." She stared at me. "You mean, if I scheduled time to process e-mail during the day, I'd get it done during the day?" She thought for a moment, contemplating whether or not to believe in this concept, and then responded, "Then I'd have to book my meetings around my e-mail time. But I have so many meetings!" I replied, "Keep doing what you're doing and you'll keep getting the same results. You have lots of meetings because you book lots of meetings. If you booked e-mail time during the day, you'd need to be more discerning about which meetings to attend." *If you don't calendar your work during the day, it won't happen during the day.* It's all about managing what you agree to do, so you can get it done with the time you have.

The truth is that you'll always have more meeting requests than you can accommodate, you'll consistently frustrate co-workers because you're not available, and you'll forever have more to do than you can do. These are realities that we all need to embrace, accept, and come to peace with. You can't change these factors, but you can change what you agree to do based on your objectives and the amount of time you have available.

Your head and your to-do list have no boundaries; they're limitless. Reality lies only in the Calendar because it has time limits. I want you to make friends with the Calendar and use it as a prioritization tool for what you can and cannot do.

Using Your Calendar to Prioritize and Plan

Imagine looking at your time as though it was money. Your Calendar is your bank account and your Task list is your credit card. Each day you deposit 24 dollars into your bank account. That's your daily allowance. Unfortunately, you'll never be able to increase it! Every time you book an appointment, you're paying a bill and your bank balance decreases. The more bills you pay, the less time you have. To balance your account, you need to reconcile what you've agreed to do on your Task list with the time you have available on your Calendar. By balancing these two, you can quickly identify if you've spent more money than you have or if your account is in balance. When you know this, you can correct your course and get yourself back on track.

The only problem with time is that you can't buy more of it! This means you need to be conscious of the precious time you have and use it wisely. If you over-commit, there's nothing you can do but renegotiate your commitments or sleep fewer hours!

When it comes to the credit card, we're all having fun using it. "Yes, I'll complete that budget. I'll call you back. We'll have dinner. I'll get that report done, finish that project, and fix the car." We're unconscious of what we're spending until the statement comes in, and then we get conscious in a hurry!

When you did the "clearing the mind" exercise, you may have felt overwhelmed as you started to transfer items from your head to your Task list. The exercise helped you clearly identify what you'd committed to do, and it was quite an eye-opener. That's why it's so important to get these commitments out of your head and into your Task list. By doing so, you can evaluate what you've spent on your credit card and prioritize how you're going to pay the bills.

Remember Eileen doing e-mail at 4 AM instead of during the day? She's going to do her e-mail anyway, so she might as well plan the best time to do it, and create a little more balance for herself.

It's very hard to know what you can and can't do if you don't know how much money you have. By planning your activities on the Calendar, as far out as you can, you're able to clearly see how much money you've spent and what is left to spend. Time and money are very similar in that regard. They both have limits, so they both require prioritization and planning to create balance.

To support you in bringing more awareness to your calendar, I'd like you to do a simple exercise. For one week, I'd like you to track how you spend your time each day and record it on your Outlook Calendar. I want you to record everything you do, and I mean *everything*. Here's an example.

- Showered and dressed: 40 minutes
- Prepared and ate breakfast: 30 minutes
- Drove to work: 25 minutes
- Waited in line to get my morning latte: 15 minutes
- Did e-mail: 30 minutes
- Received a phone call: 10 minutes
- Handled a walk-in interruption: 10 minutes.

This is a very simple exercise, but it can be extremely revealing, just like tracking how much money you spend in a week.

After you've tracked your activities for a complete week, you'll be able to analyze exactly what you spent your time doing, how long it took, and whether it truly mapped to your personal and professional objectives.

From this experience, you can determine activities you want to stop doing, activities to keep doing, quicker ways to get things done, and better times of the day to complete tasks. This exercise will also prepare you for creating your *BaselineCalendar*.

Setting Up Your BaselineCalendar

Before you prioritize and plan your Task list onto the Calendar, you'll create a BaselineCalender. A BaselineCalender enables you to identify the essential reoccurring activities that you need to perform weekly, monthly, and yearly, and ensures that you book them onto your Calendar. Essential reoccurring activities could be processing e-mail, downloading and processing voice mail, picking up your kids, and exercising three times a week. After these activities are booked on the Calendar, you can clearly see how much time you have left. This gives you a realistic view of what you can and can't do with your time. It also ensures that work activities take place at work and not at home. After you have done this, you'll prioritize your SNA's from your Task list onto the Calendar as well.

To find out what your BaselineCalendar activities are, ask yourself "How much reoccurring time do I need to allocate weekly, monthly, and annually to ensure that both my personal and business objectives get completed?" Each person has a different set of circumstances. You may have to drop off or pick up your children, you may have 120 e-mails a day and need two hours of e-mail time, and you may have five direct reports and need to meet them regularly each month for an hour. In addition, you might have annual planning meetings, staff meetings, and exercise appointments. Your specific objectives will affect what you plan on your Calendar.

BaselineCalendar Activities

Below, you will see a list of potential BaselineCalendar activities to consider.

- Processing e-mail: at least one hour a day

- Emptying additional Collecting Points: at least 30 minutes a day, depending on volume.

- Weekly Review time to update your IMS: one hour, once a week.

- Reading time: two hours, every other week

- 1:1 Meetings with your direct reports, boss, and others: decide if you want to split these appointments up or do them all in one day.

> "Energy is the essence of life. Every day you decide how you're going to use it by knowing what you want and what it takes to reach that goal, and by maintaining focus."
> —**Oprah Winfrey**

- Staff meetings: once a month, for a day
- Quarterly Strategic Team planning meeting: once a quarter for a day
- Annual Strategic Team planning meeting: once a year for a day.
- Exercise time: one hour, three times a week
- Vacations: twice a year
- Drive time to and from work and other events.
- Pick up kids at 4:30 PM on the way home: Monday, Wednesday, and Friday
- Church and community service
- Walk the dogs: three times a week

Take a moment and list the reoccurring activities you want to include on your Calendar and make sure they really represent your Meaningful Objectives, both personal and business. Realize that once you put them on the Calendar, you're making a commitment to complete them. The Calendar is a prioritization tool. Only place items on the Calendar that are critical to complete and support your objectives. Everything else stays on your Task list until it becomes a priority to calendar.

	BaselineCalendar Activity	Length of time needed	Reoccurrence
1			
2			
3			
4			
5			
6			
7			
8			
9			
10			

When you start to schedule these activities on the Calendar, you'll want to consider the best time to book them by identifying what fits into the rhythm of your business and personal life. This takes a little thinking. For example, with regard to e-mail processing, you'll want to pick a time when you're least likely to get interrupted and won't have consistent scheduling conflicts.

Carol Philips, for example, reserves from 8 to 9 AM every day to process her e-mail because she starts her meetings at 9 AM. Her staff tends to use the 8 to 9 AM time slot to get uninterrupted work done, as well. Carol schedules two hours of Strategic Next Action work time every other day. Her 1:1's happen once a month on a Thursday, and her staff meetings occur once a month on a Friday. She runs at 6 AM one morning a week, getting into the office at 9 AM. Figure 10-1 shows an example of her work week. You'll notice that she includes travel time to and from her run, client meetings, and staff meetings. This gives her a realistic view of her plans, so she knows what else she can and cannot do that day.

To book your reoccurring activities, go to the Calendar and click the Work Week icon to see a week at a glance. (To include Saturday and Sunday as part of your work week, you can make the change in the Calendar Options dialog box by clicking Tools, Options, Calendar Options.) This will support your focus on work/life balance. I'd like you to plan your BaselineCalendar using the list you created above. If you have a heavy meeting schedule, you'll need to book these new appointments weeks out. If that's the case, go ahead and plan them in the future. I know it takes courage to book your Calendar in advance, but to ensure that you complete these actions, it's necessary to schedule them. Calendar away!

Including Travel Time

I often see Calendars in which meetings are booked back-to-back. There's no way someone can be on time leaving a meeting at 3 PM and starting another at 3 PM. In Figure 10-1, you can see that Carol marks in the travel time to get to and from her meetings. This ensures that she's on time and doesn't have to rush or make excuses for being late.

You can also schedule domestic travel by scheduling drive time to and from the airport, time spent checking in, and time going through security. This ensures you know when to leave and shows how much time you have in the car and standing in security lines. This seems so obvious, but you'd be surprised how many Calendars I see in which travel time isn't scheduled. Clients figure out in their heads when to leave (often at the last minute), or they accidentally book meetings they cannot attend because they didn't mark on their Calendar the time they needed to leave for the airport. It's a simple discipline, but it helps keep your calendar realistic. Once again, more thinking on the front end saves thinking on the back end.

Including "Catch-Up Time" After Travel

When you travel domestically or internationally, not only do you want to plan out your travel time, you'll want to plan "catch-up time" to do your e-mail and voice mail when you return. You may discover that you come home with all kinds of good ideas and perspectives that you want to capture and process, so it's important to make room for these activities. You may get some of your best ideas 35,000 feet up in the skies!

People aren't realistic about scheduling catch-up time. They return from trips to back-to-back meetings and hundreds of e-mails, and then wonder why they "fall off the wagon" every time they travel. The best way to handle this is to block out large chunks of time on your Calendar when you return, so you can empty all of your Collecting Points and catch up.

I have clients who inform their staff that they're on vacation from May 15th to May 25th, but they come home on the 23rd and use two days to catch up. Get smart, plan the time you need on re-entry so you get caught up and don't have to miss a beat because of travel.

Using Out of Office Replies

When you travel, use your Out of Office (OOO) replies to clearly state what your response time will be, so recipients know when to expect a communication from you. "I'm on vacation and won't be responding to e-mail until May 28th. Please send urgent requests to 'joshp@lucernepublishing.com.' Thank you for your patience."

I had a client who was going on an extended vacation, and whose OOO stated, "I am on extended vacation from July 25th to August 25th. While I'm gone I will not be reading e-mail. If you need 'such and such,' please contact *henrys@cpandl.com*. If you need 'this and that,' contact *suzanp@cpandl.com*. If you require my attention, I will be returning on August 26th." This worked because it gave her colleagues clear information, and her staff were prepared to handle things in her absence.

Including 911 Interruptions

My clients tell me, "My calendar would be fine if I didn't get 911 interruptions." The term "911" refers to an emergency situation that you can't predict or expect. However, many of my clients can predict their 911 situations! "Every quarter, we get a virus, the system crashes, and we're down for two days. It's a real pain!"

I was working with one client who said, "I can see implementing this system just fine, but when one of those system crashes happens, it throws me off track." I asked, "How often does this happen?" He replied, "Oh, at least once a quarter." I asked, "How long does it take you to deal with it?" He sighed, "It takes two whole days out of my schedule!" I responded, "Then plan two days every quarter for your 911 interruption, and if it doesn't happen, you have more time to play with!" My point of view is that if a 911 is predictable, it's not really a 911 and you can build it into your system. Identify the 911 situations you deal with and be realistic. You know that these events will happen, so budget for them. You're going to spend the time one way or another.

If you can foresee a 911 situation, it's not really an emergency. Think about firemen for a moment. Do you think a building on fire is a 911 to a fireman? No, because firemen plan for fires and crises. That's their job and a 911 is not an emergency to them. Remember true 911's are unexpected and unpredictable.

Now, you are likely to get a few true 911 situations, so you can prepare for those as well. I include two days a month of unstructured time to handle truly unexpected situations. Of course, those situations don't happen on the day I've booked for them, but I get two days to reschedule meetings when it does happen. (That's my secret. Shhhhh, don't tell anyone because I'm not giving them up!)

As you complete setting up your BaselineCalender, consider your expected and unexpected 911 situations and how much time to book for them. This enables you to be realistic. If they happen, you have time. If they don't, you still have time.

Prioritizing SNA's Onto Your Calendar

Now that your BaselineCalendar is set up, you can start the process of prioritizing your Strategic Next Actions and transferring them onto the Calendar from your TaskPad. In the ControlPanel, as shown in Figure 10-1, you'll see the TaskPad on the right showing your Strategic Next Action categories; the Calendar in the middle, showing a week at a glance; and your Personal Folders on the left.

If your TaskPad doesn't show your categories, you'll need to change the view so they do.

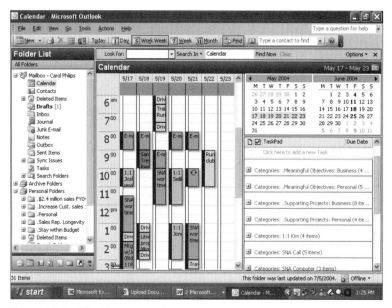

Figure 10-1   The ControlPanel

To show categories in the TaskPad:

1. Open the ControlPanel, as shown in Figure 10-1, by clicking Calendar at the left in the Outlook window, and clicking the Folder List icon.

2. Right-click the word *TaskPad*, which is in a gray bar at the top of the TaskPad list.

3. Choose Arrange By, Categories.

I'd like you to go through your Strategic Next Action categories and review each Strategic Next Action to assess when it must be completed in order for you to stay on track with your objectives. When you identify an SNA that you need to complete, go ahead and move it onto the Calendar by following these steps:

1. Right-click and drag the Task onto a specific date on the Calendar.

2. From the shortcut menu, select Move Here As Appointment With Attachment.

   An Appointment dialog box opens for the task and the task's Subject line is pre-filled with the task name.

3. In the task's Appointment dialog box, verify the date, and choose the Start Time and End Time you want for the appointment.

4. Click Save And Close.

When you drag an SNA to the Calendar, be sure to select Move rather than Copy. Move means the task will be moved from the TaskPad to the Calendar and deleted from the TaskPad. This scares some of my clients. They ask, "What if I don't do it when it's on the Calendar. I want a backup on the TaskPad." This suggests that you have an option for whether you do a task when it's on the Calendar. But the Calendar reflects your time-specific commitments, so you've agreed to do the task that day. Don't put a task on the Calendar if you're not going to do it. The Calendar tracks action items that are critical to complete. The TaskPad displays action items that you need to complete, but not right away.

Occasionally, you'll get an unexpected 911, and what you calendared will not get done. In that case, you simply drag the item to another day, or drag it back to the Task list. Pretty simple, really.

The other way of doing it is to plan reoccurring Strategic Next Action time on your Calendar. For example, you could book one hour a day for Strategic Next Action time. Instead of moving your SNA's to a specific day when you review your TaskPad, you'd leave them on the TaskPad and select due dates for the priority items. When you get to your Strategic Next Action appointment on the Calendar, you'd simply review your Strategic Next Action categories and complete the tasks that had due dates for that day.

To add the Due Date column to your TaskPad, follow these steps:

1. Right-click the word TaskPad, in the gray bar at the top of the TaskPad list.

2. On the shortcut menu, select Field Chooser.

3. Drag Due Date to the gray bar next to the word TaskPad. Two red arrows will show where you will be placing the Due Date column.

My preference is to move SNA's onto my Calendar and then mark them in red when they're completed. I have a tendency to get distracted, and if I go to the Strategic Next Action categories to find the appropriate next actions, I end up crossing off completed tasks, updating lists, and so on. To limit this behavior, I put the SNA's I need to do on the Calendar, which keeps me focused and more productive.

Are You Feeling Good About What You're Not Doing?

When you've placed your priority SNA's on the Calendar for the coming week, you'll still have SNA's on your Task list that you've decided were not critical to complete. These will remain there until you reprioritize and plan them again during the Weekly Review process, which you'll set up later in this chapter. If you've done a good job with your planning and have available time on your calendar, you can always review your SNA categories on the TaskPad and complete them ahead of time. This encourages you to be proactive.

The SNA's that remain on your TaskPad are actions you've decided don't need to be completed in the coming week. The benefit of this list is you now *know* what you're not going to do and can feel good about it! This sure beats going home at night and feeling guilty about what you didn't get done. Capturing and prioritizing your SNA's is another great benefit of using an IMS.

Making the ControlPanel Your Default View

After you've transferred your reoccurring activities and SNA's onto the Calendar, you can review your week to see how much available time you'll have. If your week is back to back with appointments, you'll know that you won't have time for chatting by the water cooler or getting distracted. However, if your Calendar is open, you'll know you have time to "shoot the breeze," work on SNA's that are on your TaskPad, or get a little distracted and have fun doing it!

Your Calendar now represents your top priorities for the week, and these are your most important agreements to keep. Therefore, you'll want to continually review your ControlPanel to make sure you honor these agreements. I recommend that you make the ControlPanel your default view so it opens whenever you start Outlook. (Don't worry, you'll still be able to get to your Inbox!)

To make the ControlPanel your default view in Outlook, follow these steps:

1. On the menu bar, choose Tools, Options.

2. On the Other tab of the Options dialog box, click Advanced Options

3. In the General section of the Advanced Options dialog box, click Browse next to Startup In This Folder.

4. In the Select Folder dialog box, click Calendar, and click OK.

Keeping Appointments with Yourself Is a Priority

After you start to book appointments with yourself, the next step is to make sure you keep them. My clients often give up their own appointments to attend meetings with other people. It seems much easier to support the requests of your staff, customers and family than it is to support your own priorities.

I hear my clients say, "I want to process my e-mail at work so I don't have to do it at home." When you book appointments with yourself, such as an appointment to process your e-mail or exercise at lunch, you're making yourself a priority. However, when you cancel these appointments to accommodate the requests of others, you're not taking care of what you need to do to accomplish your objectives. You're sending a very clear message to yourself: *Everyone else's agenda is more important than mine.* If you keep reinforcing this message, you'll eventually become resentful and tired, and you'll start blaming your organization because you're not able to keep up with your own workload and needs. It's hard to be a Superman or Superwoman when you're stressed out and overwhelmed. Make yourself a priority and you'll do a better job of taking care of others.

My most successful clients make their own appointments a priority. They know that when they take good care of themselves, they'll take good care of their customers, and staff. They're tenacious about sticking to their uninterrupted e-mail time, exercise time, planning time, and Strategic Next Action time. This practice separates those who are moderately productive from those who are extremely productive. Without exception, I've found that my most successful clients live by this discipline. It's the only way they can survive long-term. Don't give up your appointments with yourself. They help you get your job done, and get it done with balance.

Handling Meeting Requests

After your BaselineCalendar is established, you'll have less time for additional meetings, causing you to be more discriminating. The Meeting Request Model, shown in Figure 10-2, will guide you through a series of questions that are designed to help you make effective decisions regarding meetings. Remember, you'll always have more requests than you can accept, so you have to be more discerning about what you agree to do.

When I work with clients who have heavy meeting schedules—75 percent of their time is in meetings—I'll often go through each appointment on their Calendar and ask, "Does this directly impact one of your Meaningful Objectives?" This cleans out five to eight percent of the meeting requests right away. Then I ask, "Can you delegate this?" and that cleans out another two to five percent. Often, agendas can be combined by moving two meetings into one, or the agenda of a meeting can happen on a conference call, saving travel time. Also, if you have an assistant working with you, consider having that person use this model to help prioritize your appointments for you. There are many ways to work more effectively with meetings. These are just a few ideas.

Here's a closer look at the Meeting Request Model.

What Is It and Is It Actionable?

"What is it and is it actionable?" is a question designed to help you pause and reflect on what type of meeting you're dealing with. I'm sure you've received meeting requests from colleagues that are unclear. You might be asking yourself "Is it personal or business? Is it an off-site meeting or is it in the building? Is it a vendor meeting or an internal meeting?" "What is it?" Once you know what type of request it is, you can decide if you want to attend. If you think the meeting will be useful, move to the next question; otherwise, decline it.

"Your life is the sum result of all the choices you make, both consciously and unconsciously. If you can control the process of choosing, you can take control of all aspects of your life. You can find the freedom that comes from being in charge of yourself."
—**Robert F. Bennett**

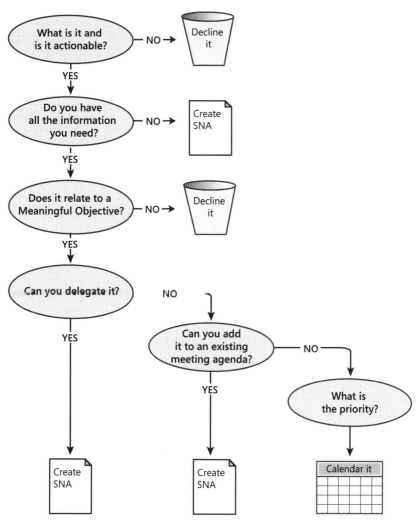

Figure 10-2   The Meeting Request Model shows you how to deal with meeting requests.

Do You Have All the Information You Need?

It's much easier to prioritize meeting requests when you have all the information available. Make sure you find out:

■ The agenda

■ Exactly what decisions need to be made that require your participation

■ Pre-meeting preparation required

- Location

- Length of the meeting

- Attendees

- Due date for the meeting

This gives you valuable information so you can make effective decisions. If you don't have this data, create a Strategic Next Action to get it. Sometimes, when you ask recipients to be more specific about what they want, they'll find alternatives and realize a meeting is not the best forum for their needs.

If you have an Executive Administrator, ask that person to request this information up front. Your administrator can create a simple template with these questions to send to requesting parties. When internal staff realize they need to answer these questions prior to getting a meeting with you, they'll do a better job of providing this information ahead of time. Once again, you're asking people to move their thinking to the front end instead of the back end, which saves cycles of action for everyone.

Does It Relate to a Meaningful Objective?

When you're clear on agenda, decisions, time, and due date, you can evaluate if the request directly maps to one of your Meaningful Objectives. If it doesn't, I'd recommend that you decline. Occasionally, there are special circumstances in which you'd accept an appointment that didn't relate to one of your objectives; supporting a colleague in reaching a goal or attending company staff events. Remember, you're not measured on the meetings you attend; you're measured on achieving your Meaningful Objectives. Stay focused on the activities you've said are important to you and don't get distracted by all the other requests on your time.

Can You Delegate It?

Clients frequently forget the option to delegate. Have you considered whether the meeting request could be passed to one of your direct reports? If someone can make decisions on your behalf, create an SNA to delegate the meeting to that person. If not, move to the next question.

Can You Add It to an Existing Meeting or Agenda?

Rather than set up a new meeting, can the agenda be added to an existing meeting that's already on your Calendar? If so, identify the SNA that you need to take to add the agenda. There's no point in creating an additional meeting if you don't have to! If this doesn't work, move to the next question.

What Is the Priority?

If you have the time and it makes sense to book the meeting, accept the request. However, if your calendar is full, you'll need to assess whether you can push the meeting out or if you need to renegotiate your current appointments to make room for it. To make these decisions, you must be clear about your objectives and deadlines, and if you have an assistant, that person will need to be just as clear.

Much like the questions in the Workflow Model, the questions in the Meeting Request Model are simple but profound, and they help you pause and think before making agreements. Our clients can reduce their time spent in meetings by 20 percent as a result of being more discriminating about what meetings they attend. It's worth taking a moment to make these decisions on the front end so you can save time on the back end. Guard your calendar and don't spend time in meetings that don't directly impact your Meaningful Objectives.

Using Colors on the Calendar to Create Differentiation

Color coding your appointments is extremely powerful because it enables you, in one glance, to differentiate among activities. There are several ways to use color. You can distinguish among meetings, such as confirmed meetings, vendor meetings, client meetings, confirmed calls, and travel time.

Carol uses her colors to distinguish between activities. Her codes are listed below.

- Blue: confirmed calls
- Orange: confirmed client meetings
- Turquoise: confirmed staff meetings

- Purple: appointments—working on objectives, e-mail, and Strategic Next Actions.

- Grey: travel time

- Green: "need to know, don't need to go"

- Yellow: personal time

- Red: completed. No actions remaining that aren't tracked

When Carol sees a phone call in her Calendar, its blue color immediately tells her that she can be in any location to complete the call, as long as she has cell phone coverage, which creates flexibility. However if she's got a client meeting, the orange color signifies that she needs to show up at a specific location, so she's got less flexibility. Gray travel time is useful because Carol can make calls during that period. The colors help her create this distinction.

Another way to color code is to distinguish between your objectives, labeling each appointment to represent the specific objective it links to. This enables you to see how much time you're spending working on different objectives, and in some cases how much time you're spending outside of your objectives.

Another powerful way to use color is to distinguish between complete and incomplete activities. When Carol completes a meeting and captures the appropriate Strategic Next Actions on her TaskPad, she then changes the meeting color on her Calendar to red so she knows the meeting is completed and has no untracked actions.

At the end of the day, when Carol reviews the Calendar, the colors enable her to immediately see what's complete and what's incomplete. If an appointment is not complete, she will track the unfinished action and mark it red or renegotiate the appointment and move it to a different day, or even back to the Task list. This creates a sense of momentum throughout the week, and it's a nice way to close the day.

To color code an appointment, follow these steps:

1. Right-click one of your appointments in the Calendar.

2. From the shortcut menu, choose Label.

3. On the drop-down list of colors, select a color or choose the Edit command to change how you classify the colors.

Unfortunately, you only see shades of grey in this book, but in real life the colors you can choose are vibrant, distinctive, and positively cheery!

My only caution with using colors is to use them consistently, otherwise they become meaningless. Before you embark on using colors, be clear how you want to employ them, and determine if you have the energy to keep using them.

Leveraging Your Time by Creating Boundaries

As an experiment, I reduced my work week several years ago to four days, and my business grew 40 percent! Now why do you think that was? That's right, I had to be 100 percent more discriminating in how I used my time because I had less of it. Creating boundaries around your time is a good thing to do because it leverages your use of it.

I have done a lot of work in non-profit, volunteer organizations. In these types of companies, volunteers often work long hours because they're inspired and committed to the cause. However, this isn't always the most effective approach. Because volunteers know they can complete a task at 8 PM at night, they give themselves more permission to be less focused throughout the day, saying, "I'll just do it later tonight." If you limit the time you have to complete a task, you become more effective in how you prioritize and plan your time. Interestingly enough, giving yourself more time doesn't help you be more productive. In fact, it can have just the opposite effect.

In several of the non-profits I've worked in, senior staff ended up implementing policies that limited the hours their volunteers were able to work, for the sole purpose of increasing their productivity. Working longer hours doesn't mean you're being any more productive. It just means that you're working longer hours. In the long run, you're not taking care of yourself and, ultimately, you won't be able to take care of your customers either.

Be careful not to fall into the trap of working long hours, thinking you're being more productive. You may just be working long hours! Scary thought, but it's definitely worth considering.

Keeping Your ControlPanel Up-to-Date

In order for your system to maintain its value, you have to keep updating it. When your data becomes out of date, it no longer supports effective prioritizing, planning, and decision making. Like most things in life, *you have to improve them in order to maintain them.*

At this point, I'd like to share a metaphor with you that will help explain how to use your ControlPanel. Compare your ControlPanel with the control tower at a busy airport. The control tower is where you direct which planes are arriving, which planes are taking off, and where the emergencies are. A control tower manages the big-picture view from 30,000 feet down to the tarmac. Similarly, your ControlPanel helps you manage everything from your objectives down to your Strategic Next Actions.

It's essential that the information the control tower receives is accurate and reflects what's happening in the skies. If the control tower makes decisions based on old information, disasters can happen.

"When you're operating out of assumptions and paradigms that are incomplete, inaccurate or distorted, there is no way you are going to get maximum quality results. Align your expectations with reality, the way things really are, and with the timeless and universal principles that create the positive results you want to achieve."
—A. Roger Merrill

Imagine that a week goes by, and you've taken on new projects, completed existing tasks, delegated new tasks, collected reimbursable receipts, made new sticky notes, and tracked a few items in your head (I know, we're all human!). If all of this information is not added to your system, you no longer have an accurate reflection of what's going on. Therefore, the decisions you make are not based on the current situation. Last week's information doesn't help you with today's situation, so you need to keep updating your system to keep it useful. The process of updating your system is called the Weekly Review.

The Weekly Review

The Weekly Review has two purposes. It ensures that your ControlPanel is up-to-date and accurately reflects your current situation, and it enables you to effectively prioritize and plan your Calendar at least once a week. This process will take you about an hour to complete.

The three steps to completing a Weekly Review are:

1. Processing and organizing all of your Collecting Points
2. Reviewing and prioritizing your Planning categories
3. Prioritizing and planning your Action categories

I'll go through these steps one at a time so you can work along with me.

1. Processing and Organizing Your Collecting Points

If you have any unprocessed data in your approved (and unapproved) Collecting Points, your ControlPanel won't be up-to-date. After you've completed processing your Collecting Points, check your head—remember, it's an unapproved Collecting Point—to make sure you're not carrying around anything by mistake! Also, check to see if you've picked up any loose papers, sticky notes, and meeting notes along the way, and process them also. This is your time to capture anything you've collected and organize it into your system.

Picking Up Actions from Past and Future Calendar Weeks   Your past and future calendar is another place clients often find untracked action steps. Go to your Calendar, view your work week, and choose the past week. Go through each appointment one by one. Ask yourself "Are there are any actions related to these appointments that aren't captured in my system?" Examples are meetings you attended, during which you wrote down next steps but didn't transfer them to your TaskPad, or conference calls you had in which you meant to follow up, but didn't. Don't be too hasty with this process. Stay present and go through each appointment until you've completed the week.

After you've captured any unrecorded items from an appointment, you can label it with the color red. This lets you know the appointment is complete and all the actions are tracked. You want your past week to be completely red at the end of this process. This lets you know everything that needed to be captured was captured and any appointments that needed to be moved were moved.

Now, look ahead to the future week and do the same process. Review each appointment and ask, "Do I have all the PowerPoint slides I need? Do I have directions and the agenda? Am I prepared for that conference call?" Again, pick up any hidden actions and record them on your TaskPad or Calendar. You can continue into the future as far as you have the courage to go, ensuring that you're prepared for what you've planned. Unfortunately, you can't turn any of these items red until they're done.

When you feel that you've captured everything and processed it into your system, you can move on to step 2.

2. Reviewing and Prioritizing your Planning Categories

Now, the prioritizing begins. The Planning categories consist of your Meaningful Objectives, Supporting Projects, and 1:1 Meeting categories.

This is your opportunity to review these Planning categories from the Control Tower instead of the tarmac, enabling you to gain a different, and much higher perspective.

Objective Categories   Go through each Meaningful Objective category, open each objective one at a time, and ask the following questions:

- Where does this objective stand today, and what's the current situation?
- Where do I want it to be? What's the outcome and by when?
- What's the most Strategic Next Action to move it forward?

In Chapter 7, you inserted links to your Metrics documents inside of your objective tasks. The purpose of doing this was to assist you in quickly reviewing where your objective stands today. I recommend that you store these metric documents on SharePoint, allowing team members to consistently update them. When you insert these SharePoint links into your objective task you will then have immediate access to the most current data.

After you've clarified the status of your objective, you can better assess what Strategic Next Action to take to move it forward. Then you can decide if you can do it in less than two minutes, delegate it via e-mail or your 1:1 category, or defer it into one of your Strategic Next Action categories.

When you've completed this process for each of your Meaningful Objectives, you'll have a much clearer view of where things stand and what you need to do to move them forward. This is a wonderful opportunity to get off the tarmac and lift yourself to a much higher view.

Supporting Projects Categories   Go through each project individually and ask the following questions:

- Where does this project stand today? What's the current situation?
- Where do I want it to be? What's the outcome and by when?
- What's the most Strategic Next Action to move it forward?

You want to be able to answer these questions quickly and effectively. To do this, you need as much supporting documentation as possible linked to the project. In an ideal world, you'd open the project and find a hyperlink to an Excel spreadsheet or a Microsoft Project document, displaying the plan along with what's completed and what's incomplete. In an instant, you'd know where the project stood. Not all projects need this level of data, but you may still want to have it handy. Also, ensure that you have any Metrics associated with the project linked into the project task. I'd recommend storing the Metrics on SharePoint.

When you've established a Strategic Next Action, do it in less than two minutes, if possible. Otherwise, delegate it via e-mail or through your 1:1 category, or defer it into one of your Strategic Next Action categories.

1:1 Meeting Categories   When you take a look at the 1:1 categories that relate to your direct reports, you're looking to review progress on objectives and discussion points and delete any items that have been completed. For the other 1:1 categories in your list, check for completed items and new agenda items. If you don't have a scheduled time to discuss these agendas, create a Strategic Next Action to make that happen.

When you get to the end of reviewing your Planning categories you've reached a good check point to stop and reflect on your work/life balance. Ask yourself, "Am I experiencing a sense of well-being?" If not, decide what you need? It may be a small thing, such as a good night's sleep or a day of unstructured time. When you've discovered what it is, record the action to make sure it happens.

Now that you've reviewed the big picture and have a better idea of where all your objectives and projects stand, it will be easier to drop to the tarmac and ensure that all your Strategic Next Actions are going in the right direction.

3. Prioritizing and Planning Your Action Categories

Your Action categories consist of your Strategic Next Actions. You will be reviewing these to delete the SNA's that you've completed, and to prioritize the actions that you'll move from the TaskPad onto the Calendar as you plan the future week.

For each Strategic Next Action ask, "Does this SNA need to be completed this week?" When you find a Strategic Next Action that must be completed, transfer it to a specific day. Decide when you want to do it, and mark the appropriate amount of time it will take. Remember, there's a 75 percent greater chance that a task will get done if it is on your Calendar instead of your TaskPad.

Scheduling Your Weekly Review

The Weekly Review will take you about an hour to complete and it happens every week. You'll need to pick a regular time to complete the review. Carol does her review 8 AM to 9 AM on Friday mornings, when her mind is fresh and her energy is good. She tried it at 4 PM on a Friday, but found it too difficult to do so late in the day. She also experimented with Monday morning, but worried about her tasks over the weekend, so Friday morning worked best for her. Pick one hour on your calendar that works for you and then drag your Weekly Review task onto that time. When it opens, turn it into a reoccurring weekly appointment. Inside of your Weekly Review, you'll find the list of all the changes you want to make to complete your IMS. To check on your progress, this will be useful to review each week.

Making Your Weekly Review a Priority

The Weekly Review process is simple and the rewards are well worth the effort. However it does take discipline. Each week, I learn something about myself doing the review. I see where I plan too much in a day, and where things took longer than I thought. I discover what kinds of tasks I avoid and how I avoid them. It's a self-revealing process that helps me to pause and reflect on my life, which I don't get to do during the week.

However, this may not be the easiest discipline to adopt. You have to stop and move your focus from the tarmac to the Control Tower, where you'll gain the higher perspective you need to complete the Weekly Review. In order to do this, you have to pry yourself away from doing e-mails and handling last-minute interruptions and deadlines. There is no perfect time to do the review! You'll always have activities that need your attention on the tarmac. You just have to stop for an hour, leave the tarmac, and gain a higher perspective to complete the review.

The Weekly Review is the first and most important discipline to adopt with regard to your IMS. It enables you to constantly evaluate your objectives and Strategic Next Actions, which helps you improves your productivity and work/life balance.

What to Do When You Fall Off the Wagon?

You are likely to fall off the wagon at some point, for any number of reasons, such as going on holiday, taking on new projects, changing jobs, undergoing reorganization, or getting the flu. You must remember that this is a process of practice and learning. All you have to do is climb back on one more time than you fall off.

The best way to get back on track is to spend time doing a Weekly Review. For most people, it's a small investment of time, considering the reward.

Using an IMS takes vigilance and discipline. It's not for the faint-of-heart, but nothing worth doing ever is. You'll be consistently improving your system, and because the results are immediate, you'll find yourself continually encouraged.

Coming Full Circle

In the beginning of the book, I described how the definition for productivity and the Cycle of Productivity were the cornerstones for your IMS. Now that your system is set up, I want to show you how that really works.

The first step in the Cycle of Productivity is "Identifying your Meaningful Objectives." This step starts on your TaskPad, with your Meaningful Objectives categories.

The second step in the cycle is "Creating Strategic Next Actions." Each week, you review your Meaningful Objectives and create Strategic Next Actions that move them forward.

The third step in the cycle is "Scheduling and Completing Strategic Next Actions." Each week, you'll transfer your priority Strategic Next Actions from the TaskPad to the Calendar so you can complete them.

The fourth and last step in the cycle is "Reviewing and Acknowledging Progress." At this point, you'll evaluate whether the completion of your Strategic Next Action moved you toward a Meaningful Objective. Then the cycle begins again!

The Weekly Review process enables you to keep moving the Cycle of Productivity forward week after week after week. As long as you keep the cycle going, you'll eventually unlock your Tasks and Subtasks, Supporting Projects, and Meaningful Objectives, and finally you'll achieve your Mission and Goals. In other words, if you consistently complete Strategic Next Actions that link to your Meaningful Objectives, you'll improve your productivity and quality of life. That is what the Weekly Review is all about; staying on track and maintaining a clear, positive focus on your objectives.

What Changes Will You Make?

Open your Calendar and open the reoccurring appointment you labeled Weekly Review. This is the task you created to capture the changes you want to make as a result of the Three Phases for Creating an Integrated Management System. Under the heading "Prioritizing and Planning," list the changes that you want to make as a result of this phase.

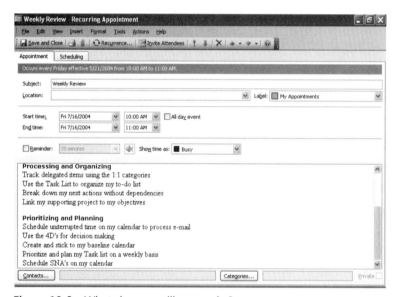

Figure 10-3   What changes will you make?

For inspiration, here's what some of our clients have to say:

1.   Use the Calendar to schedule tasks as well as appointments.

2.   Take the time to update my ControlPanel each week.

3.   Review Meaningful Objectives and Supporting Projects and create Strategic Next Actions.

4.   Plan my Strategic Next Actions using the drag-and-drop feature.

5.   Use the Due Date column on the TaskPad.

6.   Set up color codes.

7.   Book travel time on the Calendar.

8.   Do the Weekly Review.

Success Factors for Prioritizing and Planning

Here are some factors to keep in mind so you can obtain success when you're prioritizing and planning.

- Use your Calendar as the central location to track all of your daily commitments.

- Create a BaselineCalendar structure that accurately reflects the reoccurring activities you need to complete to support your objectives. Include activities such as processing e-mail, Strategic Next Action work time, picking up the kids, 1:1 Meetings, exercise time, and travel time.

- Regularly prioritize your SNA's and transfer them onto the calendar.

- Empty your Collecting Points consistently so that the information in your ControlPanel is current. When you prioritize and plan, you won't be working in a vacuum.

- Review and prioritize your Planning categories so you're managing the 30,000 foot view and gaining a higher perspective on your Meaningful Objectives, Supporting Projects, and 1:1 Meetings.

- Prioritize your Action categories, planning your Strategic Next Actions onto your Calendar to ensure that they get done. This enables you to be realistic about how much time it takes to get the job done, and it supports you in moving toward your objectives.

- Use color codes to create distinctions and add value to your Calendar.

- Schedule uninterrupted time to complete your Weekly Review. Make this appointment a priority. If necessary, set it up to do with a colleague or your executive administrator. It's the most important practice you can do. It's the glue that holds your system together.

- Review your Calendar for work/life balance, and identify what you need to do to maintain and sustain equilibrium.

- Keep your appointments with yourself so that you can take care of yourself and do a better job of taking care of others.

You have to continually improve your system in order to maintain it. The Weekly Review ensures that you keep your system up to date and that you operate within the limits of your Calendar. This keeps you realistic about what you can accomplish. Remember, you can't do everything, but you can do anything, as long as it fits into your Calendar. Respecting your Calendar makes it easier to respect your agreements.

I've used my IMS for more than 24 years now, and I continually fine-tune it to make it better and more effective for me. Have fun with your IMS. Integrate as much of your personal and business life into it as you can. The more you use your IMS, the more useful it will become. Remember, using your IMS isn't about doing more. It's about improving the quality of your life.

Afterword

I hope this book has inspired you to make many positive and wonderful changes toward being more productive and taking care of yourself and your family.

These changes don't have to be big. In fact, effective changes can be small. For example, if you focus on creating Strategic Next Actions without dependencies, that alone will make a difference. If you set up your E-mail Reference System and schedule an hour a day of e-mail processing time, that too will make a difference.

When you've successfully implemented these changes you can return to this book and create the next level of change. We have many clients who take our programs over and over because there are many facets to this content, and productivity is an area you can always improve.

Remember, your IMS is not about *doing* more e-mail, working longer hours, answering phones, setting up systems, and filtering meeting requests. These are all important aspect of productivity. However, at the end of the day, your IMS is about improving and maintaining the quality of your life.

An interesting question to ask yourself is, "How does my system help me 'be present'?" When you turn off your computer, are you still thinking, "When do I need to finish those expenses?" "Did that proposal get written?" Or can you quietly count the raindrops, watch the snowflakes and really *be present* with those moments?

I encourage you to use your system to manage all of your daily tasks so you can get them off your mind. You'll then be present with the people you love and all the people you come in contact with during the day.

Before I sign off, I want to return to the beginning, where we started: The top 10 limiting beliefs, in Chapter 1, which sabotage your intentions to improve productivity and work/life balance. I learned that the belief "I don't have enough time to do all the things I want" wasn't true. Because of that belief, I'd managed my life from my to-do lists rather than from my calendar. Consequently, I broke agreements, worked longer hours, and spent very little time "being present." I was a "doer" but didn't have time to "be," and I wasn't sure I really knew what "being present" was anyway.

Over time, I discovered that I could do anything I wanted to do, as long as it fit into my calendar. This caused me to simplify and to prioritize what was really important to me. I learned to say "no," and to make myself and my appointments more important than taking care of others. I discovered how to slow down, take a breath, and be present. To my surprise, both my own, and my team's, productivity increased enormously.

When you look back over your life, you won't remember all the times you did your e-mail standing in the grocery line and during meetings. You'll remember who you were and the difference you made. Make yourself a priority, and use your IMS to serve you and your company. In the long run, you'll be more successful! Remember, it's not just about doing. It's about living and experiencing the quality of your life.

Go forth, and take back your life!

Contact us at:

McGhee Productivity Solutions
info@mcgheeproductivity.com
Phone: (303) 573-0723
www.mcgheeproductivity.com

Index

Microsoft Press

Work smarter—conquer your software from the inside out!

Microsoft® Windows®
XP Inside Out, Second
Edition
ISBN: 0-7356-2044-X
U.S.A. $44.99
Canada $64.99

Microsoft Office
System Inside Out—
2003 Edition
ISBN: 0-7356-1512-8
U.S.A. $49.99
Canada $72.99

Microsoft Office
Access
2003 Inside Out
ISBN: 0-7356-1513-6
U.S.A. $49.99
Canada $72.99

Microsoft Office
FrontPage® 2003
Inside Out
ISBN: 0-7356-1510-1
U.S.A. $49.99
Canada $72.99

Hey, you know your way around a desktop. Now dig into the new Microsoft Office products and the Windows XP operating system and *really* put your PC to work! These supremely organized software reference titles pack hundreds of timesaving solutions, troubleshooting tips and tricks, and handy workarounds into a concise, fast-answer format. They're all muscle and no fluff. All this comprehensive information goes deep into the nooks and crannies of each Office application and Windows XP feature. And every INSIDE OUT title includes a CD-ROM packed with bonus content such as tools and utilities, demo programs, sample scripts, batch programs, an eBook containing the book's complete text, and more! Discover the best and fastest ways to perform everyday tasks, and challenge yourself to new levels of software mastery!

Microsoft Press has other INSIDE OUT titles to help you get the job done every day:

Microsoft Office Excel 2003 Programming Inside Out
ISBN: 0-7356-1985-9

Microsoft Office Word 2003 Inside Out
ISBN: 0-7356-1515-2

Microsoft Office Excel 2003 Inside Out
ISBN: 0-7356-1511-X

Microsoft Office Outlook 2003® Inside Out
ISBN: 0-7356-1514-4

Microsoft Office Project 2003 Inside Out
ISBN: 0-7356-1958-1

Microsoft Office Visio® 2003 Inside Out
ISBN: 0-7356-1516-0

Microsoft Windows XP Networking Inside Out
ISBN: 0-7356-1652-3

Microsoft Windows Security Inside Out
for Windows XP and Windows 2000
ISBN: 0-7356-1632-9

To learn more about the full line of Microsoft Press® products, please visit us at:

microsoft.com/mspress/

Self-paced training that
works as hard as you do!

Microsoft® Windows®
XP Step by Step
Deluxe, Second
Edition
ISBN: 0-7356-2113-6
U.S.A. $39.99
Canada $57.99

Microsoft Office
Project 2003 Step by
Step
ISBN: 0-7356-1955-7
U.S.A. $29.99
Canada $43.99

Microsoft Office Excel
2003 Step by Step
ISBN: 0-7356-1518-7
U.S.A. $24.99
Canada $35.99

Microsoft Office
FrontPage® 2003
Step by Step
ISBN: 0-7356-1519-5
U.S.A. $24.99
Canada $35.99

Information-packed STEP BY STEP courses are the most effective way to teach yourself how to complete tasks with the Microsoft Windows operating system and Microsoft Office applications. Numbered steps and scenario-based lessons with practice files on CD-ROM make it easy to find your way while learning tasks and procedures. Work through every lesson or choose your own starting point—with STEP BY STEP'S modular design and straightforward writing style, *you* drive the instruction. And the books are constructed with lay-flat binding so you can follow the text with both hands at the keyboard. Select STEP BY STEP titles also prepare you for the Microsoft Office Specialist credential. It's an excellent way for you or your organization to take a giant step toward workplace productivity.

Microsoft Press has other STEP BY STEP titles to help you get the job done every day:

Home Networking with Microsoft Windows XP
Step by Step
ISBN: 0-7356-1435-0

Microsoft Office Word 2003 Step by Step
ISBN: 0-7356-1523-3

Microsoft Office Outlook 2003 Step by Step
ISBN: 0-7356-1521-7

Microsoft Office System Step by Step—2003
Edition
ISBN: 0-7356-1520-9

Microsoft Office PowerPoint 2003 Step by
Step
ISBN: 0-7356-1522-5

Microsoft Office Access 2003 Step by Step
ISBN: 0-7356-1517-9

To learn more about the full line of Microsoft Press® products, please visit us at:

microsoft.com/mspress

What do you think of this book? We want to hear from you!

Do you have a few minutes to participate in a brief online survey? Microsoft is interested in hearing your feedback about this publication so that we can continually improve our books and learning resources for you.

To participate in our survey, please visit:

www.microsoft.com/learning/booksurvey

And enter this book's ISBN, 0-7356-2215-9. As a thank-you to survey participants in the United States and Canada, each month we'll randomly select five respondents to win one of five $100 gift certificates from a leading online merchant.* At the conclusion of the survey, you can enter the drawing by providing your e-mail address, which will be used for prize notification *only*.

Thanks in advance for your input. Your opinion counts!

Sincerely,

Microsoft Learning

Microsoft | Learning

Learn More. Go Further.

To see special offers on Microsoft Learning products for developers, IT professionals, and home and office users, visit: *www.microsoft.com/learning/booksurvey*